Coffins on Our Shoulders

Coffins on Our Shoulders

THE EXPERIENCE OF THE PALESTINIAN CITIZENS OF ISRAEL

Dan Rabinowitz

Khawla Abu-Baker

UNIVERSITY OF CALIFORNIA PRESS
Berkeley   Los Angeles   London

University of California Press
Berkeley and Los Angeles, California

University of California Press, Ltd.
London, England

Library of Congress Cataloging-in-Publication Data

Rabinowitz, Dan, 1954–.
[Dor ha-zakuf. English]
    Coffins on our shoulders : the experience of the Palestinian citizens of
Israel / Dan Rabinowitz, Khawla Abu-Baker.
        p.   cm.
    Includes bibliographical references (p.) and index.
    ISBN 0-520-24441-9 (cloth : alk. paper) — ISBN 0-520-24557-1 (pbk. :
alk. paper)
1. Palestinian Arabs—Israel.   2. Palestinian Arabs—Israel—Social
conditions.   3. Palestinian Arabs—Legal status, laws, etc.—Israel.
4. Palestinian Arabs—Israel—Politics and government.   5. Israel—
Ethnic relations.   6. Arab-Israeli conflict—Influence.   7. Social
integration—Israel.   I. Abu Baker, Khawla. II. Title.
DS113.7.R3413   2005
305.892′7405694′090511—dc22   2004022691

Manufactured in the United States of America

14   13   12   11   10   09   08   07   06   05
10   9   8   7   6   5   4   3   2   1

This book is printed on New Leaf EcoBook 60, containing 60% post-
consumer waste, processed chlorine free; 30% de-inked recycled fiber,
elemental chlorine free; and 10% FSC-certified virgin fiber, totally
chlorine free. EcoBook 60 is acid-free and meets the minimum
requirements of ANSI/ASTM D5634–01 (Permanence of Paper).

Dedicated to our mothers, Sarah and Nada, and to the aunts and uncles they lost in Eastern Europe during the Holocaust and in Palestine in 1948, respectively

Contents

Preface

The idea to write this book came up before the rift that opened between Israel and the Palestinians in the Occupied Territories and inside Israel in September 2000. When we began working on the manuscript, few believed that the arena it describes could deteriorate so quickly and turn into the dangerously bleeding wound that it has become in recent years.

Coauthoring a book, a complicated task under any circumstances, required in our case the spanning of interpersonal, cross-gender, cross-cultural, and cross-ethnonational perspectives. It became a mental journey whose intensity and outcomes took us completely by surprise.

If this odyssey in any way improved our capacity to understand the complex reality that we attempt to represent here, it happened because friends and colleagues helped along the route. Many have been generous with their time and insights. Members of both our families consented to reopen in our presence some traumatic pages from their personal memories and the national histories in which they participated. We are grateful to the staff at Mar Elias College in 'Iblin, to the parents of the late Asil

'Aslah, and to Asil's classmates, who shared their grief and opinions with us following his death in October 2000. We are indebted to students and their leaders in colleges and universities up and down the country who helped us track the undercurrents on campus that are prevalent among their generation. Marwan Dwairy, Khawla's partner, and Iros Rabino-witz, Dan's partner, followed the project with interest and care from the outset. Their comments at many stages were invaluable, helping us to clarify and streamline our analysis and argument. Khawla's daughters and Dan's children afforded us invaluable glances into the world of Palestinian yuppies and Israeli youths, respectively.

We wish to thank Jim Clark and Naomi Schneider, both at the University of California Press, for believing in this project and for the energy, consistency, integrity, and common sense with which they helped to bring the present volume to the world. California's Jacqueline Volin, Bonita Hurd, Justin Hunter, and Sierra Filucci worked on the final stages to prepare it for print. Without them the book would have been lacking in flow, accuracy, and style. We also wish to thank Joe Monteville and the Center for Strategic and International Studies in Washington, D.C., for a grant that helped this project in its early days, and Salman Natour for permitting us to translate and quote from his speech in memory of those who died during the tragic events of October 2000.

Many other friends and colleagues contributed time and insight to this project. These include, in alphabetical order, David Abrahams, Sirab Abu-Rabi'a, Uri Ben-Eliezer, Matti Bunzl, Yiftah Dekel, the late Muhammad Hamza Ghenayem, Akram Haniyeh, Haim Hazan, Hanna Herzog, Salem Jubran, Courtney Jung, Dov Khenin, Tanya Luhrmann, 'Adel Mana', Zvi Me'ir, Joel Migdal, Nisim Mizrahi, Hannah Naveh, Ori Nir, Areej Sabagh, Marshal Sahlins, Gideon Samet, Nadera Shalhoub-Kevorkian, Aliza Shenhar, Yehouda Shenhav, George Stockings, Yesha'ayahu Tadmor, and Michelle Zackheim. Responsibility for the views expressed, as well as for any faults and errors, remains wholly ours.

This English edition is a restructured, expanded, and updated version of the Hebrew and Arabic editions published in 2002 and in 2004, respectively, by Keter Publishing in Jerusalem and Madar in Ramallah (Rabi-nowitz and Abu-Baker 2002, Abu-Baker and Rabinowitz 2004). A German edition is forthcoming in 2005. The order of the authors' names on the covers alternates from edition to edition. We wish to indicate that this is a shared project, and that both of us should be considered as principal authors regardless of the order of names on the cover.

Note on transliteration: We have used *The Chicago Manual of Style*'s rules for Arabic transliteration throughout.

Dan Rabinowitz, Khawla Abu-Baker
Tel Aviv and Acre, July 2004

Introduction

Mar Elias College in the village of 'Iblin is a church-run high school serving Palestinians—Muslims, Christian, and Druze—from western Galilee and beyond.[1] In late June 2000 some fourteen hundred youths, teachers, clerics, proud parents, and other family relations packed the main auditorium for the annual graduation ceremony. As they took their seats, the school choir formed on stage and started singing. The first song was "Mawtini" (My homeland). Written in the 1930s by Ibrahim Tukan, "Mawtini" has major emotional significance for every Palestinian and is second only to "Biladi Biladi" (My country, my country), the semiofficial Palestinian national anthem. As soon as the first sounds of "Mawtini" were heard, everyone fell silent and stood up. The crowd remained standing for the next song too. It was Samih al-Qasem's "Muntasib al-

Qama" (The standing tall), sung poignantly by the choir as the graduates entered. The words were:

Standing tall I march,
My head held high,
An olive branch held in my palm,
A coffin on my shoulder,
On I walk.

The marching graduates, draped in caps and gowns, stirred the audience, who joined the choir with singing and applause. The standing ovation continued until the graduates all reached their designated rows in the front.

The impressive show of respect for "Mawtini" and "Muntasib al-Qama" assumed a new significance minutes later, when the educational counselor, an Orthodox Christian minister, embarked on a sermon that had unmistakably religious overtones. To his dismay, he soon discovered that the spontaneous outburst triggered earlier by the anthems had dissipated. The mixed crowd listened politely but remained seated. Taken aback, the minister stopped in midparagraph, raised his eyes from his notes, and addressed the silent auditorium in a reprimanding fashion. "It is customary to stand up to honor the words of God," he said. The audience stood up dutifully, and he proceeded.

The singing of "Mawtini" and "Muntasib al-Qama" was congruent with other elements of the ceremony that celebrated the tenacity, endurance, and resolve of Palestinians against all odds. Clearly, the event was an opportunity for public affirmation of a growing national awareness, a sentiment many in the Palestinian minority and most Jewish Israelis had not been fully cognizant of until recently.

The graduation ceremony in 'Iblin illustrates a wider phenomenon that this book, based on observations and interviews conducted between 1999 and 2004, seeks to describe and analyze: the emergence among the Palestinian citizens of Israel of a new sociological generation that we label the Stand-Tall Generation. Its representatives and leaders, many of them women, display a new assertive voice, abrasive style, and unequivocal substantive clarity. They have unmitigated determination, confidence, and a sense of entitlement the likes of which had only seldom been articulated previously by Palestinians addressing the Israeli mainstream.

Members of the Stand-Tall Generation were born in Israel in the last quarter of the twentieth century. They made their political debut following the general elections of 1999 and came of political age with the tumultuous events in the Occupied Territories and inside Israel in October 2000. They are the grandchildren of those who went through the fateful war of 1948 as young adults, and they are the children of those born in the 1950s and early 1960s who spearheaded the politicization of the Palestinian minority in Israel in the 1970s and 1980s.[2]

The members of the Stand-Tall Generation echo the demands of their forebears to change the character and formal definition of Israel from "the state of the Jewish people" to "the state of all its citizens"—demands that have set the tone of the political campaigns of Palestinians inside Israel since the mid-1990s. But the simple dictum of "the state of all its citizens" no longer covers the entirety of the quest for change. Disillusioned with the prospect of ever becoming equal citizens in Israel, members of the Stand-Tall Generation are no longer interested in being marginal hangers-on of the Zionist project. They tend to see citizenship as a collective entitlement, not just a personal affair. They seek deep historic justice and meaningful incorporation into a transformed Israel—notions this book explores at some length.

Samih al-Qasem's powerful image of youngsters with coffins on their shoulders, determined to make the ultimate sacrifice for land and nation, is not unique to Palestinian culture. Rituals that glorify death are part of nation-building efforts everywhere. Like Palestinian poetry, the Zionist cultural canon is replete with calls on men and women to die in glory so the nation's dignity and independence can be preserved. Natan Alterman's famous poem "The Gold Platter" is one emblematic example.[3] In it, a young man and woman who have emerged from battle approach a tearful woman who personifies the nation, fall at her feet, and die. Their last words, uttered to the mother-nation as they perish is that they—like others killed in war—are "the golden platter on which the Jewish state was given to you." Haim Guri's poem "Here Are Our Bodies Laid

Down," written after thirty-five Israeli soldiers were killed by Arab fighters on a hill south of Bethlehem in early 1948, likewise glorifies death by using the perspective of the dead.[4] By 1970, the canonized valorization of death was solidified and robust enough to begin attracting an antihegemonic wave of sociopolitical critique.[5]

The emergence of the Stand-Tall Generation is not simply an internal affair within the Palestinian community. It carries consequences for minority-majority relations relevant to Israel at large. In terms of social theory, it touches on issues currently pertinent to sociologists, political theorists, anthropologists, and lawyers preoccupied with ethnic relations in liberal democracies.

Mainstream theories of liberal democracy are premised on the individual as the fundamental bearer of rights and privileges. They focus on persons as free agents who share social goods and who, through political participation, shape the physical and social universe they live in.[6] But what about those who cannot or will not enter the realm of politics as free individual agents? Habermas's recent notion of deliberative democracy, a variation on the theme of a politics of choice and freedom, presents a vivid illustration of their conundrum.[7] Premised on individual choices, deliberative democracy does not properly account for those who enter politics to defend rights and entitlements that they associate with their collective universe. In fact, members of ethnic minorities, indigenous or immigrant, who enter politics in liberal states often do it in pursuit of goals quite different from those sought by members of hegemonic majorities. Latecomers to the society for which the system was initially developed, ethnic minorities often challenge the basic tenets of the system, exerting inner tensions that could force it to transform.

The recent prominence of indigenous ethnicity and ethnonational strife within states and regions in central and eastern Europe, Southeast Asia, and parts of Africa, coupled with the rapid expansion of immigrant minorities in the West, has triggered a wave of renewed interest in comparative approaches to the problem and various theoretical insights into it.[8]

Kymlicka's influential early work on this issue is premised on the recognition that states can prey upon nonhegemonic minorities, and on

the conviction that when they do, the main responsibility of liberal democracy is to defend the individual members of such minorities from the
tyranny of the majority.[9] Initially, this trajectory played down the political quest of many ethnic groups, including indigenous minorities, for
meaningful cultural identity. The right to secure cultural continuity was
rendered immaterial unless it came to rescue personal advancement. In
the long run, the argument went, genuine integration would eclipse the
quest for cultural autonomy. Members of ethnic minorities who grew up
in a liberal democracy inevitably would recognize the advantages of liberalism and gradually would assign culture and identity less political
import.

Kymlicka's later work joins that of others who pay more attention to
the complexities involved with the politics of culture and try to tackle it
through more sophisticated notions of multiculturalism and considered
tolerance.[10] Still others are more inclined to highlight the inherent tension
between depoliticized individual equality of the type stressed by conventional liberal-democratic philosophy and the emphasis on cultural
distinction and collective identity that ethnic minorities so often val-
orize.[11] The dilemmas preoccupying the Palestinian citizens of Israel
when it comes to active participation in Israeli politics present a lucid
example of this conundrum.

Social scientists writing about Israel have produced a substantial body
of research that focuses on Israel's Palestinian citizens. Elia Zureik and
others have taken the marginal status of the Palestinians within Israel as
the defining feature of Israel, depicting it as a colonial settler-state.[12] A
convincing case has likewise been made regarding the structural and
institutional features of Jewish hegemony, dating to as early as the 1950s,
which were designed to contain the Palestinian citizens, thus producing
what Ian Lustick has called the Israeli system of control.[13]

Key decisions made by judges in Israel's Supreme Court of Justice in
their occasional capacity as chairs of the central elections committees
have been used by Yoav Peled to demonstrate the mitigated citizenship
that Israel affords its Palestinian subjects. Restrictions made on Palestinian candidates and parties, Peled shows, stand in clear contrast to the
unhindered access enjoyed by Jewish Israelis to most aspects of the com-

mon good.[14] A different view, whose main proponent is Sami Smooha, reflects a more lenient approach to Israel and Zionism by labeling it "ethnic democracy."[15] The argument here is that, while primarily geared toward maintaining the superiority of Jewish Israelis, Israel nevertheless grants Palestinian citizens formal rights and some access to power and resources, and that this qualifies it as a democratic state.[16] We challenge this narrow view of democracy, arguing that Israel is but a nominal, minimal democracy.

The Palestinian community in Israel is a collective loaded with external pressures and fraught with inner tensions. To begin with, Palestinians are a majority turned minority. Prior to 1948, the total population living within the territory that would later become Israel—that is, within the territory delimited by the Green Line determined in 1949—can be estimated as 1.5 million. Approximately 900,000—three-fifths—of these were Palestinians. By the time the 1948 hostilities were over, however, 85 percent of these Palestinians had been uprooted and were refugees, mainly in adjacent Arab states.[17] Currently numbering over a million, Palestinians now represent less than a fifth of Israel's population and are in constant search of empowerment and political expression. To complicate things further, their quest for equality and genuine inclusion in Israel takes place even as they seek a clearer role within the Palestinian fold—a predicament Emil Tuma is said to have described as "holding two watermelons in one hand." Given that their state is still at war with their mother nation, their predicament is likely to remain even when a formal settlement between Palestine and Israel is finally achieved.

Three-quarters of the communities defined by Israel's Bureau of Statistics as "low income" are Palestinian.[18] With an average of more than five persons per household, Palestinian families in Israel have 50 percent more mouths to feed than Jewish Israeli ones have. The average rate of unemployment in Palestinian communities inside Israel in the early 2000s was 15 percent, reaching 20 percent in some communities. This level is approximately 60 percent higher than unemployment ratios in Israel at large.[19] In many Palestinian communities, a disproportionately high portion of the population depends on social security payments to make ends meet.[20] This notwithstanding, Palestinian local councils, which serve approximately 12 percent of the population of Israel,[21] receive only 8 percent of the total budget allocated by the central government to local authorities—50 percent less per capita than Jewish Israeli councils receive.[22]

Israel's land regime is a tool for and an outcome of mass usurpation of Palestinian land.[23] Land allocation policies designed by the Israel Land Administration, in which the Jewish National Fund maintains a constitutional majority, consistently ignore the needs of Palestinian communities. Palestinians, while representing over 16 percent of the entire population, own merely 3.5 percent of the available land.[24] The proportion of the area under municipal jurisdiction of Palestinian towns and villages is even smaller, only 2.5 percent. With land allocation policies, Israeli institutions and officials consistently marginalize Palestinians. Many Israelis, for example, would see suggestions to allocate land for new Palestinian settlements as repugnant.

Economic stagnation, underdevelopment, unemployment, and poverty in the Palestinian community are inextricably linked to long-standing government policies of neglect and discrimination. All Israeli administrations, with the sole exception of Rabin's government in the early 1990s, left Palestinian towns and villages outside the loop when assigning subsidies and development incentives.[25] Palestinians are excluded from a variety of welfare benefits and state-subsidized mortgages reserved for army veterans and new immigrants.[26] The exclusion of Palestinians from essential economic spheres such as banking, import and export franchises, and advanced technology further contribute to economic marginalization.[27] Most of the employed Palestinians commute daily to Israeli towns, thus underscoring the character of many Palestinian settlements as dormitory towns. Some sectors of the economy that once attracted a large number of Palestinian workers, such as construction and textile manufacture, have proven particularly vulnerable to economic and political change triggered by neoliberalism and globalization.[28]

Palestinian citizens remain unwanted guests in the Israeli economy, members of a community whose needs and claims are deemed irrelevant to what mainstream Israel defines as its worthy national goals. In a major departure from genuinely democratic processes, government policies that concern the Palestinian community are perpetually determined by Jewish Israeli experts, rather than by representatives of the community itself.

The establishment of the state of Israel in 1948 signaled the loss of educational autonomy for the Palestinians. Israel established a centralized system that treated the school system as a means of ideological control, consistently weakening all traces of Palestinian identity that might have lingered in it.[29] Fifty years on, the educational objectives and the programs designed for Palestinian schools still fail to reflect the community's identity as a national minority, part and parcel of the Palestinian people. Instead the structure and content of the schooling system amount to a futile attempt to produce submissive citizens with no sense of political identity. Budgets are pitiful and physical facilities are abysmal, often unsafe. The choice that individuals and families have concerning which school to attend is limited.[30]

A comparison of how Palestinian citizens of Israel and Jewish Israelis are treated when detained by the police indicates that Palestinian detainees are significantly more likely to end up being charged with a crime. In fact, decisions made at all levels of the law enforcement system—police investigation, state prosecution, and judgments handed down by the judiciary itself—consistently indicate disproportionately harsh treatment of Palestinians.[31]

Israel reflects the national aspirations, collective memory, and cultural values of its Jewish majority. Its dominant narratives stress the legacy of the Jewish Diaspora, the Holocaust, and the rebirth of the Jewish nation through the Judaization of physical, cultural, and spiritual space. But in the experience of Palestinians citizens, Israel's ascendance, seen by its Jewish citizens as a supreme manifestation of historic justice, is associated with grave familial and communal loss; with blanket curtailment of civil liberties, particularly under the military governorate up to 1966; and with wide-scale land appropriation—in short, with the systematic marginalization of the Palestinians in their own homeland.

The state's acknowledgment of the legitimacy of Palestinian cultural difference does not arrest marginalization,[32] and certainly does little to integrate into the canon the Palestinians' collective memory and sense of history. Any reference, direct or indirect, to the normative core of the state can only alienate its Palestinian citizens, reducing them to strangers in their ancestral homeland. At best, they are tolerated as fringe individuals, recognized as part of a collective only at times of traumatic events like war, terror attacks, or widespread demonstrations. This syndrome, known in other ethnically divided states, becomes a painful irony once we recall that Palestinians lived in Palestine long before the onslaught of Zionism and the establishment of the state of Israel.

Despite the formal and explicit commitment to equality included in Israel's declaration of independence, the state has yet to recognize the suffering that its Palestinian citizens, their kin, and their community endured in 1948.[33] Israelis, who perhaps require this denial to construct a semblance of normality, nurture the belief that 1948 is over and done with—a sealed case that bears no relation to current events and that can be conveniently treated as irrelevant to the future. Nothing, we argue throughout this book, could be further from the truth.

An adequate understanding of the emergence of the Stand-Tall Generation hinges on a sound analysis of the wider context of Israeli-Palestinian relations in the 1990s. The effect of the Oslo Accords of 1993, their partial implementation on the ground, and the events that followed the attempt in late 2000 to reach a settlement between the warring parties is dealt with in detail later in the book. For now, suffice it to say that the failure of the negotiations at Camp David in July 2000, the well-publicized visit of then opposition leader Ariel Sharon to East Jerusalem's Temple Mountain (Haram al-Sharif) in East Jerusalem two months later, and the eruption immediately thereafter of the popular and violent uprising known as Intifadat al-Aqsa played a crucial role in the politicization of an entire Palestinian generation, within Israel and elsewhere.

When the wave of protest that swept through the Occupied Territories in October 2000 spilled across the Green Line—which divides Israel from the West Bank and Gaza[34]—into Israel, it immediately became apparent that this time the Palestinian citizens of Israel would mobilize unprecedented support for their brethren in the territories. The next two weeks saw mass demonstrations staged in Palestinian communities up and down the country, many of which were brutally suppressed by an unprepared and ill-equipped police force. Within two weeks, thirteen young demonstrators—twelve of them Israeli citizens—were killed by police gunfire. Hundreds more were wounded. Many feared the situation was spiraling out of control, into open ethnic conflict.

In his discussion of sociological generations, Karl Mannheim suggests that members of an age cohort who, between the ages of seventeen and twenty-five, go through a dramatic—sometimes traumatic—constitutive experience, develop a common political and sociological worldview.[35] We believe that the events of October 2000, while certainly not the first juncture at which members of the Stand-Tall Generation ever found themselves occupying a single experiential universe, was a defining moment of sociogenerational proportions.

The clarity with which the members of this generation identify themselves with Palestinian national identity, and the ease with which they discard genuine affiliation with Israel, presents a clear departure from the ambivalence that typified their parents' generation in these matters. The confused illusion that guided—or obscured—the hopes of earlier generations to be included in the Israeli project has now been replaced with a sober view of the reluctance by most mainstream Israelis to see Palestinian citizens as equals.

Like other sociological generations, the Stand-Tall Generation is not uniform. There are Palestinian teenagers who view the new consciousness of their peers as dangerous and futile, and Palestinians in their seventies and eighties who strongly identify with its spirit of defiance. Some Palestinians see the elimination of the Green Line and the emergence of a binational Palestinian-Israeli state as the ultimate long-term goal.[36] Other Palestinians are committed to a two-state solution, hoping that Israel would concomitantly redefine itself in ways that might enable them to live with its core values and get an equal share of its resources. In the aftermath of the shock created in October 2000, some seek disengagement from the Jewish Israeli mainstream, while others are convinced a better future hinges on better cooperation with moderate Israelis. Whatever their ideological positions, and however effective or futile their agency has so far been, members of the Stand-Tall Generation seem determined to redefine their situation within Israel, modifying the very nature of the state in the process.

Within Israel's Jewish majority, patterns of thought concerning the Palestinian minority are also going through profound revisions. After decades of misrecognition and denial of Palestinian sensibilities, Israelis now awake to what for some of them is a frightening reality. The new dynamics of identity and belonging apparent in the Palestinian fold threaten to upset the control mechanisms—which, until quite recently, went unchallenged—thus raising Israeli fears of Palestinian irredentism. These apprehensions, while obviously far-fetched, must not be taken lightly. The emotional energy they might unleash could undo the fragile inner balance holding Israel together.

The political worldview of the Stand-Tall Generation, shaped by the reality of Israel's occupation of the Palestinian territories since 1967, is wedded to the paradox created by that war. On the one hand, the decisive military outcome persuaded many Palestinians to accept the long-term presence of the Jewish-dominated state. On the other hand, renewed contacts with Palestinians in the West Bank and the Gaza Strip, and with diasporic Palestinians and the Arab world at large, exposed the Palestinian citizens of Israel to geographic, cultural, and political universes in which Israel is a relatively negligible entity.

The 1967 war and the ensuing conquest bred the Israeli policy of "open bridges," enabling contact and commerce with Jordan and, through it, with the Arab world. It also brought an influx of hundreds of thousands of Palestinian laborers into Israel, entailed large-scale land expropriation for Jewish settlements throughout the territories, and provoked Palestinian guerillas to execute terror attacks against Israelis in the territories in Israel proper. These processes gradually altered the status of the Green Line, temporarily blurring its significance. Before construction began on the separation wall in 2004, the rigid borders of pre-1967 Israel became fluid markers, their influence on future military and political developments questionable.

Is the Green Line impassable or penetrable? Does it function as a real border, or is it only a virtual convention denoting an interstitial reality? Does it engender separate political and social entities or fuse them together? Is it still there? Is its disappearance and reemergence part of a historic process, whereby Palestine—as defined by the League of Nations and surrendered to a British mandate after World War I—becomes an

extended zone of contestation, with two national communities strug-
gling for identity, resources, and control?[37] Will the obtrusively inhuman
wall—erected ostensibly to stop suicide bombers but in effect a means to
punish the Palestinians and a preemptive step against a territorially
viable Palestinian state—change the course of history?

Identifying the true meaning of the Green Line is a cardinal question
for both Israelis and Palestinians.[38] Are the Palestinian citizens of Israel
really a separate group with a distinctive history, a discernable sense of
identity, and an independent vision of the future?[39] Or is such a distinction nothing but the reification of the artificial separation that Israel created within Palestine, a schism the Palestinians can never accept? Is the
tendency that we identify among the Stand-Tall Generation—to down-
play Israel as a focus of identity and to stress their Palestinian consciousness—a further step toward finally robbing the Green Line of its political
and cognitive import?

Liberal Israeli Zionists need the Green Line so as to render all that lies
beyond it as temporary conquest. This exempts them from having to confront the historic legacy and lingering guilt associated with the military
conquests and ethnic cleansing Israel perpetrated in 1948. Projects such
as ours, we like to think, may help subvert such denial.

Baruch Kimmerling and Joel Migdal argue that the Palestinian nation
emerged in a series of anticolonial struggles: the peasant (fellaheen)
revolt of the 1830s, the anti-British revolt a century later, and the first
intifada, which began in 1987.[40] Intifadat al-Aqsa, with its seemingly
inexorable energy, was a reminder that the first intifada, in which the
Palestinians first demonstrated their capacity to exert political will in
spite of an insidious occupation, lacked two major players: the Palestinian diaspora and the Palestinian citizens of Israel. Intifadat al-Aqsa in
many ways paved the way for these two segments to return to the
national arena and reclaim their role in the quest for self-determination.

Identity is a contested, fragmented, varied entity. Those who turn to
this jointly authored book for a simplistic answer to the question, Who
are the Palestinian citizens of Israel today? are bound for disappointment. In matters of identity, simplistic questions and essentialist defini-
tions often prove redundant. It is, as Homi Bhabha amply demonstrated,

a realm of imaginary construction in which components are in synergetic tension and negotiation with one another.[41] Even globalization, the specter of which hovers in the Middle East as it does elsewhere, has no clear thrust in these manners, strengthening local ethnonational identities in some instances, mitigating them in others.

The first part of this book (chapters 1–3) is a sociohistorical analysis of the Palestinian citizens of Israel that demonstrates that the Stand-Tall Generation was preceded by two earlier ones. The first of these, whose story is presented in chapters 1 and 2, is the generation of survivors—Palestinians who, in the aftermath of the dramatic war of 1948, found themselves trapped in a state they never wanted, let alone invited. The second, described mainly in chapter 3, is the generation that has spearheaded the Palestinians' civil struggle inside Israel since the 1970s.

Our generational analysis historicizes this struggle. It illustrates how the state attempted to control the community's intellectual energy and political awareness in a futile effort to cultivate docile, depoliticized, submissive subjects. One aspect of this was an exercise in labeling, in which the state successfully subsumed the Palestinians under the designation "Israel's Arabs" or "Israeli Arabs." Another entailed techniques designed to control, isolate, and incarcerate the Palestinians in both time and space, to borrow Renato Rosaldo's suggestive imagery.[42] This included obliterating the relative autonomy enjoyed by the Palestinian educational system under British rule, removal of the Palestinian community from state-sponsored schemes of development and economic growth, tight control of cultural and literary processes, and consistent stifling of public discourse.

The second part of the book (chapters 4–6) sketches the profile of the Stand-Tall Generation in light of recent events and uses this historical perspective to offer a different vision for Israel's future. Israel's main dilemma concerning its Palestinian citizens is whether to include or control them. This dilemma is vividly illustrated in two diametrically opposed documents produced in late 2000. The first document is an unsolicited report about the Palestinian citizens of Israel, presented to Prime Minister Ehud Barak in November 2000 by twenty-six researchers from various Israeli academic institutions.[43] Advocating the replacement of the current Israeli system of control with a strategy of accommodation and cooperation, it presents a radical, post-Zionist departure from the accepted dogmas of Israel. The second document is a summary of a year-long seminar sponsored by the Interdisciplinary Center of Herzliya in 2000.[44] Known in Israel as the Herzliya Report, this document frames the relationship between the Palestinian minority and the Jewish majority primarily as a demographic struggle, then goes on to detail the means by which hegemony can be perpetuated. Explicitly seeking to reduce the role of Palestinian citizens in shaping the character and agenda of the state, it calls for limitation of the rights of Palestinian individuals and communities.

Comparing these two documents is more than just an academic exercise. Both reports put the Palestinian citizens of Israel at center stage, recognizing that decisions pertaining to their fate will have ramifications for the very essence of the state—for its stability and chances of prosperity. The academics' report advocates a redefinition of Israeli citizenship in ways that will breed a democratic transformation of the state itself. This view, which declines to accept ethnonational affiliation as the primary key to full citizenship, sees the current situation, in which the two communities move in separate circles, as inherently dangerous. It calls for a series of substantial changes in the very definition of the Israeli project, predicting that failure to effect them could soon make the tough events of October 2000 a tame prologue to far more troubling occurrences. If it continues to adhere rigidly to its ethnonational core as a Jewish state, the authors of this report say, Israel might become entangled in a syndrome recently branded as "the dark side of democracy."[45]

The Herzliya Report, in contrast, proposes tightening state control of the Palestinian minority. This approach, which was plausible for many Jewish Israelis even before October 2000, has since become more popular. It lures many who fail to recognize the racist overtones that guide it and the heavy moral and political price tags that it carries. It signals the surrender of any prospect for a truly liberal democracy, and a retreat toward dubious sociopolitical configurations that resemble *herenvolk* democracy of the type known in South Africa under apartheid.

The debate within the Israeli mainstream concerning the future of democracy is no longer between zealous ideologues representing opposing poles of the political spectrum. It is now conducted in the mainstream and involves a wide cross-section of the secular movements that have led Zionism since the 1920s, including liberal-minded members of Labor, Likud, Meretz, Shinuy, and others. Palestinian spokespersons of the Stand-Tall Generation have yet to gain access to many of the platforms where this debate takes place. Their very presence, however, on some of these platforms, and the clarity with which they see their own position, already plays an important role in the debate.

Soon after we began our joint work on this project in 1999, we realized that we had been born within weeks of each other to two families from Haifa. The Abu-Shamlas and the Abu-Bakers, Khawla's maternal and paternal kin, moved to Haifa from Ya'abad, a village near Jenin in the West Bank, in the early 1920s—precisely when the Bodankins, Dan's maternal kin, arrived from the Ukraine. The two families put down roots in Haifa, benefiting from its rapid growth under British rule. Then came the war of 1948 and the subsequent establishment of Israel, which sent the two families on diametrically opposed trajectories. The Abu-Shamlas and the Abu-Bakers were displaced, and they lost most of what they had. The Rabinowitzes became integral to the professional and social echelons of a state that had some of the fastest and most consistent growth rates in modern history.

The intersection of our families' stories fascinated us. We probed, collected new details, and posed more questions to ourselves and our relatives as we went along. At first we were uncertain whether a juxtaposition of our respective backgrounds and life stories had a place in a book primarily designed to discuss sociohistorical processes. Gradually, however, and with the help of colleagues, friends, and editors, the value of these stories was brought into relief. We realized that, while our respective families had never been particularly political or otherwise involved in the grand scheme of Middle Eastern history, the anecdotes that emanate from them, spanning five generations—from our respective grandparents, parents, siblings, peers, and children, all the way to Khawla's first grandchild, born in 2003—present insightful illustrations of the historico-political arena we analyze. We decided to include them. The result is a bifurcated account of divergent histories reflecting the dynamics of the personal and the political in a war zone, a version of how identities and destinies in Palestine and Israel were shaped before and in our time.[46]

The book thus features two intersecting narratives. One is a socio-historical account of the Palestinian citizens of Israel. It reads, by and large, as a linear chronological progression and is presented visually in blocks of justified text. The other narrative, justified to the left only, has segments of the stories of our families interjected into the main narrative in chronological order.

Juggling these two narratives was not only a matter of finding the appropriate graphic technique, but it also reflects sensibilities that are central to current social theory and practice. They deal with the relationship between what we selectively observe, collect, and gloss as "data," and the ways in which we formulate them into arguments and, ultimately, abstract them into theoretical postulations. This major anthropological preoccupation since the 1980s is, of course, inspired by, and is an inspiration for, recent debates in literary criticism, philosophy, and history.[47]

Michel de Certeau describes stories as spatial practices, bearing reminders of our journeys to and fro in our constructed environments.[48] Persons occupy space, inhabit it, and move through it, turning it into place and imbuing it with meaning. Stories have value inasmuch as they convey this process, illustrate it, and give it shape.[49]

In a work dedicated to intersubjectivity in ethnographic writing, the anthropologist Michael Jackson illuminates some aspects of the journeys that writers take from personal narrative and subjective anecdote to abstract essays and scientific monographs.[50] It is a practice, he indicates, that goes back to the rise of modern science in the seventeenth century, when authority began to shift from direct testimony and immediate experience to abstract, less personal, panoptic discourse and the essay gradually replaced the story as an authoritative rendering of reality.

Theodor Adorno, who believes that essays do not ignore narratives but treat them and subsume them, approves of this modernizing trend. He sees essays as testimonies to the value of subjective experience, of irony, and of a personal angle in a world captivated by objectified, thematic argument. He thinks, moreover, that essays can bridge art and science.[51] Others are less inclined to celebrate this fusion. Walter Benjamin's concern is that the propensity of the positivist scientific revolution toward the abstract and the general robs us of the valuable human capacity to exchange experiences.[52] Jackson, who echoes this view, sees renditions of personal experience as constituting "a form of truth," rekindling the spirit of an era in which "wisdom and knowledge had not parted company."[53] And he reminds us of Hanna Arendt's poignant remark that stories are important because they can "reveal meaning without committing the error of defining it."[54]

Stories are an essential component in people's search for faith, for some provisional guidance. They make life bearable by reconciling us to the ways things are. Essays, on the other hand, purport, in the final analysis, to point at how the world should and perhaps could be. Making prudent use of the space that opens between the spontaneous inspiration of the storyteller and the considered argumentation of the essayist, and attempting to construct coherent and consistent narratives that will remain at peace with an empirical reality out there, is indeed a fundamentally exciting challenge for the social sciences.

Integrating the stories of our families into our essay invoked an array of fascinating issues. First, when the context is as politically charged as in the case in hand, the relationship between storytelling and essay writing becomes particularly loaded. All the more so when coauthors come from the opposite sides of the ethnonational divide that they explore and seek to analyze. Moreover, in our case, the stories integrated in the essay are those of the essayists themselves. Finally, we had to face the conundrum of coauthorship: the challenge of fusing two voices into a coherent, credible ensemble.

Johannes Fabian stresses the importance of the choice of tense and person in any given narrative.[55] Our choice was to present ourselves— Khawla, Dan—as the pivots of the stories of our families, to use past tense, and to refer to each of us in the third person singular (Khawla did this; Dan did that). We of course could have constructed a narrative in two separate, identified first-person singulars (I saw this, I felt that).[56] Such a strategy would have imbued the text with a more personal, committed flavor. Had we done so, however, we would have placed our readers, particularly Israelis and Palestinians but also others who identify with either side, in a situation they are all too familiar with: having to judge one narrative as more convincing, at the expense of the other. Using third-person singular for each of us enabled us to cultivate a voice that, while admittedly detached, personifies the spirit of our project: our narrative presents a Palestinian endorsing a representation configured by an Israeli, and an Israeli embracing a rendition constructed by a Palestinian.

Researching and retelling the stories of our families offered us a surprising second look at history. It was a journey that taught us, and, we like to think, those who have read the Hebrew and the Arabic editions of this book, how geopolitical realities—the strife these realities bring and the hope they sometimes inspire—play out in the experience of the family into which one is born and that one then perpetuates.

Amira Haas, whose articles for *Haaretz* have rightly earned her recognition and acclaim in Israel and beyond, cautions against the allure of storytelling.[57] She is frustrated, she says, with being linked to a metastory about peace. Nothing in the bigger picture she has been writing about from Gaza, Ramallah, Jerusalem, and Tel Aviv in recent years, she says, suggests that peace is in the making. On the contrary, the reality she has been writing about is one of entrenched occupation, structural conflict, and protracted bloodshed. It is her editors and readers who insist, in spite of her, that she writes "stories," and that these "stories" are about "peace."

Haas's complaint is a cautionary tale. It warns against confusing the substance, tone, or texture of a story with reality out there. The stories we incorporate into this book are not the best illustrations of what reality is like. Neither are they the most accurate representation of what it might have been or should be. Rather, they are included because of their capacity to help readers come to terms with versions of the past that are alien to them, and to do so even if they cannot quite determine whether these versions are real, conservative, exaggerated, consciously beefed-up, unconsciously imagined, or even fantasized. It is people's propensity to hear, apprehend, and accept personal anecdotes of yesteryear, we feel, that may help them think more positively about the future.

Chapter One

'Aarif Abu-Shamla was born in 1903 to a well-to-do rural family in Ya'abad, a village near Jenin in the West Bank.[1] An only son to his parents, he nevertheless left home at the age of eighteen and headed for the rapidly developing coastal town of Haifa.[2] He was not alone there. Other members of his extended family from Ya'abad and other villages in the northern part of the West Bank had settled in Haifa before. His aunt, who had married a man from the neighboring village of Keri, offered him a room in her apartment on Stanton Street in downtown Haifa, near the Shabib Café and the port.

Haifa was a natural choice for a young man of 'Aarif's ambitious character. Jenin and Nablus, the two Palestinian towns nearer his home village, were modernizing very slowly and offered limited scope for employment and progress.[3] Haifa, on the other hand, was developing quickly under British rule, destined to become a regional industrial center in the service of the empire.[4]

'Aarif found work in the customs office at Haifa port. A cornerstone of Britain's vision for the region, the port was growing rapidly in the early 1920s. Industrious, authoritative, but at the same time collegial and well liked, 'Aarif met success, becoming a manager in the customs service before he turned thirty. His position enabled him to help friends and relations find employment in Haifa. In fact, the clan-based solidarity they had all known in Ya'abad and its neighboring villages soon became a feature of their social world in Haifa too. They worked together, lived close to one another, and went out at night in a crowd. 'Aarif, who was known as an exquisite *dabka* dancer and who played a fine tune on the recorder, was a central figure at those gatherings.[5]

In 1923, 'Aarif married Maryam Sit-Abuha from the village of Keri. Their union was one component in a three-part marriage exchange, in which 'Aarif's two sisters married Maryam's two brothers, both of whom were merchants in Haifa.[6] A third brother had land and sheep in Umm al-Zinat, a village outside the town on the western slope of Mount Carmel.

'Aarif and Maryam settled in a large rented apartment in Stanton Street. In 1924 they had a baby daughter, Najiyah, the first of their seven children. Another daughter, Nazmiyah, born in 1938, remembers growing up in a bustling city. Haifa was lively particularly during the Muslim festive seasons, when villagers from all over northern Palestine would come to buy and sell. When her grandmother and aunts came into town to shop or obtain medical care, they stayed with the family. Another childhood memory Nazmiyah carries is that of Fatmah and Amaneh, her favorite teachers at al-Jam'iya Primary School.[7]

Nada, 'Aarif and Maryam's fifth child—Khawla Abu-Baker's mother—was born in 1936. She too went to al-Jam'iya on al-Nasrah Street.[8] One of her teachers there was the daughter of Sheikh 'Az al-Din al-Qasam, the martyred symbol of Palestinian nationalism whose death at the hands of British troops after an extended manhunt in 1935 was one of the triggers of the Arab Revolt of 1936–1939.

Nada recalls that Jews and Palestinians in her native Haifa lived in close proximity in mixed neighborhoods, mixed apartment buildings, and even shared flats. Her own parents, Maryam and 'Aarif, who sometimes let rooms in their six-room apartment, had a Jewish family—a couple and their nineteen-year-old daughter—as lodgers for a while in the 1940s. Nada recalls the two families as having separate routines and customs and maintaining only limited contact with one another. The Jewish lodgers, who were religious, consistently declined to eat the food prepared by Maryam. Only on Muslim holidays did they give in, politely tasting the festive dishes their landlady prepared. Nada remembers watching the Jewish man praying in the morning, leather bands wrapped around his arm. Like many Arab Jews who came to Palestine from Middle Eastern countries, this family spoke fluent Arabic. The Abu-Shamlas called them Yahud awlad 'Arab.[9]

Muhammad Abu-Baker was born in Ya'abad in 1924. When he was five, his mother passed away. At fourteen, tired of arguing with his father, he decided to join his kin in Haifa. One of them, a cousin, was 'Aarif Abu-Shamla, who fixed him up with work in the customs service. But Muhammad did not like the harbor. He soon left, got a job in a laundry, learned the trade, and later opened a laundry business of his own. His breakthrough came when the British army contracted him to clean and press uniforms of officers and servicemen based in and around Haifa.[10]

Muhammad's younger brother Mahmoud soon followed him to Haifa, where he became a porter, carrying loads off ships. The two siblings rented a room together from a fellow Palestinian, Na'im Abu-Sham.

·   ·   ·   ·   ·

By the early 1920s, the Arab community in Palestine was going through a process of modernization and urbanization, developing the elements and institutions of an organized civil society. As part of an open Arab Middle East, the Palestinians were responding to twentieth-century

European colonialism with their particular brand of protonationalism. Like other Arab national movements, it too was modeled after the post–Ottoman Turkish version of the ostensibly primordial ethnic state advocated by the Young Turks and personified in Kamal Ataturk.

Like other Arabs engaged in national movements, the Palestinians were groping for a sense of solidarity and nationhood under British rule. The events in Jerusalem and elsewhere during the Wailing Wall Revolt of 1929 and the Arab Revolt of 1936–1939 have since been identified as the defining moments of political consciousness and grassroots mobilization.[11] Throughout the period, however, citizens associations were developing in Palestinian cities—in the older centers like Jerusalem and Nablus and the up-and-coming coastal towns like Jaffa and Haifa. The role these processes would soon play in the political socialization of the Palestinians is seminal to the argument of generational development we bring here, and it merits some elaboration.

The British authorities had a relatively liberal policy toward citizens associations, particularly in the rapidly developing cities on the coastal plain. Trade union associations, women's organizations, political parties, sports clubs, youth movements, and paramilitary groups were allowed to operate relatively freely.[12] But the effects of the liberal policies of the British Mandate must not be overstated. The political socialization of the Palestinians is the legacy of a continuous, long-standing struggle, one that had begun in 1869, when the Ottoman education law became the formal foundation for state education in Palestine. In fact, education remains to date a locus of contention between the state and the Palestinian community, an arena where the right and the means to determine goals, curriculum, and administrative structures are hotly contested.[13]

The first step taken by the British that had a significant effect on education in Palestine was the transformation of the language of instruction in all schools from Turkish to Arabic. This came in response to a demand that Palestinian leaders and thinkers had been voicing for decades.[14] But important as it was, this transformation failed to redefine the supreme objective of the system—namely, the cultivation of loyalty to state and empire. To be sure, it was not replaced by any effort to stimulate national Palestinian consciousness. Rather, the British government imposed censorship policies that curbed the political activities of teachers both at school and after hours. Teachers were forbidden to express solidarity with political parties, let alone seek official membership. Educators were required to obtain permission from the state to publish books and articles and were not allowed to belong to many social movements. The British tolerated affiliation with sport clubs, branches of the British Council, and committees and local groups dedicated to improving the quality of life in the villages, all of which operated under strict British supervision. But an education law passed by the British in 1932 empowered the director general of education to fire teachers classified as "disloyal to the government." Few were in fact fired on such grounds: the implicit threat was enough to deter most teachers from activities that might have been construed as "disloyal."

Palestinians were part of an open Arab Middle East—a fluid, prestate situation, in which a person could take breakfast at home in Haifa, have lunch in Beirut, spend the night in Damascus, and the next day head for Baghdad. The Arab National Council, founded by Palestinians on the eve of the commencement of the British Mandate, supported the unification of "Greater Syria," including parts of present-day Israel, Syria, Jordan, and Lebanon, under the Hashemite king Feisal. The council's ideology was disseminated primarily through high school teachers.[15] Journals such as *Al-Nafais, Al-Assriyah, Al-Kafalah,* and *Al-Muntada* soon became important tools that linked political leaders and intellectuals in Palestine, Syria, and Lebanon, and that monitored developments in the educational system. Many of the investigative reports and complaints published in them were in fact written by teachers using pseudonyms.

Other publications were sponsored by private schools, including *Mejlat Kuliyat Terra Santa* (the *Terra Santa College Journal*) and *Mejlat Kuliyat al-Quds Lileshubban* (the *Al-Quds College Journal*), which gained some influence in local politics. Teachers, students, and alumni regarded them as platforms for the expression of political positions and national aspirations; these journals also provided an outlet for historical research unencumbered by imperial censorship. For most of these journals, circulation was not confined to the constituencies of the specific sponsoring institutions. The information, expressions of national sentiment, and call for politicization that they contained reflected and enhanced new forms of consciousness among Palestinians at large.

Though Palestinian class stratification was clear and rigid, and social gaps between urban Palestinians in the coastal towns and peasants in many countryside communities was considerable, the Palestinian community soon mustered an effective, anti-British national struggle, with strikes and protests in 1929 and, later, in 1936–1939 becoming key historical events.[16]

In the 1920s and 1930s, Palestinian intellectuals intensified their demands for changes in educational curricula. Their main point was that existing educational programs damaged Arab national values, fostered docile attitudes toward the British Mandate, and humiliated the Palestinian community. The British authorities rejected these demands, and the Palestinian leadership responded by resorting to alternative educational means in an attempt to introduce their own political ideas into the system. Poetry primers, required in school programs as early as first grade, were an important component of this effort, with Palestinian innovators successfully inserting Palestinian poetry into programs and curricula for most age groups. This was the Palestinian version of a widespread process in the Arab world whereby Arabic poetry became a major tool of political education and consciousness.[17]

Arabic radio broadcasts conveyed political messages to Palestinian youth at least as early as 1936. The poet Ibrahim Tukan, during his short-lived tenure as the director of the British-run Arabic radio station, contributed significantly to this effort. During his term, radio broadcasts transmitted lessons and lectures for schoolchildren modeled on content formulas developed by the national leadership. The British supervisors were quick to suppress this.

The Palestinian scout movement, established before World War I as an auxiliary force to aid the Ottoman army, retained its military form and structure under British rule. In this it was no different from scout troops throughout the British Empire and beyond. The content of its activity, however, was confined by the British authorities to the educational sphere, to the extent that, when the Arab rebellion broke out in 1936, the government prohibited the scouts from wearing uniforms. As is often the case with such attempts by colonial governments, the ban backfired, stimulating deeper commitment among Palestinian youths to the national cause. During the 1936–1939 rebellion, the scouts in fact undertook a number of nationalist tasks, including supervision of the Palestinian general strike and the anti-British economic boycott. The national leadership also used scouts to relay messages and convey materials to schools and political gatherings, including poems and patriotic texts banned by the British.

·   ·   ·   ·   ·

Asher (Oscar) Bodankin was born around 1883 in Pinsk, in the border zone between Byelorussia and Poland. He attended school in Pinsk, where he stood out as a bright, quick pupil. In 1908 he married Manya (Miryam) Veriyer, like him a native of Pinsk. Soon after their marriage, the couple migrated eastward into the Ukraine and settled in Kiev, where Asher had relatives and a good range of employment opportunities.

Asher was known for his sharp sense of humor and his keen interest in music. He once traveled two days by train to Odessa to see the renowned opera singer Feodor Shaliapin perform. Upon arrival in Odessa he discovered that all tickets at affordable prices had gone. Desperate to attend the concert, he paid what little money he had to a stagehand, who allowed him to enter a backstage corridor. To get a side view of the stage, however, he had to climb a rope dangling from the ceiling. He tied a large knot in the rope and viewed the concert seated on it.

Asher and Manya's eldest daughter, Nehama, was born in 1911. Their second daughter, Sarah—Dan Rabinowitz's mother—was born in 1918. When the family lived in Kiev, Asher's younger sister, Batsheva, lived with them, taking care of Nehama and Sarah when Manya was at work or shopping.

The Ukraine was badly hit by the extended period of unrest that swept the region in 1918. After the October revolution, Kiev became the

site of a bitter civil war between the revolutionary Bolsheviks and the
White army. Control over the city oscillated between the armies several
times. During the fighting in the spring of 1918, Asher and his family,
along with other relatives and neighbors, took shelter in the basement
of their apartment building. Gunfights raged outside between local
defenders and hoards of desperate and hungry soldiers whose affiliation was not even clear. Those in the basement were terrified that their
hideout would be discovered, and that the building would be looted
and the inhabitants robbed and murdered. Sarah, an infant less than six
months old, cried with hunger, and her mother, Manya, was unable to
console her. At one point, some of those huddled in the basement
demanded that Manya lie down on the infant to muffle her cries and, if
need be, that she choke the baby altogether. The family resisted. A terse,
hushed argument ensued. Fortunately, the voices of the soldiers outside
grew fainter before the argument came to a head. Sarah was saved.

In 1920, Asher and Manya left Kiev for a short spell in their native
town, Pinsk, before moving on to Stolin, where Asher found work as
chief accountant in a logging company. During their spell in Stolin, he
became interested in Zionism and the idea of going to Palestine. At one
point a Jewish National Fund emissary came to Stolin. He delivered a
stirring speech to the community, at the end of which he pitched the
crowd for donations to the fund. On their way home, Asher, who had
given generously, confronted his daughter Nehama, then ten or twelve
years old. Staring at the gold ring on her finger, he demanded to know
why she had not given it away. Eighty years later, Nehama recalled her
answer to him: "But Father, have you forgotten? I am just a child!"

For Asher, Zionism was both a fundamentally important ideology
and a practical solution to personal and familial strife. He saw the move
to Palestine as an opportunity to put an end to the family's wanderings
between Poland and the Ukraine and to start a better life in Palestine.
Manya, however, was unimpressed. She thought the notion of going "to
the desert" was a risky affair, and she took a while before deciding.
Eventually, however, she gave in. Her daughters Nehama and Sarah are
still convinced that the decision to opt for Palestine saved them from
the fate that befell the rest of their family—annihilation by the Nazis.

By the end of 1924, Asher Bodankin had saved a thousand pounds sterling, thus qualifying for the desired status of a "capitalist emigrant" to Palestine, as defined by the British. The family set off, traveling by rail through Warsaw to the Black Sea, then by ship to Haifa, where they arrived in January 1925. By that time, Haifa had become a stronghold of Jews from Pinsk. The Bodankins decided to join it and settled in the town. Asher's sister Bracha, who also made the trip to Palestine with her family, settled in Ra'anana in the coastal plane not far from Tel Aviv.[18] Another sister, Batsheva, the one who had looked after Nehama and Sarah in their early childhood in Kiev, and another brother, Berl, stayed behind in Poland.

Asher and Manya found an apartment near Jaffa Street in Haifa's German Colony, where their youngest son, Avraham, was born soon after their arrival.[19] Nehama and Sarah recall a sense of alienation, fear, and disassociation in the company of their Palestinian neighbors. In 1929, when Palestinians staged anti-British demonstrations and riots in the main cities, Jewish families in downtown Haifa often locked themselves in their apartments, fearing Palestinian violence. On one occasion the Bodankins joined another family who lived in a more massive neighboring building, where they all stayed for several days until the violence abated.

Nehama and Sarah attended Hareali School, a private school in the Germanic tradition established in Haifa in 1912. When she was sixteen, Sarah and some of her classmates joined the Jewish fighting force the Haganah. Their duties included standing guard at the entrance of the regional commander's office and delivering messages as couriers. Sarah was later trained in Morse code, and she served in the Haganah's communications platoon in Haifa.

Jewish immigrants in Haifa, particularly those who had professional training back in Europe, were able to capitalize on the dramatic process of development that took place there between the two world wars. New jobs were offered in industry and in the growing British bureaucracy. Businesses established by Jewish entrepreneurs and even British-owned firms tended to prefer Jewish employees, and Asher soon became chief accountant at Saker-Bromberg, importers of metal products from

Europe. He worked hard, gained a measure of economic independence, and, in the 1930s, managed to make an old dream of his come true: he sent Sarah and Nehama to obtain higher education in Europe. Nehama went in 1931 to study commerce at the Pitman School in London and later took French in Strasbourg. Sarah, who inherited her father's love of music, set out in late 1935 for Vienna, where she had been offered a place at the state academy of music. She was studying in Austria at the time of the 1938 Anschluss and has a vivid memory of Hitler's entry into the city in March of that year.[20] A few months later, at the eleventh hour, she hurriedly returned to Palestine.

World War II saw Palestine becoming a vital logistics and command base for the Allies. Massive British military presence stimulated growth and economic prosperity, but once again dividends were unevenly distributed. Jewish firms, organizations, and individuals benefited infinitely more than their Palestinian counterparts. Clearly, the Jewish community—the Yishuv, as it was called—made better use of the new political and economic circumstances to prepare for the future.

In the early 1940s, Asher tried to venture into business. He bought land, borrowed some money, and started building an apartment house in Hadar Hakarmel, a residential part of midtown Haifa. The initiative failed. Burdened by debt, he found himself at the mercy of a usurious loan shark. He lost his savings paying back the money and ended up extricating himself from the adventure by the skin of his teeth, left with only one apartment of the dozen in the building he had financed. Soon after, in 1943, although only in his mid-fifties, he died of a heart attack.

Meanwhile, as World War II raged all over Europe, the news of the fate of the Jews that slowly trickled in was too horrific to believe. The Bodankins in Haifa learnt that Asher's sister Batsheva, by then married and the mother of three, as well as Asher's brother Berl and his wife and children, had all been murdered by the Nazis in 1941 or 1942. In 2001, at the age of ninety, Nehama spoke of the loss of her beloved aunt as the "unhealed wound of my life." To this day, she said, she wakes up at night, haunted by horrifying images of what the final moments must have been like for Batsheva. She did learn that Batsheva had been brutally separated from her three daughters by the Nazis shortly before they all perished.

Three of Manya's sisters and their families were also murdered by the Nazis. A fourth sister, Anna, was expelled with her husband and their youngest daughter from Pinsk in 1939. The three spent the war years wandering in central Asia and in Europe, eventually arriving in Palestine in 1948. Anna's second daughter remained in Pinsk and was murdered by the Nazis. Her son, who was active in the Bund, a non-Zionist Jewish movement, was arrested by the Soviets and then handed over to the Germans, in whose custody he subsequently died.[21]

Two other sisters of Miryam survived the war—one lived in Kiev, the other in Bubrovsk. The seventh sister reached Israel in her old age, in the early 1970s.

·   ·   ·   ·   ·

In the aftermath of World War II, as the extent of the Holocaust became evident, an enormous wave of sympathy for the Jewish people engulfed the West. The standing of Zionism in Europe and North America was transformed—an occurrence that would have a fateful effect on the geopolitical reality of the Middle East. Governments as well as public opinion in the West now identified territorial Zionism as the inevitable political destiny of the Jewish people. This newly found global support for Zionism relieved some of the European guilt associated with the history of the Jews in Europe, including the Holocaust. In fact, the advent and success of the political program of Zionism in the coming years allowed Europeans to clear their conscience and set about their real priorities: the rebuilding of the continent and the regeneration of economic prosperity.

A political climate supportive to Zionism thus allowed the Jewish Agency for Eretz Yisrael (established in the first year of the century to coordinate and manage Jewish immigration and colonization in Palestine) and a number of other organizations associated with the Zionist establishment to work efficiently with displaced-persons camps in Europe. At these camps, they recruited hundreds of thousands of refugees for immigration to Israel and service in the Israel Defense Forces (IDF).[22] The British were ambivalent but, on the whole, cooperative. The restrictions they imposed on Jewish immigration from Europe beginning in

1946, and the incarceration camps they set up for illegal Jewish immigrants in Cyprus and in Palestine itself were circumvented by the Jewish community. Taking advantage of the partial and often ineffective nature of most British actions against arms stockpiling and mobilization, the protomilitary structures established by the Yishuv were gaining strength. Sporadic British moves in this cat-and-mouse contest, some of which produced encounters that still feature in the pantheon of Zionist symbols as heroic countercolonial episodes, did little to change the general picture. The 1940s witnessed consistent arms procurement by the Jewish forces in an intensive effort to be as ready and as well-equipped as they could possibly be in the impending struggle against the Palestinians.

The Palestinian response, in the meantime, was slow and sluggish. Most Palestinians were not alert to the implications of the Zionist plan. Few anticipated that historical inertia, which normally guarantees the inherent rights of native communities, could ever be destabilized. A firm, self-evident belief in natural justice numbed the Palestinians to the geopolitical upheaval that was brewing in the wings. The Palestinian leadership under Haj Amin al-Husseini, convinced that its stand was not only politically prudent but also inherently just, systematically rejected all proposals for territorial compromise with Zionism.[23] The independence gained at various stages since the 1920s by Egypt, Syria, Jordan, Lebanon, and Iraq had a profound influence on Palestinian thinking. The Palestinians, the leaders as well as the rank and file, had no reason to fear that their national future would be different from that of other Arab peoples.

On the eve of the fateful events of 1947–1948 the Palestinians thus had a false sense of security premised on the illusion that the future could only be an uninterrupted repetition of the present and the past. This was the politicocultural outlook of a generation of Palestinians that would become, virtually overnight, the tragic victims of the war of 1948.

The partition plan adopted by the General Assembly of the United Nations in November 1947 allotted the Jewish state eleven thousand square kilometers, mostly in areas where a Jewish majority already prevailed.[24] This territory was in fact home to some 520,000 Jews and 320,000 Palestinians. While it was clear that the remainder of Palestine would become an Arab state, the exact character of this state was never determined. The British wanted to confer the land on the Hashemites, a dynasty originating in Arabia that already ruled Transjordan under the British aegis. Other Western powers were more inclined toward a Palestinian state, possibly with Jerusalem as an extraterritorial enclave to be governed by the international community.[25]

The Palestinian refusal to accept any form of partition of their homeland was absolute—an adamant position that looms over the Israeli-Palestinian dispute to the present day. Many Israelis continue to view this refusal as a plausible explanation for the 1948 war. They often use it as a blanket justification of Israel's subsequent conquest of territories far greater than its share according to the U.N. plan and as the cause for the "inevitable" removal of the majority of Palestinians from these parts. For their part, some Palestinians refer to the partition plan's borders as a possible basis for future territorial compromise.

The resolution by the U.N. in favor of partition on November 29, 1947, triggered an immediate wave of Palestinian guerilla warfare against Jews, with hits and skirmishes in various parts of the country. December 1947 and early 1948 saw both sides using gunfire, explosive charges, car bombs, and roadblocks in an attempt to get the upper hand.

Immediately after the approval of the U.N. partition plan, Haifa, with seventy thousand Palestinians and seventy thousand Jews, went through a trying period. Gunshots and terror attacks scarred the city, and the Palestinian population felt increasingly insecure. Stories about massacres of Palestinians perpetrated by the Jewish Haganah and the Jewish right-wing underground Irgun Tzvai Leumi (Etzel) reached Haifa from the villages. It was rumored in the Palestinian fold that the Jews would plant false information about an impending attack in a particular village, thus enticing Palestinian men from neighboring villages to rush to the rescue, leaving their own homes vulnerable to the real attack. Palestinians began leaving their homes in villages around Haifa in search of more secure locations.

Insecurity prevailed in Haifa's Palestinian quarters. In most cases the topographic advantage of the Jewish neighborhoods, situated uphill, enabled armed combatants to observe targets in the Palestinian areas and shoot at them at will.

.   .   .   .   .

Explosions and the sounds of sharpshooter rounds became background noises for the Abu-Shamla family. In theory, the British army banned Jews from entering Palestinian quarters and vice versa. To this day, however, many Palestinians are convinced that, in the weeks before their final departure, the British were actively supporting Jewish actions against the Palestinians in Haifa.

One day in late 1947, Muhammad Abu-Baker and his brother Mahmoud were sitting with a group of friends at a store in downtown Haifa. A van went past them several times, but, having heard the driver speak Arabic in a local dialect, they did not register this as suspicious. Suddenly they saw the man abandon his vehicle at the top of the road, allowing it to roll out of control in their direction. Everyone understood what was about to happen and ducked for cover. Mahmoud, however, stayed in the middle of the road, yelling at the top of his lungs, perhaps to warn others: "The Haganah has invaded the street, the Haganah has invaded." The car bomb rolled down the street and exploded, destroying two residential buildings and a number of stores. Some twenty Palestinians were killed and many more were injured. The blast hurled Mahmoud twenty feet away. He landed on the road, caught under concrete beams that fell from a collapsing building. Brought to a hospital in Haifa in critical condition, he was later transferred to a hospital in Jenin, nearer his family, where he remained for almost eighteen months. Fifty-odd years later, at the age of seventy-five, Mahmoud still has respiratory problems caused by the injury.

In December 1947 and in early 1948, the number of gunfire clashes in Haifa increased. Palestinians now lived in fear for their lives. 'Aarif persuaded Maryam to take their six children and seek refuge with relatives in the village of Rumanah near Ya'abad, which they did. Three months later, however, Maryam became impatient with uncertainty and returned with her children to Haifa. "Our fate will be just the same as everyone else's," she said fatalistically. Soon after that, her seventeen-year-old son, Mohammad, joined the Arab Rescue Army (Jesh al-'Inqadh).[26]

•   •   •   •   •

The first quarter of 1948 saw sporadic actions on both sides develop into an all-out war. The Jewish community, while outnumbered by the Palestinian population, was otherwise better prepared. The Holocaust had solidified a sense of urgency and a realization that collective self-reliance is not only a good strategy but also, in certain historical circumstances, a blueprint for survival. This realization defined a sense of communal solidarity and willingness for personal sacrifice that enabled civilian and military institutions to achieve a high level of centralized organization. An effective comprehensive mobilization of the community ensued. Unlike the Palestinians, who knew from past experience that they could take temporary shelter in neighboring countries if war broke out, Jews in Palestine were convinced they had no real alternative but to stay put. This of course would have historic consequences. What began in late 1947 as a retreat of mainly urban Palestinians seeking temporary shelter with relatives and friends until the violence subsided became, with Israel's military successes in mid-1948, a systematic ethnic cleansing.

•   •   •   •   •

Toward the end of April 1948, leaflets circulated by the British in the Arab parts of Haifa promised the Palestinian residents an imperial guarantee of safety if they would leave for Lebanon or Syria. Escorted army trucks were made available to those who wanted to go, and some made their way east in small convoys. Najiyah, 'Aarif's and Maryam's eldest daughter, her husband, and their two children left for Syria under British escort. They would later find their way back to Jenin, in the Jordanian-controlled West Bank. Maryam, whose siblings had property in Haifa and refused to leave, chose to remain with them.

At the end of April 1948, the Haganah had taken over most Palestinian neighborhoods in Haifa. Using loudspeakers, the British army announced that anyone wishing to protect themselves should leave their homes immediately and head toward the port. Jewish snipers fired sporadically as Palestinians rushed toward the harbor. Maryam grabbed her smaller children; took their birth certificates, a set of clothes for each, a blanket, and some money; and, after locking her apartment carefully, walked with them toward the harbor. Her son Muhammad, by then a regular member of the Arab Rescue Army, refused to join them. Her eldest son, Ahmad, who had recently married his maternal cousin, was torn between his own family and that of his wife, whose parents had recently left for Syria. The last encounter Maryam had with Ahmad was a dramatic, frantic exchange in the middle of the road in downtown Haifa. She implored him to stay with her in Haifa, but moments later he was off with his wife to join her family in Syria, where he would remain a refugee for the rest of his life. Maryam, who never saw her eldest son again, grieved their separation until her death years later. Ahmad's relatives in Israel have yet to meet his offspring, who are still living in refugee compounds in Syria.

Maryam took her children to the pier. Her husband, 'Aarif, joined the crowd a little later. The British officers ushered the masses toward a barge, which, anchored at the pier, appeared to be a part of it. Then suddenly the barge was afloat, possibly being towed by another vessel. The surprise was total. Most of those aboard had never sailed before. Many did not grasp that the British were in fact taking them away from their hometown.

Maryam became seasick as the unexpected journey started, and she could not look after her children. Nazmiyah, one of the older daughters, took hold of her baby sister, Hiyam. But before long Nazmiyah, too, was ill and started vomiting. The crew on board the barge took care of Hiyam until the raft reached Acre.

Despite their desire to stay in Haifa and guard their property, Maryam's siblings—four brothers and a sister—were forced to leave everything behind and join the others at the harbor. By the end of that fateful day, all members of the extended family had become refugees. Some who managed to cross the front line and find their way to their native village on the West Bank were expelled a second time when the IDF took it a few weeks later. This time they went as refugees to Irbid in Transjordan. The property the family had in Haifa and in Umm al-Zinat

was lost. 'Aarif's sister, concerned about her physically disabled husband, was apprehensive of the lot awaiting them as refugees in Acre. She decided to return to their parental home in Ya'abad, where she hoped it would be easier for her and her kin to look after her husband. Nazmiyah would not see Fatmah and Amaneh, the primary schoolteachers she so admired and who disappeared during the war, ever again.

Muhammad Abu-Baker, twenty-four at the time, also arrived at Haifa port, where he found many relatives, neighbors, and acquaintances. Before he left, he managed to lock his store, but he failed to take any possessions with him. He was convinced that their absence would be short-lived, and that he would return to normal life in Haifa soon. Pushed to and fro with the others on the pier, he finally found himself sailing to Acre. In the commotion on the vessel, an infant fell overboard. Muhammad, not a particularly good swimmer, jumped after her, grabbed her, and was himself rescued by others who pulled him and the infant back on board.

．　　．　　．　　．　　．

By late spring and summer 1948, the Israeli thrust was clear: to secure as much land as possible with as few Palestinians on it as possible. This objective was attained in ways that far exceeded expectations. By the end of the war, the Israel Defense Forces had conquered some nine thousand square kilometers over and above the area earmarked by the U.N. plan for the Jewish state. Some 750,000 Palestinians who formerly lived in the twenty thousand square kilometers that eventually remained under Israeli control became refugees. More than four hundred Palestinian villages and a number of thriving urban communities were no more.[27]

These losses constituted what Palestinians refer to as al-Nakbah, the catastrophe. Those Palestinians who remained under Israel's jurisdiction after the war numbered some 160,000—less than a fifth of the territory's original Palestinian population. The urban middle class vanished almost entirely, leaving behind mainly uneducated and often landless peasants.

Half of them were displaced persons—internal refugees whose native communities had been destroyed, now forced to start over as poor, humiliated guests in Palestinian communities that somehow survived.[28] The demographic and geographic shock was shattering. Those Palestinians who remained and then became citizens of Israel were reduced to a generation of survivors.

.   .   .   .   .

In 1939, shortly after Sarah Bodankin returned from her truncated sojourn at the academy of music in Vienna, she met Leonard (Lenny) Rabinowitz, a young lawyer who had recently arrived in Haifa from South Africa.

Born in Johannesburg in 1912 to a Lithuanian Jewish family that had come to South Africa in the 1890s, Lenny was part of the first cadre of young Zionist leaders in South Africa. One of the founders of Habonim, along with Louis Pinkas, Colin Gluckman-Gilon, Saul Friedman, and others, Lenny joined the first wave of new immigrants from South Africa to Palestine.[29] He first arrived in the country in 1935 as a journalist assigned to cover the South African delegation to the first Maccabiah—an all-Jewish sports competition modeled after the Olympic games organized in Palestine, then Israel, once every four years as of 1931. During this visit he met the educator Dr. Arthur Biram, founder and director of the Hareali School in Haifa, who persuaded him to join the school as an English teacher. Lenny agreed and remained in Haifa. His parents and seven siblings stayed in South Africa. The youngest, Herbert, came to Israel with his family in 1960, as did two of Lenny's nieces and a nephew later on.

When Lenny met Sarah in late 1938, he was working as an attorney for Solomon and Lifschitz, a leading law firm in Haifa. He was active in the Notrim (sing. Noter) framework—a small, mobile Jewish defense force operated with British consent. As a Noter he took part in "tower and stockade" operations, in which an entire new Jewish frontier settlement would be erected overnight on land purchased by the Jewish

Agency, using prefabricated wooden elements for a perimeter fence and essential structures. He was particularly proud of having taken part in the dramatic first ascent in 1938 to Hanita, a kibbutz located on a mountain ridge near the Lebanese frontier. At Solomon and Lifschitz, Lenny became an expert in land issues and was often sent to handle land purchase negotiations between the Jewish Agency, local groups of Jewish settlers, and Palestinian landowners.

Lenny and Sarah were married in September 1939 in a double wedding. Nehama, Sarah's elder sister, was married on the same occasion, to Moshe Blaizer, a native of the veteran Jewish agricultural settlement of Kfar Tavor in Lower Galilee. The ceremony took place on the evening immediately after Yom Kippur, days after the start of World War II.

After her return from Vienna in 1938, Sarah had a number of piano recitals and played in some chamber music ensembles. By and by, however, she abandoned her dream of being an internationally known pianist. After her marriage in September 1939, she began giving piano lessons, and, between 1940 and 1947, she gave birth to Daphna, Asher, and Carmel. Her duties as a mother and teacher, along with her appearances in local, small-scale concerts, filled her life. Lenny continued work as an attorney with Solomon and Lifschitz until 1947, when he was offered a position in Binyan, a mortgage company established by the Zionist Federation of South Africa to provide building credit for construction projects in Palestine.

By the time the 1948 war broke out, Sarah and Lenny Rabinowitz were living in a rented two-room apartment on Kidron Street on Mount Carmel. The war, however, never truly reached the family's apartment. Battles fought in Haifa during April 1948 took place in the lower sections of the town, far from the residential neighborhoods on the mountain. The curfew imposed by the British during the summer of 1947, and again just prior to their final departure in May 1948, is inscribed in the family's memory more vividly than gunfire exchanges, bombs, or other forms of clashes between Jews and Palestinians. Sarah recalls how Lenny, who owned a private car, occasionally had to make his way to the office downtown in a convoy, escorted by British armored vehicles.

The mass departure of Palestinians, who within a few days in late April and early May 1948, became nameless refugees, is not really a part of the family members' recollections. The facts must have trickled into their consciousness by way of rumor, newspaper reports, and radio broadcasts. Those who had gone, while not quite neighbors, were after all fellow residents, clients, and providers of services. But since the family saw no crowds of refugees actually fleeing or being expelled, the harsh reality was conveniently omitted from their consciousness.

The years 1947–1948 were difficult ones for Lenny and Sarah, and not only because of the war. Lenny found little interest or joy in banking, and in early 1948 he decided, in consultation with the management, to terminate his work at Binyan. Having left first Solomon and Lifschitz and then the mortgage company, he was ill at ease. Life in the small apartment was crowded. The three children slept in one small bedroom; Sarah and Lenny made their bed every night in the living room, where Sarah also gave her piano lessons in the afternoon. Lenny, a lean, modest, shy man, was more of a reserved English gentleman than a coarse Israeli Sabra.[30] His comportment did not match the image of the new Israeli, a sociocultural construction speeded and accentuated by the war. His contribution to the military effort was marginal and had peaked a decade earlier, with his rather unglamorous affiliation with the British-sanctioned Notrim force. If anything, his sense of marginality was only sharpened by the war.

He was not alone. The Zionist canon, depicting an unproblematic, burgeoning national project miraculously transforming and uniting diasporic Jews, was in many ways a myth. The Jewish community in Palestine and later Israel had many men and women who did not fit in. Like others, Lenny brought with him from his previous home a foreign accent, foreign attire, and other cultural baggage that made him stand apart from the ideal image of the Sabra. This new icon, manufactured by a new elite that utilized it as a stepping-stone for social advancement, was never cast in his shape.

But Lenny's vulnerability went beyond his misalignment with the mythological image of the new Israeli. There was something hesitant and insecure about him, a vulnerability exacerbated by war, occupational crisis, and the responsibility of providing for three small children (the youngest was four months old when the war erupted) at a time of great uncertainty.

In the summer 1948, the tension in Haifa eased off. Almost the entire Palestinian population had gone. The war had been essentially decided. The remainder of that fateful year still saw an Israeli campaign of conquest, ethnic cleansing, and transgression, but most incidents took place in territories that lay beyond the boundaries of the Jewish state assigned by the 1947 U.N. partition plan. That summer, Lenny and Sarah took their children for a long visit to South Africa. It was more than merely a vacation or an opportunity to visit family. Their sojourn in Johannesburg lasted more than six months and was partly an attempt to convalesce, regroup. Daphna, their eldest daughter, who turned eight when the family was in South Africa, attended grade three at the primary school in Rosebank, a suburb of Johannesburg.

But a new state had been established in Palestine, and a new bureaucracy was rapidly replacing old British institutions. Lenny's friends—including his childhood mate Colin Gilon (then still Gluckman), recently appointed as state attorney general; Haim Cohen, who became chief legal adviser to the government and later a Supreme Court justice; Joe Kokiyah, appointed district attorney of the Jerusalem district; and others—sent dispatches to Lenny in South Africa urging him to return and join the budding legal system of the new state. The familiar Zionist combination—the urge to be a part of the national project and the desire to seize an opportunity for personal advancement—was in play again. In April 1949, Lenny, Sarah, and the children returned to Haifa. Lenny was appointed district attorney of the Haifa district.

Sarah and Lenny, unsettled by professional and personal crisis earlier in 1948 and by a spell abroad that failed to yield an alternative to life in Palestine, looked at a brighter future after their return to Israel. Lenny had a senior government position much more suitable for him than anything in the private sector. Sarah was poised to make the most of Haifa's rapid growth and consolidate her practice as a music teacher. The Jewish community had a sense of solidarity, optimism, and a new confidence in its ability to shape its destiny. It was the start of a new era, with the promise of a better life for all.

In spite of this recovery—or perhaps because of it—the narrative of 1948 adopted by the family remains fragmentary and incomplete. Jewish heroism in the war, for example, is absent from it. It is as though the war, whose legacy became a central building block for Israeli identity, had taken place elsewhere or had been fought by others. Somehow it seems to have bypassed the family's emotional universe.

Significantly, the family's narrative also lacks concrete awareness of the Palestinian tragedy. The disappearance of tens of thousands of people who, not so long before, had been colleagues and clients, or even strangers sharing the same streets and landscapes, never fully registered and does not seem to have exacted emotional costs such as regret or a sense of responsibility or guilt. The moral paradox inherent in the building of a new triumphalist society on the ruins of another was never tackled. Rather than defining itself against the tumultuous historical events it had experienced, the family downplayed them and forgot them. Like the members of Sarah's family who had been murdered by the Nazis but whose deaths were somehow muffled in her own memory, the events of 1948 were largely silenced. There were no exalted tales of Jewish bravery, nor was the Palestinian calamity explicitly denied. Instead there were thick lumps of silence.

Chapter Two

The Abu-Shamlas reached Acre as part of a continuous stream of displaced Palestinians the day it was captured by the Israeli forces. The
men were rounded up and arrested. 'Aarif and his son Mohammad,
who at thirteen looked older than his age, were no exception. For three
long months Maryam turned up every morning at the police headquarters to plead for her son until she finally convinced the officers in
charge to let him go. Most men, including 'Aarif, were detained for
more than eighteen months. No indictments or legal proceedings of any
kind were ever filed.

Nada, twelve at the time, and her younger sister Nazmiyah, recall
how in their first few days in Acre, thousands of incoming displaced
Palestinians gathered in the al-Jazzar mosque in the old city, sleeping
in the courtyards and on the floor of the great hall. At first they all

believed it would be only days before they were allowed to return to their homes. The army, however, had other plans. The road from Acre south, toward Haifa, was blocked; the old walled city was cordoned off and isolated from the newer quarter, trapping those in and around the mosque. Initially, travel out of town was impossible: it required special travel permits from the army, and none were being issued. Soldiers fired shots at anyone attempting to escape or otherwise break the harsh rules that the IDF imposed on the conquered town. Only the sea route north, to Lebanon, was kept deliberately open.

Shortly after the IDF took over, it found Palestinian residents of Acre who had stayed put despite the hostilities and appointed them as members of a board of trustees. The board assumed responsibility for providing the incoming flow of displaced families with food, shelter, and other basic needs. On a number of occasions, members of the board broke into empty homes of Palestinians who had fled to Lebanon and made them available for displaced families. Nazmiyah recalls that the family, along with their paternal aunt and other relatives from Haifa, some thirty people all told, slept in a large room of a Palestinian house that had been opened by the board.

With time, this temporary measure tended to become a permanent solution. Its consequence can still be felt in some of the more impoverished and rundown quarters in mixed towns inside Israel today.[1] More than fifty years later, many of the displaced families are yet to fully recover from the social, economic, and emotional trauma of 1948.

In the spring and summer of 1948, many Palestinian refugees and displaced persons were malnourished, sometimes hungry. In Acre many lived on bread and olives. Only the more affluent families, mainly local ones who had remained in Acre, could occasionally afford the luxury of canned meat or other forms of more substantial nourishment. The International Red Cross, the presence of which began to be felt in Acre soon after the hostilities abated in late spring, gave away ration cards to help regulate the distribution of basic foodstuffs. With time, these ration cards, called by the Palestinians Kart Mu'an, became a precious thing for the internally displaced—the first form of documented identification officially sanctioned by the state of Israel.

.   .   .   .   .

In the immediate aftermath of the war, Palestinian refugees in Palestine/Israel, Lebanon, Syria, Jordan, Gaza, and beyond were preoccupied primarily with the realities and hardships of survival. Families were fragmented and impoverished, uprooted from their birthplaces and communities of origin. Survival required unrelenting effort. Getting through the bitterly cold, snow-filled winter of 1950 in temporary domiciles, finding food for children, looking for work, and scraping together an income were all-consuming tasks.[2] Uncertain of the fate of their dispersed kin, people were losing hope of reunification. Many were shocked, unable to fathom why they personally and the nation as a whole were being subjected to such a cruel fate.

The hope of many refugees and displaced Palestinians that help would come from Arab states which would turn around their destiny was quickly dashed. Instead they began to realize that the war they had just lost was destined to have irreversible and lasting outcomes. Those in refugee camps outside Israel were preparing for long-term, even though temporary, life in exile. Those within were reluctantly beginning to come to terms with being subjects of a state imposed on them, one that transformed them from an indigenous majority to a trapped minority.[3]

From its early days, Israel extended formal citizenship to the Palestinians who remained within its borders. The Palestinians were included in the first population census in 1949 and were given the right to vote and be elected to the Knesset, Israel's parliament, in the first general elections that same year. This notwithstanding, Israel also subjected them to a host of dominating practices. One was a discursive move involving the state's introduction of a new label to denote them: the hyphenated construct "Israeli Arabs" ('Aravim-Yisraelim) or, sometimes, "Arabs of Israel," ('Arviyey-Yisrael).

The new idiom Israeli Arabs, while purporting to be no more than a technical, bureaucratic label, evidenced a deliberate design. A clear reflection of the politics of culture via language, it intentionally misrecognized the group's affinity with and linkage to Palestine as a territorial unit, thus facilitating the erasure of the term *Palestine* from the Hebrew vocabulary.[4] The term puts "Israel" in the fore, constructing it as a defining feature of "its" Arabs.[5] The Palestinians, already uprooted in the physical sense of the word, were also transformed into a group bereft of history.

Moreover, the term *Israeli Arabs* invokes spatial diffusion. *Arab* is a term applied to hundreds of millions in highly diverse groups from the Atlantic to the steppes of central Asia. The Arabs may have common cultural denominators, but they have no unitary territorial focus. *Israeli Arabs,* which obliterates any suggestion that the group in question is related to a territory, is a label the ethnoterritorial project called Israel could easily embrace.

The label *Palestinians,* on the other hand, signifies an obvious link to a specific territory—the one where Israel had been established. Most Israelis of course refuse to recognize that the land in which they live was until recently the communal home of Palestinians. The notion that the land they see as theirs is the national home and cultural cradle of others is anathema to them, one that breeds amnesia and denial.

The adoption of the nomenclature *Israeli Arabs* was just one element in a web of multifaceted hegemonic processes that were unfolding in the 1950s. The generation of survivors, the label we suggest for those Palestinians who remained within the state of Israel after 1948, denotes a new demographic, geographic, and political reality. Approximately 85 percent of the Palestinians who, prior to 1948, had lived in the territory that would be subsumed within the state of Israel, were now outside it. With hundreds of communities turned into rubble and ash, the capacity of the survivors to defend their rights or otherwise maintain their individual and collective sense of dignity was decimated. The personal, familial, communal, economic, and cultural rupture was indeed extreme.

·   ·   ·   ·   ·

With her husband 'Aarif and her thirteen-year-old son, Mahmoud, in jail; her eldest son, Ahmad, a refugee in Syria; and her second son, Muhammad, who had left with the defeated Arab Rescue Army, somewhere in Jordan, Maryam was alone with her daughters in Acre. Coping with poverty and hunger, she soon found, was every bit as oppressing as the pains of separation. Coming from a relatively well-to-do urban family, she had never imagined herself as an employee. With nothing better available, however, she had to find a job. She managed to put it off for a few months, but finally came to terms with her reality and joined other displaced women who found employment as fruit pickers in olive and orange groves near Acre. The groves, which had belonged to wealthy Palestinians prior to the war, had since been seized by neighboring kibbutzim and individual Jewish farmers, who then employed Palestinian refugees to work in them. As an urbanite, Maryam came to work draped in a black veil, insisting on covering her face with the cumbersome cloth despite the blazing heat.

Nazmiyah remembers that, during the hard times that characterized their early days in Acre, she sometimes joined her mother picking fruit while her older sister Nada took care of little Hiyam. Winters were cold, and there was very little clothing. Most of what they wore came from distributions by the Palestinian board of trustees. Blankets came from the Red Cross. Schools started functioning properly only in the autumn of 1950, some eighteen months after the family moved to Acre.

Women, particularly single ones and those whose husbands were away, were especially vulnerable to attack. A Christian neighbor of the Abu-Shamlas, a woman from al-Ma'aalik Alley in the old city, was alone at home with her young son and daughter while her husband went to Lebanon to arrange for them to move there. Shortly after his departure, three Jewish soldiers broke into her apartment and gang-raped her. She screamed for hours. Her neighbors, woken by her yells, listened in the dark, too terrified and helpless to attempt a rescue. Healthy men were all in prison; those at home were elderly or ill, and were subject to a tightly enforced night curfew. None had weapons, and they all knew that Israeli soldiers, once threatened, would shoot without warning. The following day some of the neighbors who had been mute witnesses to the nocturnal atrocity departed for Lebanon.

Since Maryam had no financial and familial support to speak of, her anxiety for her daughters and their future intensified. Whenever she

heard the footsteps of Jewish soldiers walking nearby, she hid Nada
and Nazmiyah behind mattresses for fear they might be raped. Many
parents hastily married off young daughters to ensure that they would
be protected from such violence. Three twelve-year-old girls from the
immediate neighborhood were thus betrothed and immediately left
their families to join their husbands in the camps in Lebanon.

Like many displaced Palestinians, Maryam was given to depression
that gradually became chronic. Overwhelmed by hardship and anxiety,
she and her neighbors would meet each evening after work to lament
their bitter fates. The daily gathering became the main emotional outlet
for these sad women—the only avenue they had to ease the pain that
defined their recent personal and familial lives and transformed them
forever. Forty-five years on, members of the second and third generations, men and women still suffering the consequences of their parents'
depression, seek help at the therapeutic clinic that Khawla, Maryam's
granddaughter, runs in Acre.

.   .   .   .   .

While the hostilities were largely over by the autumn of 1948, Israel nevertheless imposed military rule on all Palestinians under its jurisdiction.
This system of control, premised on British Emergency Regulations, subjected the Palestinians to a vast array of draconian restrictions.[6] It enabled
military district governors to confine them to specific areas, the boundaries of which could be arbitrarily redefined, and vested the military with
most civil powers. Permits to travel outside the village and the region,
work permits, planning permits for the construction of homes and other
buildings, family unification certificates, and many others now depended
on the governor's approval.

The generation of survivors watched despondently as the state constructed an elaborate structure of legal and judiciary instruments designed to consolidate the transfer of conquered Palestinian lands to Jewish ownership.[7] Knesset laws, particularly the Absentee Property Law
(1950) and the Acquisition and Compensations Act (1953), along with a
number of significant modifications to preexisting British laws, created a

coherent legalistic veneer to the wholesale appropriation of Palestinian assets.

For hundreds of thousands of Palestinians who were now refugees in Arab states, the Absentee Property Law (1950), designed primarily to rule out their chances of holding on to legal rights in land, was a particularly heavy blow. This law, however, was also harsh on internally displaced Palestinians who, having been expelled or having fled during the war, had managed to find sanctuary in other Palestinian communities inside Israel. Defined under the new law as "present absentees," Palestinians included in this oxymoronic category found their assets officially classified as abandoned property.[8]

They soon learned this term had dire consequences. Property labeled "abandoned," it turned out, was automatically placed in the control of the custodian of absentees' property—a state official at the powerful and efficient Ministry of the Treasury. In the agricultural periphery many Palestinians watched helplessly as their fields and houses, now legally appropriated by the state as abandoned property, were given to kibbutzim, moshavim, and later, new towns developed by the state.[9] In more metropolitan urban centers such as Jaffa, Haifa, Lid, and al-Ramleh, properties were made available to the new immigrants arriving in vast numbers from Europe, Asia, and North Africa.

Between 1949 and 1953, most Bedouin residents of the Negev were forcibly removed from their ancestral territories. Some were cast across the border, either into the hills of Hebron in the Jordanian-controlled West Bank or the southern Arava Valley. Others were removed to the desolate triangular region lying roughly between Be'er-Sheva, Arad, and Dimona. In 1950, Israeli authorities completed the expulsion of Palestinian residents of Majdal (Ashkelon) in the south, Ikrit and Biram in the north, and other villages elsewhere.[10]

·   ·   ·   ·   ·

Some time after they arrived in Acre, Maryam was granted permission to visit Haifa for a few hours. She arrived at her house on Stanton Street and discovered that Israeli looters had broken into it. Mattresses had been cut open and the entire contents of the food closet spilled on the floor.[11] The pillaged home aggravated Maryam further, intensifying her depression and her sense of loss. She summoned whatever strength she had, collected family pictures and children's clothes that she found scattered in the apartment, and prepared to leave. This time she could not even lock the door, which had been broken by the looters. She found a rope, tied the door shut, and raced away, desperate to make it back to Acre before her travel permit expired at nightfall.

A few months later she returned to Stanton Street, only to find it occupied by a family of Moroccan Jews whom the government had housed there. The new residents "allowed" her to enter and look for the remainder of her things. She found none of her belongings, and the new inhabitants could not provide a clue as to what had become of them. She stood there, a hapless stranger in her own home. Did she decide when to go? Was she asked to leave? Kicked out? Whatever happened in her apartment that day, her visit added one more layer to her sense of rage and loss. She returned to the circle of refugee women in Acre with yet another trauma to be woven into their laments.

Having returned from South Africa to Haifa in 1949, Lenny and Sarah Rabinowitz and their children lived in the same rented apartment they had occupied before the trip, on Kidron Street on Mount Carmel. Daphna, who was ten years old, remembers her first sight of snow during the freak winter of December 1950, when she slid on a makeshift sledge down Moriah Avenue near home.

The apartment was small, and the couple dreamed of acquiring a better one. One day in 1951 the telephone rang in Lenny's office. It was an old friend, a lawyer who had connections with the office of the custodian of absentees' property in Haifa. "Lenny," he said, "if you're looking for trouble, poke your nose into number 19 Panorama Road." Lenny, who could not leave the office in the middle of the morning, immediately called Sarah, who took only minutes to catch a bus. When she arrived at the address, she found a splendid stone house with four apartments. The one on the ground floor had six rooms and a huge balcony overlooking Haifa Bay. The house, it turned out, had been con-

structed in the early 1930s by a Christian German industrialist who
lived in it until World War II started. In Palestine as elsewhere, once the
war broke out all Germans were declared enemy subjects, to be arrested
or deported. Their properties, including 19 Panorama Road, were
seized by the Custodian of Enemy Property.

The ground-floor apartment, which was particularly attractive to
Sarah, had been used by the British during the war to house senior
army officers. When the war ended, the place was rented to British
clerks and businessmen. At the time Lenny was tipped off by his
friend, the lodgers who had used it last were about to leave and
return to England.

Sarah called Lenny and told him what she saw. When he was done
with work that afternoon, he headed straight to Panorama Road. The
apartment was locked and empty. He went around the back, found an
external staircase that led to the large balcony, threw a blanket atop an
old mattress he found there, and spent the night. He knew an overnight
stay had legal consequences that could prove significant should someone else turn up and make a bid for the apartment. In the morning he
wasted little time in calling the custodian's office, filed an offer for the
apartment, and got the keys as well as the custodian's official provisional permission to move in. The actual process of purchasing the
apartment lasted more than a year and was officially sealed long after
the family had moved in. The sum required by the state as purchase
payment was huge by the couple's standards, and the deal could be
concluded only with the help of Lenny's older siblings in South Africa.
Some of the money was granted by them as a gift, some as an advance
against Lenny's share in the modest inheritance that would be left by
their elderly parents.

By and by, the Israeli army began issuing more travel permits for Palestinian citizens. Some were ad hoc, others longer term, allowing people
to enter towns and rural settlements in the Jewish regions for several
hours every day. Maryam's friends persuaded her to seek work as a
laundry hand in Jewish homes in Haifa. It would, they said, be an easier and more secure job than picking fruit. Maryam agreed, sought such

employment, and found it. For several years her work became the main source of income for the family.

'Aarif found it trying. Having been released from prison in late 1949, he was unemployed for almost five full years—a fate shared by many Palestinian men, particularly those who, like him, had been displaced during the war. The humiliation caused by unemployment was compounded by the fact that his wife was now the main breadwinner. The talented flute minstrel, the hero of the dabka dances in prewar Haifa, became a bitter, agitated man.

Maryam learned how to slip through Wadi A'ara across the Green Line into the West Bank, now under Jordanian rule.[12] She visited her brother and sister in Rumanah, saw her daughter in Jenin, and looked up her husband's relatives in Ya'abad. During one of these hurried visits, she met her son Muhammad, who had joined his kin after a few years of wandering in Lebanon, Syria, and Transjordan. On her next visit to Ya'abad, Maryam took her baby daughter, Hiyam, along. This enabled her to stay with her relations a whole week, during which she found an opportunity to ask her brother to give his daughter Lutfiyah's hand in marriage to her son Muhammad. Her brother consented, and a complicated operation to have the young couple take legal residence in Israel began.

First Lutfiyah was brought to Haifa by the Red Cross. Then the family applied for a reunification permit for Muhammad so the marriage could take place. The permit was finally granted, and Muhammad, who returned from the West Bank, married his cousin Lutfiyah in Haifa. A few months later, however, the government discovered that some of his documents had been forged. Lutfiyah was already pregnant, but the government was unyielding. Muhammad was unceremoniously deported to the West Bank. His son, 'Aarif, who was born in 1951, spent the first part of his life without his father. Their first reunion, organized by the Red Cross, was not until 1960. Once reunited, Lutfiyah and Muhammad chose to stay away from Israel, taking residence in Tubas on the West Bank.

.   .   .   .   .

One of the consequences of 1948 was that many Palestinian families, now shattered and dispersed, had to decide which segments of the kin group would have a chance to reunite and who would stay estranged. International agreements did not facilitate complete family reunification. In fact procedures ratified by Israel, designed primarily to dilute the Palestinian population, often discouraged reunification. For one segment of a given family to be allowed to return, others were forced to give up their hopes to do the same. This predicament in many ways prevails to date. In fact, many Palestinians fear that if a peace agreement is signed between Israel and Palestine that does not include a comprehensive solution encompassing all refugees, the problem will be perpetuated.

The Palestinians who remained within the state of Israel after the war of 1948 were in a difficult situation. Humiliated by the defeat, shocked and disoriented by its consequences, they were also restricted by and dependent on the state in virtually every aspect of their daily lives. Military rule, while obviously the most visible and physically oppressive mechanism of control, was not the only one. It was augmented by the increasingly influential security service (later renamed the General Security Service, known by its Hebrew acronym *Shabak*) and by special segregated sections of most ministries designed to govern the Palestinians as a de facto separate category of citizens.

In the early decades following 1948, the Palestinian citizens of Israel displayed three main political trajectories:[13] an inclination toward Israeli-Arab politics, which sought to assert a pacified, nonconflictual presence within the Israeli system and earn whatever political and economic rewards the state might care to offer individuals and kin groups; the Communist trajectory, which preferred to frame collective grievances in terms of a class struggle and tended to seek help and protection from the Soviet bloc; and the nationalist trajectory, which, inspired by pan-Arabism and Nasserist ideologies, preferred to forgo immediate benefits, accentuate the national character of the local struggle, and wait for a comprehensive victory of Arabism that would earn the Palestinians full political redemption.[14]

Ghanem's analysis of the main ideological trajectories is probably correct. It may even be the case that popular support for these political trajectories was evenly distributed, reflecting politicized sensibilities evident within the Palestinian fold since the 1920. This notwithstanding, our own characterization of the generation of survivors hinges on the distinction between political awareness, which was indeed diverse and rich, and political agency, which at the time was choked by external circumstances.

It was the limitations set on agency, not poor political awareness, that shaped behavioral patterns of Palestinian adults in the 1950s in the face of Israeli power. The first priority was to survive, even if it meant bottling up existential bitterness and rage. Representatives of the state were greeted humbly: *Naʿam ya sidi* (literally phrased, Yes, my elder) is one representative idiom—a phrase connoting alienated courtesy, fear, and contempt, all disguised in proper formal parlance. Behind closed doors different utterances reflected hopes that the need for submission to this detested fate was only temporary. The proverb *Hakmak zalmak tishki hamak lamin?* (When the one who rules you is also he who abuses you, where can you carry your complaint?) captures this tension most succinctly.

Much has changed since the 1950s in terms of political agency and empowerment among the Palestinian citizens of Israel, as well as in the rules of Israel's politics. The stifled circumstances that prevailed at that time, however, crystallized a pattern of majority-minority relations and minority-state relations that die hard.[15] In some respects, the tension defining this pattern persists.

·   ·   ·   ·   ·

Some five years after he became a refugee in Acre, Maryam's husband, ʿAarif, had a chance encounter with the Israeli man who, years earlier, had been his supervisor at Haifa port. The man, who had been under the impression that ʿAarif had become a refugee in Lebanon or Jordan, immediately invited him to return to work. ʿAarif agreed and was soon placed in charge of a storage space for timber. To ease his access to the old-new workplace, ʿAarif was given a one-room cabin at Shemen Beach, near the southeastern edge of Haifa harbor. He added another level to the structure, planted a garden, and brought his family from

Acre. The Abu-Shamla family started a new chapter of their displacement, this time in Haifa, their hometown.

A few years later, when ʿAarif's Jewish benefactor from the harbor passed away, the family was once again forced to evacuate their home and leave. This time they did not go far: ʿAarif improvised a makeshift apartment, two rooms made of corrugated iron, part of a compound that housed some twenty families of Palestinian employees of Haifa harbor. Most structures were made of scrap materials and lacked running water, electricity, and any other infrastructure. It was unbearably hot in summer and freezing cold in winter. But it was near the port, and the family had space enough to raise some fowl, cultivate a small vegetable garden, and maintain a semirural existence in the industrial heart of Haifa.

In May 1967, as Israel prepared for what would be come the 1967 war, the municipal council of Haifa declared that the proximity of the metal shacks to Haifa port exposed the compound's residents to security risks the council was unprepared to take, and it issued evacuation warrants. Soon the police arrived and ordered them to pack and leave. A woman who had given birth the day before was carried out on her bed as bulldozers razed her home to the ground. Nazmiyah was pregnant at the time. Her husband and their four children hastily packed their belongings onto a van and found temporary shelter near a mosque in nearby Halisa, a predominantly Palestinian neighborhood. ʿAarif and Maryam were invited by a Palestinian woman in Halisa to stay in a storage space below her apartment. ʿAarif became an immigrant-refugee for the fourth time in his life.

. . . . .

Israel's chief citizenship law—the Law of Return, passed in 1950, was a simple yet effective legal ploy. Its main effect was to annul the inherent right to citizenship normally granted to individuals born within a given territory. Instead of prioritizing birthright as the main avenue to formal citizenship, the law stipulated that a person born in Palestine was eligible for citizenship only if he or she had never sojourned or taken refuge in areas controlled by those opposed to the establishment of Israel and its existence. This of course had massive ramifications: hundreds of thousands of Palestinians who, during the hostilities in 1948, had fled their homes, however fleetingly, or had been driven out by Israeli forces, were now deprived forever of their right to citizenship.

Other sections of the law defined an easy way for certain others to obtain Israeli citizenship: every Jew, wherever he or she was born, was welcome to become a citizen. In one stroke Israel's legislature thus robbed most local Palestinians of their birthright and presented the right to citizenship on a silver platter to every Jewish person who wished to accept it. The Law of Return remains to date the main determinant of the right to immigrate and become naturalized in Israel. As such, it remains the chief legal impediment facing Palestinian refugees wishing to return to their ancestral homeland.

Not surprisingly, Palestinians who found themselves under Israeli jurisdiction in the early 1950s had little faith in the Israeli legal system and few means to seek recourse. Most Palestinian lawyers, judges, and political leaders were exiled or expelled during the war. Many of those who stayed nurtured the hope that Israel might prove to be a passing episode and, thus, were hardly prone to attempt to take advantage of its legal system. Some in fact recall the sense of gratitude they felt at the relatively mild version of discrimination they were facing. Many were stuck with the misguided wish that Arab states and the U.N. would come around, address their plight, and rectify their situation.

When Palestinians did submit claims in Israeli courts, they had only a limited chance of succeeding. Israeli courts consistently failed to take into consideration their collective situation and their history. Instead, judges were happy to accept the arguments put forward by the state, particularly the defense establishment, against the Palestinians. A long series of rejected Palestinian appeals ensued.

The electoral participation of the Palestinian citizens of Israel in the early decades of the state likewise followed a pattern of conformity and obedience. The generation of survivors turned up at the ballot box in numbers, faithfully casting votes in favor of the ruling Zionist parties.

Their hope that the victors would share some of the spoils with those who voted for them was often shattered.[16] In the realm of civil rights and liberties, many of the relatively lenient rules passed by the British were soon changed, shoring up the power of those in charge. For example, a clause in the emergency regulations (1945) that prohibits schoolteachers from political activism was incorporated wholesale into the Israeli legal code. Teachers who took part in political demonstrations or helped disseminate political flyers, articles, or other publications were summarily dismissed. Palestinians began to realize that the education system was used to eradicate their national, cultural, and historic identity in an attempt to depoliticize them.

. . . . .

Sarah Rabinowitz has fond memories of the 1950s. While by no means opulent, life in the large apartment on Panorama Road with three children, and later even four, was comfortable. A woman who looked after the children and did the cleaning stayed in the apartment with them.[17] The family owned a private car and had season tickets to the philharmonic orchestra. Gatherings with friends, including attorneys and judges from Haifa and the capital, Jerusalem, took place around the fireplace in the large reception room in winter and on the balcony in summer. Lenny was a member of Haifa's Rotary Club and later among the first members of the golf club in Caesarea. The children, like their mother, went to Hareali School. In 1957 Daphna was chosen to represent Israel in the international youth forum organized by the *New York Herald Tribune,* an annual conference in which representatives from three or four dozen countries, one youth from each, visited the United States for two months. The delegates did individual lecture tours in various parts of the United States, then came together for a series of joint public events in New York and Washington, D.C. A photograph of the group of delegates taken on the White House lawn, published simultaneously in the *New York Herald Tribune* and in newspapers back home in Israel, shows Daphna, wearing an embroidered Yemenite shirt, smiling down at President Dwight Eisenhower from the top of her six-foot frame.

Sarah and Lenny's second child, Asher, named after his maternal grandfather, inherited his mother's talent for music. He played the cello at Memorial Day and Holocaust commemoration ceremonies at school and performed with the Gadna (cadet corps) orchestra.[18] In 1960, dressed in khaki and wearing an Israeli sun hat *(kova tembel)*, Asher, armed with his cello, featured for a split second in Otto Preminger's epic pro-Zionist production of Leon Uris's *Exodus*. Asher's younger sister, Carmel, played the recorder, put on skits at the annual meeting of the Association of South African Immigrants held in the Hulda Forest, and starred in a production of a play by Haim Nahman Byalik staged at school. And in June 1960, five-year-old Dan took the stage at a nursery-school Independence Day play, where he played a new immigrant arriving at the shores of Israel. In the first act, wearing tattered clothes and an old cap of the sort more frequently seen in Europe, his character was a stereotypical Diasporic Jew, arriving empty-handed and distraught at Haifa port. By the third act he was transformed into a proud peddler wearing sparkling blue-and-white attire, pushing a wagon load of haberdashery and wearing a confident Zionist smile.

In 1958 Daphna was conscripted into the IDF, where she served as an officer in the legendary paratroopers brigade from 1958 to 1960. The splendor of her uniform, complete with lieutenant stripes, red beret, and occasionally a rifle, made a deep impression on the children of the neighborhood. The spectacle, however, paled in comparison to the one that would take place periodically a few years later. In 1960, after a successful decade as district attorney, Lenny was appointed as a judge in Haifa's district court. Once a month, on a Wednesday, a police patrol car would pull up in front of the house, immediately attracting the attention of the children playing in the street. The driver, in full police uniform, would wait until he caught a glimpse of Lenny crossing the front garden, then leap out of his seat in time to open the car door and respectfully usher the judge into the passenger seat. The car would then set off to the police academy at Haifa Bay, where Lenny lectured police officer cadets on the principles of law and government.

For Lenny the appointment to the district court signaled a return to land issues—an area of the law he had been involved with as a young attorney in the 1930s.[19] He found much interest in this field and, in the 1960s, wrote verdicts that were crucial to the fates and fortunes of many Palestinian families. Most Palestinians appeared before him as defendants in cases initiated and conducted by the district attorney, to answer charges of unlawful possession and cultivation of state land. More often than not, the defendants had been cultivating fallow land or fields that had been owned collectively with relatives or neighbors who became refugees in 1948, and that, in light of the new laws passed by Israel, were now defined as state property. The Haifa district court dealt with the bulk of the legal action that ensued from this concerted administrative campaign to transfer rights to more than a million acres from Palestinian ownership to Israeli control.

Recent research indicates that Lenny, as a judge, was somewhat more sympathetic toward Palestinian defendants than his colleagues were. All district judges in Haifa occasionally ruled against the state. However, some of Lenny's verdicts cited in Geremy Forman's fascinating doctoral dissertation (Forman 2004) indicate that Lenny was a particularly outspoken critic of the state. He pointed out disingenuous conduct on the part of the district attorney's office, condemned the use of inaccurate and even false evidence, and openly rebuked the district attorney's overzealous prosecution of cases in which the evidence was flimsy (2004: 156–59, 175–77). Forman shows in fact that, in November 1960, Lenny's rulings prompted Minister of Justice Pinhas Rozen and his director general, Joseph Kokia, to seek Lenny's removal from land cases. When the Haifa district court rejected this maneuver, the director general tried to cajole Lenny into compliance in a more direct and personal manner. In an official letter sent on November 21, 1960, Kokia openly suggested to Lenny that he might want to consider softening his criticism of the state as reflected in his recent verdicts (158, 159, n. 438).

Hindsight and lessons learned about the machinations of the legal and administrative aspects of Israel's land regime, however, indicate that Lenny's dissenting voice was a lone liberal cry in the wilderness that could do little to undo the new laws' structure. In fact, paradoxically, his exposure of the blatantly unethical and illegal measures so often taken by the state may have strengthened the state's claim of due process. Lenny's verdicts could easily be interpreted as saying that, if only the judicial process could be conducted fairly, the gross injustice behind the political will and legislative work that engendered the land regime could be absolved.

And so it came to be that, in spite of his critique, this soft-spoken, tolerant, and modest man, a genuine example of leniency and consideration in his personal conduct and in his other judicial work, was a perfectly reliable component of a smoothly operating administrative machine designed to justify and regulate dispossession. Israel could rely on its judges without hesitation. Reasonable and righteous civil servants—and Lenny was a righteous man if ever there was one—judges tend to conform to what they understand to be the guiding values and the spirit of the system that appoints them. Their perception of legal idioms, hegemonic legal interpretation, and the intentions of the system, together with a genuine belief that law reflects the democratic institutions that express the people's will, tends to curb and limit their scope of justice. The instincts of those who earnestly attempt to marry court decisions with the principles of natural justice are easily eroded.

·   ·   ·   ·   ·

The determination with which the Israeli military moved during the hostilities of 1948 to chase the Palestinians off their land was reflected in the persistence with which Israeli historiography attempted to obliterate the presence of pre-1948 Palestinians from the physical landscape and from collective memory. Only the Palestinian citizens of Israel, along with a handful of Jewish Israelis who refuse to forget, insist on recognizing this void as an absence.

Palestinians who were born as citizens of Israel know all about the generation that was ravaged in 1948. People, they say, have roots: they cannot be truncated like dry logs. The memory of them cannot just vanish. The spirit of those forced to go, and of their fields and houses now burnt and demolished, lag behind. For their children and grandchildren, members of the generation of 1948 are living links to history and national identity. The human shadows of that war—those missing from their old communities, those living miserably and harshly in Lebanon, Syria, the West Bank, the Gaza Strip, and Jordan—still haunt the memory. Not surprisingly, the refugees of 1948 have become living repositories of Palestinian destiny. Keepers of the material and symbolic keys of homes they locked in haste, their broken hearts claim the right to return with a persistence that is not easily swayed. They stubbornly refuse to vanish.

Khawla, while visiting a bookstore in Amman, Jordan, in the mid-1990s, was asked by the elderly shopkeeper where she was from. "From Israel," she said. Indignant, the man corrected her, exclaiming, "Palestine." Khawla replied with empathy that if it could make a difference she was prepared to say "Palestine" not once but thrice each time she was asked. The keeper, obviously a Palestinian refugee, concluded softly, "We must not forget."

The incident echoes the efforts of Palestinians in Israel to incorporate the world they lost in 1948 into the labels they forge for self-identification. Some call themselves "Arabs of the inside" (Arab al-Dakhil); others say "Arabs of 1948" (Arab Tamanyeh Wa'arba'in). Both idioms represent the bifurcated identity created by al-Nakbah. The *inside* denotes a place. *Nineteen forty-eight* rekindles time. The combination of the two engenders and preserves the common memory of loss.[20]

The catastrophe of 1948 was not only an endpoint for the Palestinians but also a starting point for much that came later: memories, deliberations, and debates; acceptance and rebellion; hope and recurrent disappointment. Whether forced to live as stateless refugees abroad or as citizens inside Israel, many of the generation of survivors still bear the stamps of places they were born in. Many have adopted surnames that refer to their community of origin, now long destroyed or forested over: Damouni, Mi'ari, Majdlawi, 'Akawi. . . .

The generation of survivors had limited ability to launch effective political opposition. The most conspicuous effort, the Arab Nationalist al-Ard movement, was suppressed in the late 1950s through a series of restrictive administrative measures and court decisions.[21] Other outfits made sporadic attempts to derail the state by blowing up agricultural machinery and structures, only to be crushed unceremoniously by the agencies in charge of state security. The disintegration of the organizational infrastructure the Palestinians had prior to 1948, and the effective system of control developed by the state, frustrated most initiatives, preventing them from carrying out effective operations.

The most significant sparks of real political resistance against the state during the early decades were lit by the Communist Party and, subsequently, by ultranationalist Palestinians loyal to pan-Arabist ideologies such as the Ba'ath Party and Nasserism, particularly individuals affiliated with Abna al-Balad (Sons of the Land). Here again, however, laws enforced by the military government restricted most activity, suffocating and preventing genuine seeds of political change.

One thing that could never be suppressed completely was literary articulations of the widespread sense of loss and longing. Political poetry became a major vehicle for expressions of collective memory and for the preservation of national morale. Regulations devised and enforced by the military governors, restricting freedom of speech, compelled poets such as Tawfik Ziyad, Mahmoud Darwish, Emil Habibi, Emil Tuma, Rashid Husein, and later Samih al-Qasem and Hana Abu-Hana to write and publish underground. Many were kept under house arrest or in administrative detention. Some of the detainees used stints in prison to compose new works that earned them recognition as "poets of the struggle." In the absence of other avenues of expression, intellectual and literary work assumed particular cultural and moral import. Many felt that mundane routine activity such as work, raising children, repairing a home, and even expressing oneself in Arabic constituted political statements of struggle and survival. People talked of "improving our conditions" decades before they could dream of, let alone openly demand, equal rights.

In 1959, years before he was elected to the Knesset and then made mayor of Nazareth, Tawfik Ziyad wrote in the name of those whose lives were dedicated to the preservation of the covenant with their homeland:

> O my people, a generous and fresh bough,
> O dearer than my very soul,
> We preserve your covenant.

We refuse to surrender to torture in the prison,
To the chains and window bars of evil.
We are prepared to suffer poverty and hunger,
Until we liberate the moon that has been crucified.

We will return to you the justice that was robbed,
We will recall the morrow from the darkest throes of greed
So no one can any longer buy or sell you,
O dearer than my very soul,
We are preservers of your covenant.[22]

.   .   .   .   .

In 1948, when Muhammad Abu-Baker came to Acre as a refugee, he found sanctuary in the house of one Mahmoud al-Ya'abdawi, a relative from his native village, Ya'abad. Al-Ya'abdawi, who was employed as a cook at the Acre jail, fed the many fellow villagers who took refuge in his home with leftovers he brought from work. Young Muhammad began helping his host, and at one stage even became a supplier of food for the jail.

At fourteen, 'Aarif's and Maryam's daughter Nada was tall and beautiful and looked older than her years. Maryam was concerned for Nada's safety, and when twenty-six-year-old Muhammad Abu-Baker asked 'Aarif, a member of the same village community he had originated from, for Nada's hand in marriage, 'Aarif and Maryam immediately consented.

Somehow, Muhammad managed to purchase in Damascus a fine dowry, including household articles and pure silk clothing. It was important for him to show that, even as a refugee with no family support to speak of, he could provide for Nada. Compared to that of other refugees, his standing was indeed quite stable. Nada, who was far from fully cognizant of what her new role as a married woman would entail, was thrilled with the chance to wear makeup at the wedding.

After they were married, Muhammad and Nada decided to settle in Ya'abad, across the border from the West Bank, now held by Jordan. Aided by villagers who led them to hidden footpaths and back roads, they managed to steal across the border. But their attempt to live in Ya'abad was brief. Nada soon realized that leading a rural lifestyle with no running water or electricity was an experience so radically different from the life she knew in Haifa and Acre that it simply would not work for her. The couple then moved to Jenin, where Nada's oldest sister, Najiyah, was living with her family. But Muhammad had trouble finding work, and a few months later the couple was back in Israel after another clandestine crossing. It was Muhammad's fifth migration, Nada's fourth.

Maryam and 'Aarif were still living in the old walled city of Acre, and Nada and Muhammad rented a small apartment close to them, in al-Ma'aalik Alley. Three years later the young couple moved to Harat al-Yahud (the Jewish quarter), a section of the old city named after an ancient synagogue. There, in subsequent years, six of their seven children would be born: Shahrazad, Khawla, Da'ud, Ahmad, Asma, Basma, and Baker.[23] Shahrazad, Baker, and Da'ud died when they were young. Like her mother, Maryam, Nada now had her share of grief and loss. Like her mother, she too found an outlet for her pain in reciting poetry that spoke of loved ones who were gone, never to be seen again.

In the festive seasons, Nada would treat her children to new shoes and clothes bought in Acre's "New City," now mostly under Jewish ownership.[24] Fashion in these stores was in step with the times—as were the prices. Khawla recalls her admiration for her mother, who, as a native of Haifa, spoke Hebrew well enough to handle the Jewish vendors at the stores. She too wanted to learn Hebrew, a language few Palestinians knew well or respected at the time, and speak it like her mother.

And throughout the 1950s, every Tuesday morning a little old Palestinian woman named Um-Morris would come to the Rabinowitz household at 19 Panorama Road, now renamed Yefe Nof Road. Smiling submissively, Um-Morris would spend her mornings washing, rinsing, and hanging clothes and linen in the backyard. She was, in all probability, the first Palestinian woman Dan ever saw, a Palestinian assigned to the Sisyphean task of rubbing out the stains and spots produced continuously by the new landlords.

Chapter Three

O children of our neighborhood,
they've taken our land,
cursed our history,
smashed our heads,
killed our cattle.

Muhammad Ali Taha

The neighborhood children whom Muhammad Ali Taha addresses in this verse are Palestinians born after al-Nakbah (the catastrophe) of 1948. The painful poem is a reminder of the dreadful reality that befell their nation following that war. Having lost control of their territorial assets and livelihoods, the Palestinians were now in danger of having their heritage and sense of identity eroded too.

The neighborhood kids represent, metonymically, a generation of Palestinians who were born as citizens of Israel in the 1950s. These children matured in the shadow of the wars of 1967 and 1973 and came of political age with the events of Land Day (Yawm al-Ard) in March 1976. Theirs is the generation that led the civil and political struggle that has defined the Palestinian community in Israel since the 1970s. We authors are the same age. Khawla Abu-Baker is clearly one of them.

.   .   .   .   .

Khawla, the second daughter of Nada and Muhammad Abu-Baker, was born in January 1955. Nada was eighteen at the time. The seven years that had elapsed since her family's displacement from Haifa and reset-tlement in Acre had enabled her to gradually adjust to their new pre-dicament. And while she was relatively successful in building a new extended network of acquaintances and friends in Acre, her heart in many ways remained in Haifa.

Harat al-Yahud (the Jewish quarter) in the old city of Acre, where the Abu-Bakers lived for almost three decades, was a microcosm of post-1948 Israel. In it lived displaced Palestinians from neighboring towns and villages, alongside veteran residents of Acre who had stayed put in spite of the hostilities. It was also the site of the void created by those forced to flee to Lebanon and Syria, which had been filled by the un-welcome presence of newly arrived officials and policemen, many of them Druze, who were stationed in Acre to govern and police the town. There were Christian and Muslim Palestinians alongside new Jewish immigrants who arrived with the mass influx into Israel in the early 1950s. Neighbors looked after one another's children, sometimes even nursing them to allow young mothers to shop or go to work. Khawla thus has Druze, Muslim, and Jewish "mother's milk siblings."

The dominant language in Acre's old city was Arabic, but other Mid-dle Eastern and European tongues were part of the scene too. One of the neighbors was an elderly Jewish woman known as Um-Shiya, named after her son Shiya, who lived in one of the new Jewish neigh-borhoods outside the walls and who was an acquaintance of Muham-mad Abu-Baker's.[1] Um-Shiya's eyesight worsened as she grew old, making her dependent on her neighbors for many household chores. She often waited for the Abu-Baker children to return from school, then asked their help with threading a needle or finding an item she could not locate. The children did not always understand her language and were sometimes scared of her. But Shiya's pleas with Muhammad that the family keep an eye on his mother, and the occasional candy offered in exchange for services rendered, kept the kids in line. Khawla recalls

Um-Shiya's house as being different from the Palestinian residences she was familiar with. The furniture was foreign, the voices emanating from the old radio remote and incoherent. Strangest of all, however, was the quiet in the old woman's empty, lonely apartment. Having an older person live alone is anathema to Arab culture, where the elderly are venerated and seldom left without familial care.

Muhammad invested all his energy in a new laundry he opened in Acre, which was successful. His expanding clientele included local Israeli police officers, who regularly brought their uniforms to him for cleaning and pressing. Palestinians who observed the amicable relations he maintained with these officials began asking him to intervene on their behalf with the authorities. He was soon elected regional delegate to the Association of Trade and Industry, and joined Acre's Rotary Club, where he was among the first Palestinian members. His daughters Shahrazad and Khawla sometimes accompanied him to meetings at the club, to eat European cakes and listen to debates in Hebrew.

Muhammad wanted to provide his children with the very best and was a keen believer in Western culture and modernization as keys to progress. His motto was *"Kul franji branji"* ("Everything Western is good"). His children thus attended Terra Santa School, a private school run by the Franciscan order Custodia de la Terra Santa. In the early 1960s the language of instruction there was English, and graduates wrote British matriculation exams.[2] Exceptionally alert and clever, Khawla started nursery school at two and a half, began first grade at five, and graduated from high school at seventeen. She spoke Arabic at home, English with the priests at school, and French in private lessons given by the nuns.

Muhammad and Nada were sociable, and their door was always open to relatives and friends. But the pain caused by the rupture of both their families of origin in 1948 was always there. They felt it particularly during holidays, when Muhammad made a point of telling his children about family relations they had never met. His remembrances and stories were always set in his ancestral village on the West Bank. He spoke of it with the melancholy reserved for people and places lost forever.

'Aarif, Nada's father, always visited his daughters and their families on holidays. His wife, Maryam, however, seldom accompanied him on these visits. For her, the holidays intensified the grief of separation from her two sons, her daughter, and her siblings. Instead of seeing living relatives, she and other older Palestinian women signified festivities by visiting cemeteries and praying near the graves of loved ones.

.   .   .   .   .

The institutional reality that the state of Israel constructed around its Palestinian citizens had explicit and implicit facets. There was of course the security service Shabak, affiliated directly with the prime minister's office. Kept as an unmentionable twilight apparatus until the early 1990s, it was largely absent from the administrative reality of the state and remained outside public discourse. In contradistinction, the military regime that was established to control parts of the country where the Palestinian citizens were concentrated—mainly Galilee and the "Triangle," a densely populated Palestinian region just east of Tel Aviv—was explicitly and openly intrusive. Other means of control included specialized and separate departments within the Ministries of Education, Welfare, Interior, and Religious Affairs, which purported to cater to the "particular needs" of the Palestinian community. The operations of these departments were often premised on a paternalistic vocabulary of justification promoting "modernization" and "progress" of a sector inherently assumed to be primitive and backward.

The security service, the military governorate, and the specialized departments in other cabinet ministries were fertile grounds, each in its own way, for the emergence and development of an insidious reality of collaboration and cooperation on the part of Palestinians. A close relationship existed between state agencies that dispensed routine services to Palestinians and the ruling Labor Party, which sought their votes in elections.[3] This soon created a deep dependency of whole Palestinian communities on the party. It strengthened the leverage of the party's prominent Palestinian members in their own communities, militated heavily against genuine empowerment, and kept at bay the demand for collective rights. Parties not included in the Labor-centered coalitions that held power from 1948 to 1977 were unable to offer their Palestinian supporters help in terms of government services or budgets, and had an obvious disadvantage when it came to recruiting members and voters. The Israeli Communist Party, which became increasingly attractive to Palestinian citizens on ideological lines, was not invited to join parliamentary coalitions. While never formally outlawed, it nevertheless remained marginal for mainstream Israeli politics for decades.

Liaison between the state and the Palestinian citizens of Israel in the first decades after 1948 was established mainly through government-appointed village *mukhtars* (headmen).[4] Many were chosen after convincing regional Labor Party technocrats that they were authentic community leaders who could secure votes for the party through their personal authority over fellow villagers and clan folk. Others were favored because of their willingness to act as proxies on behalf of absent Palestinian refugees in deals involving the transfer of property to the state. The dubious legitimacy they supplied to the emerging land regime was rewarded with a variety of political and personal favors, including positions in the civil service, infrastructural improvements in areas where their kin lived or had assets, rights in property, and sometimes even cash.

．　　．　　．　　．　　．

Muhammad joined the Communist Party briefly, but soon got cold feet and quit. Convinced that "walls have ears" and that no person was safe from careless gossip and malicious informers, he tried to keep political opinion and critique of the state to himself. His laundry was next door to a bookstore owned by an active member of the Communist Party, and the two had an exchange agreement: Muhammad did his neighbor's laundry and in exchange received a copy of every new book that arrived. Muhammad was proudly amused with how he managed to clandestinely bring copies home before Shabak agents would show up at his neighbor's shop to take them off the shelves. This was one source of the family's impressive book collection. Khawla's own reading would later be supplemented by the library at school, where she found books in Arabic from Egypt, Lebanon, Syria, and Jordan alongside literature in many European languages.

Some of the local teachers hired by the Franciscan school held political views that barred them from employment in schools more closely supervised by the Israeli Ministry of Education. Some of them occasionally held political discussions with students in the schoolyard. At times the Shabak pressured the school to fire teachers deemed overly political. The students, who lost significant educational figures in this manner, were witness to firsthand evidence of Israel's censo-democracy.

In 1966, three students at the Terra Santa School in Nazareth who tried to cross the border into Jordan were shot by an Israeli border patrol. Palestinian youngsters up and down the country, long enraged with being monitored and with the heavy-handed treatment their community was subject to by the authorities, staged angry demonstrations. The protest vented frustration with the way some Palestinians played into the hands of Israel, through acquiescence as well as active collaboration. Many youngsters dreamed of getting away, knowing this would probably jeopardize their prospects of ever returning. Some actually did it—none more conspicuously than the poet Mahmoud Darwish, who exchanged Haifa for life in exile in the late 1960s.

Members of the Abu-Baker family traveled a few times to the Mandelbaum Crossing in East Jerusalem, under Jordanian rule until 1967, for short reunions with relatives from the West Bank.[5] In 1961, after extended efforts, the International Red Cross arranged a long-anticipated meeting for Muhammad and his family with Ahmad, his aging father, who still lived in Ya'abad near Jenin. The whole family traveled to the crossing to be introduced to their patriarch. When the moment came, Muhammad burst into tears. It was the first time any of his children had ever seen him weep.

The relatives from Ya'abad brought olive oil and bread in order to give Muhammad's children a taste of their ancestral land. But the meeting was cruelly brief, lasting only half an hour, with everybody hard pressed to chose between conversation topics. This was the first and last encounter of Muhammad's children with their grandfather Ahmad, who died in 1965, just two months before the next scheduled reunion at the Jerusalem crossing.

In 1966, Muhammad traveled to Turkey to meet his brother Mahmoud, who had been working in Kuwait for many years. Their meeting, after eighteen years of separation, was emotional. Muhammad and his neighbors often spoke about the difficulties of life in *ghurba* (exile). For him, Acre too was *ghurba*. Home would always be Ya'abad and Haifa.

The Rabinowitz family home on Yefe Nof Road never had an explicitly ambitious or competitive atmosphere about it. Perhaps there were few additional goals that the family could realistically aspire to. In 1960, when Lenny was appointed as a district judge—the second-highest tier of the Israeli judicial system—he was forty-eight. The composition of the thirteen-strong Supreme Court of Justice at the time meant that his chances to advance there were not promising. Sarah taught the piano at home, a practice she maintains in the early twenty-first century, well in her eighties.

Tame ambitions notwithstanding, the social status and prestige enjoyed by the family were rising. The waiting list of children hoping for a place in Sarah's busy schedule was growing with each academic year. With time, new cadres of teachers, mostly women, joined the Dunyah Weizmann Music Conservatory, where Sarah was a leading figure. Many looked up to her as a role model and mentor. Students were attracted to her personal charisma and sincerity, admiring her ability to simultaneously be attentive and insist on discipline. Lenny, now a judge, was a member of the board of trustees of the Technion, Israel's leading technological university, located in Haifa. He also served as chairman of the Parents Association of Hareali School in Haifa, and later as chairman of the school's board. He served as president of the Haifa Rotary Club and was for many years a trustee for a major institution for the blind, for the Israeli Philharmonic Orchestra, and for the Council for the Preservation of Historic Buildings. His involvement in such projects, rewarded regularly with public honors and citations, persisted after his retirement from the bench in the late 1970s and lasted until he passed away in 1990.

.   .   .   .   .

Zionism is an overarching ideological canopy that conflates the national project with the interests of a particular elite. In this, it is identical to hegemonic subsets everywhere. The ruling Labor Party, state agencies, the Knesset, the judiciary, and other institutions formed a cohesive, sanctimonious web continuously reaffirmed by an ethos of self-evident patriotism. Considering themselves for many decades to be above criticism, these institutions were fondly viewed by many Israelis as irreproachable. The role assigned to them by the national narrative ensured that the interests they served remained largely unnoticed.

As elsewhere, this tendency was brought to perfection by the middle classes. The early decades of the state thus saw the Israeli middle class consolidated around a well-disguised set of self-evident assumptions and choices consistently construed and defended as apolitical. The secret charm of the bourgeoisie, its ability to produce an idealized consensus that conceals the influence of power relations and keeps ubiquitous political structures outside public scrutiny, was at full force.

.   .   .   .   .

Hareali School, which Sarah attended in the 1920s, and which was where Lenny taught briefly as a young man and where all four of the couple's children attended school, was a bastion of this spirit. For example, it consistently refused to allow emissaries of most youth movements to visit its campuses or otherwise recruit its students. Hashomer Hatzair and Hanoar Ha'oved Vehalomed, both of which were associated with the socialist left; Benei Akiva, which was linked to the National Religious Party; and Beitar, part of Menachem Begin's right-wing Herut Party were all kept away: they were too "political." Instead, the school positively encouraged its entire student body to join the ostensibly apolitical Scouts Movement. The fact the Scouts served as an explicit channel into the Zionist settlement project was overlooked as long as the movement refrained from formal association with any political party. Likewise, the school was instrumental for the consolidation throughout Israel of the militarist Gadna corps (youth battalions) dedicated to teaching basic military skills to high school students.[6] The highly political character of these institutions, so obvious in retrospect, was routinized and naturalized to the point of misrecognition by those they came to inculcate.

Khawla excelled in mathematics and physics. At the end of eighth grade, her parents, both of whom had spent their youth in Haifa, wanted to enroll her in the sciences track at Hareali School there. Muhammad traveled to Haifa with her school record to start her registration process, and came back with the good news that the application seemed successful. She needed, however, a supporting reference from the Terra Santa School in Acre, where she had just completed her primary education. This, however, proved difficult. The principal, who wanted to keep his best students and strengthen the community, was reluctant to let Khawla go. If she stayed, he promised, he would establish a science track for her and her contemporaries. The family gave in. Khawla stayed in Acre, joining thirteen others in the first cohort of graduates of the school's physics and mathematics track.

Had Khawla's bid to move to Hareali been successful, she would have joined the cohort that graduated from the school in 1972—the cohort to which Dan Rabinowitz belonged. As it happened, the 350-strong cohort of 1972 at Hareali had but a single other Palestinian student.[7]

·   ·   ·   ·   ·

The ostensibly apolitical assumptions that underwrote the Israeli middle classes portrayed Israel as a personification of the Jewish Diaspora: a small and isolated collective surrounded by malicious enemies. With time, this fundamental cosmology was buttressed by an elaborate series of persuasive and self-evident clichés that stifled all debate. A robust web of interdependent effigies emerged that has enabled all Israel's leaders, from Ben-Gurion to Ariel Sharon, to represent the state as a progressive, peace-seeking entity stretching a reconciliatory hand to the Arabs only to have it inexplicably rejected. Even today, most Israelis tend to see their history and destiny along these lines. This immovable belief in the mythic image of the small and peaceful nation became particularly salient during the weeks just prior to the war of 1967.

·   ·   ·   ·   ·

In the buildup leading to the 1967 war, Israeli authorities declared a cluster of military bases in Kurdani, just outside Acre, to be a restricted military zone. Palestinian families who lived nearby, mostly poor families who had migrated to the area from the Jordan Valley in the early 1920s, were evicted.[8] The evacuees were given temporary shelter at the Terra Santa monastery, where Khawla's school was located. The memory of their arrival is the first that Palestinian children who attended the school, including Khawla, have of that war.

When the war erupted, Muhammad and Nada Abu-Baker gathered their five children for a chilling talk. All of them were still heartbroken over the loss, two months earlier, of Baker, the couple's youngest child, who died in an accident at a neighbor's home. Shahrazad was fourteen, Khawla was twelve, Ahmad was nine, and the twin girls, Asma and Basma, were seven. With war approaching, Muhammad and Nada told them, each one must learn how to identify himself or herself as an Arab. That meant memorizing their full official names in line with proper Arab custom: given name, followed by father's name, and name of the paternal grandfather and his paternal line, six generations back. Khawla still recalls memorizing the whole chain: "*Ana bint 'Arab* (I am the daughter of Arabs). *Ismi* (My name is) *Khawla Ahmad Da'ud Taha Yasin Abu-Baker, min Harat al-Yahud talat 'ashar, Akka* (from the Jewish

quarter, house number thirteen, Acre)." With memories of 1948 etched
in their minds, Nada and Muhammad were not taking any chances.
Should the approaching war result in further expulsion or dispersal,
they wanted to make sure their children knew how to make themselves
known to Arabs and get assistance.

As the war approached, schools prepared bomb shelters and performed evacuation drills. The nearest thing to a shelter anywhere near
Khawla's school was an adjacent church. Otherwise the old city had
no public protection for its mostly Palestinian residents. When the
warning sirens went off on the morning of June 5, 1967, the Abu-Bakers
took refuge in a large room with exceptionally thick walls on the
ground floor of their apartment. They were joined by other neighbors
and spent many hours discussing the situation, playing games, and lis-
tening to the news on a transistor radio.

The first reports from broadcast stations in the Arab states were
euphoric. Tucked away together in the apartment, the Abu-Bakers and
their neighbors all believed that Arab armies were closing in on Tel
Aviv. Parents started to prepare their children for a reunion with relatives in the West Bank, Lebanon, and Jordan. Soon, however, the real
situation on the frontiers, so radically different from the versions aired
on the radio, was revealed. At the war's end, Khawla's music teacher, a
Scottish priest, unfolded a map of the Middle East and relayed to the
children what he had heard on the BBC. Indicating the new positions of
the Israel Defense Forces (IDF), they realized Israel was now in control
of the entire West Bank. Khawla understood that, while she might be
able to finally meet her relatives in Ya'abad, the circumstances of this
reunion would be unlike what she had hoped for.

In the weeks immediately before the 1967 war, Dan and his schoolmates
in Haifa, aged twelve and thirteen, volunteered to help prepare hospitals and senior citizens facilities for the impending hostilities. They
stuck masking tape in crisscross patterns on glass windows to prevent
flying glass in the event of air raids and helped clean the shelters. More
than their female peers, the teenage boys impatiently anticipated military action. Foreign Minister Abba Eban's tireless diplomatic efforts to

forestall the war annoyed them. In their view, his visits to the capitals of Europe and America to meet with world leaders reflected a hesitant, reconciliatory mentality that many in Israel in those days associated with the Diaspora. The youngsters worried that all this talk might cancel out the promise of excitement with the impending war. Buoyed by a sense of historic justice that would soon evolve into self-righteousness, Israeli collective consciousness was leaving no space for an alternative assessment of the situation.

·   ·   ·   ·   ·

When the second week of June arrived, Israel was euphoric. At a price most saw as trifling—a short spell in bomb shelters and a relatively small number of casualties—a prize was won that Israelis perceived as nothing short of miraculous. Within a week the Arab armies were in ruins. Israel tripled the size of the territory it controlled. The IDF took Temple Mountain and many other holy sites. General Yitzhak Rabin, chief of general military staff, stirred hearts in a poetic speech atop Mount Scopus in which the victory was presented teleologically as the just culmination of Jewish history. Beginning with biblical splendor, his speech spanned the forced Diaspora, the persecutions and the Holocaust, the 1948 war of independence, the unrelenting Arab hatred, and finally, this most recent salvation by a young and moral army. The speech, however, was at the same time a prelude to future reconciliation based on Israeli might—a task Rabin and his generation would later learn was easier said than done. But at the time, a sense of strength prevailed, breeding a new cult of heroism.

The price paid by the families of some seven hundred dead Israeli soldiers and by the thousands of maimed and injured men—and everyone knew someone who was hurt—was covered over by a wave of jubilation. The many thousands of dead and wounded Arabs, some of them civilians; the new wave of Palestinian refugees who crossed the Jordan River into Jordan; and the heavy price that future generations of Palestinians and Israelis would pay for the results of this war could not have been further from the hearts and minds of those who listened to Rabin's speech on the radio or read it in the papers in Israel and abroad.

Israel's conquest of the West Bank, Gaza Strip, Golan Heights, and Sinai Peninsula in June 1967 reconnected the Palestinian citizens of Israel with their brethren in the Arab world in a paradoxical, convoluted way. On the one hand, the rift between the "Arabs of the inside" and the others, a rift that had been such a central part of their existence between 1948 and 1967, was suddenly bridged. On the other hand, the manner this came about, through a resounding Israeli military victory, was devastating. If anything, the 1967 war highlighted the military might and political stability of the Israeli project, convincing even the staunchest Arab optimists that Israel was here to stay.

.   .   .   .   .

The occupation of the West Bank changed the summer vacation routines of the Abu-Baker children, who now could join their cousins for days and weeks spent in the fruit orchards and tobacco fields of Ya'abad on the West Bank. Relatives took twelve-year-old Khawla to the hills near the village to show her the site where Sheikh 'Az al-Din al-Qasam was killed by British troops in 1935, enlightening her about his role in their joint heritage.[9] Shahrazad and Khawla were reunited with their cousin 'Aarif, son of their maternal uncle Muhammad and his cousin Lutfiyah, who had lived with them in Acre as a child before he and his mother joined his father in Tubas on the West Bank in 1960. On visits to Tubas, their uncle Muhammad showed them literary journals and political periodicals published in the Arab world. Unlike anything she had encountered before 1967, Khawla now learned Arab high culture firsthand. Leafing through the Jordanian textbooks that her cousins used at school was an eye-opening experience for her.[10] It made her ask questions, cross-check sources, compare different sets of information, and understand that truth is anything but monolithic.

Relatives and friends in the West Bank believed that the Israeli conquest would be short-lived. They had trouble understanding how Palestinians within Israel had never taken arms against the Israelis. Some accused their own relatives, now holding Israeli citizenship, of being collaborators with the enemy. This did not stop them, however,

from asking kin in Israel to mediate with Israeli bureaucracies. Muhammad's brother Mahmoud, who by then had left Kuwait and returned to
Palestine with his wife and two children, lived with them in Acre for a
while before eventually settling in Ramallah.

The new reality forced many Palestinians to consider complicated
issues of identity, belonging, place, and citizenship. On both sides of the
Green Line, Palestinians were reevaluating what it was that they called
"home." One of the workers in Muhammad's laundry moved with his
family from Acre to the Gaza Strip to join relatives who had been expelled in 1948. Muhammad himself considered the possibility of a
return to Ya'abad. But Nada, who recalled her failed attempt to live
there in 1950, refused. A city woman, she knew that she could not
adjust to village life and the pervasive demands of a large and dominant rural clan.

Dan grew up in Haifa, following a trajectory that was in many ways
predestined. He attended Hareali School on Mount Carmel for his primary, secondary, and high school education; joined the Hacarmel Scout
Troop, designed specifically for Hareali kids;[11] attended Gadna sessions; and spent three years at the Hacarmel tennis club, and a longer,
more significant period with the Maccabi Haifa men's basketball club.
There were adolescent girlfriends and lovers in the permissive, carefree
pre-AIDS days.

The new geographical expanses incorporated into the Israeli system
of control as a result of the 1967 war stirred a whole generation of
Israelis into renewed interest in the physiography of the country. These
were the days before the information revolution. Israeli television was
on the air three hours each night; cinema advertisements emphasized
when films were in color as opposed to black and white. Youngsters
read books and talked about them. People listened to music on the
radio. And walking tours and hikes were an essential element of
Israeli culture.

In December 1971, Dan took advantage of his parents' absence from
the country for a few weeks and went on a ten-day excursion in the
desert. He spent a week at the Ein Gedi Field Study Center as a volun-

teer on an archaeological dig, then another week on the beach in Eilat. The freedom and independence was addictive. He began collecting topographic maps, soon becoming an enthusiastic consumer of information about routes and nature sites off the beaten track. Detailed information was relayed in telephone conversation, scribbled hurriedly on notes taken while speaking to other travelers he met at bus stations, and gleaned from papers and pamphlets published by organizations such as the Society for the Protection of Nature in Israel or by the kibbutzim movement. For newly emerging religious Zionism, this territorial experience soon became part of its messianic ideology, exalting the divine Jewish right of return to the entire biblical land of Israel—Eretz Yisrael. The secular middle class, subscribing to a more pragmatic ideology, was not impressed. Instead, it saw the physical experience of the newfound territories as an austere exercise in the realm of learning. Hikes and the culture of nature were framed as politically neutral. The hidden politics of the self-evident celebrated another victory.

At the end of his senior year in high school, Dan had a first fling with the radical left. He took part in a series of ideological meetings sponsored by Matzpen in Haifa and Jerusalem; their messages, however, did not leave an indelible impression on him. His motivation for attending probably had more to do with the marine blue eyes of a certain young woman from Haifa than with a genuine thirst for combating false consciousness. And in the last summer prior to the beginning of his conscription service in the IDF, he became a devotee of Guru Maharaji—an Indian boy who cleverly marketed himself as a source of spiritual enlightenment, trading the love of many thousands of Western followers for an impressive fleet of polished supercars.

Spirituality notwithstanding, Dan, like his other male friends, eagerly awaited his induction into the ultimate blood rite that caps the Israeli manhood cycle. When his time for conscription arrived, he first joined a Nahal group, intending to join a new kibbutz in the Golan Heights.[12] Soon, however, he left the Nahal and instead joined the air force's prestigious pilot's course. Successful in the initial stages, he was forced to leave the course six months into it because of a slight heart deficiency. The balance of his service was spent in the educational corps—lecturing to soldiers about the historical significance and geographical features of the parts where they were stationed. Most of this he did in the IDF's Central Command, where he became intimately familiar with the physical terrain and archaeology of the West Bank, the Jordan Valley, and the hills of Hebron and Bethlehem. His assignments also included gigs at the headquarters of the seven districts of Israel's military government in Gaza and the West Bank.

What Dan completely failed to fathom was the political significance of the occupation and of his own incorporation into it through his conscription into military service. He voted for leftist parties like Moked in 1974 and Sheli in 1977, but the significance of his role as an instrument of occupation managed to escape him.

Khawla did well in her matriculation exams in 1972 and was planning her next move. Her teachers and family encouraged her to study medicine at the Technion in Haifa, which she was inclined to do. But the anticipated switch from being the favorite outstanding student at the supportive Terra Santa school in Acre to being one Palestinian woman among thousands of Jewish Israelis, mostly men, in a large, anonymous institution troubled her. The Technion, while excellent academically, was unfamiliar ground, and the transition to Hebrew as the language of instruction was daunting. Her sister Shahrazad was engaged and about to be married, and Khawla herself had just met Muhammad May, a young pediatrician about to graduate from medical school at Hebrew University in Jerusalem, who soon asked her to suspend her studies and marry him. The proposal emancipated her from the need to brave her anxieties about the Technion. In the summer of 1973, two months before the October war, she and Muhammad May were married.

Muhammad, a man with deep political convictions, was a Nasserite. He had been one of the founders of the radical al-Ard movement banned by Israel's Supreme Court from taking part in the Knesset elections in the early 1960s.[13] Muhammad later became a pioneering member of the Council for the Defense of Arab Lands. He was born in Birweh, a village situated near the main road between Acre and Safad in western Galilee. When Birweh was destroyed in 1948, Muhammad's family became internal refugees. They first took shelter in Abu-Snan, a predominantly Druze village nearby, eventually settling in the village of Makar, east of Acre. Another son of pre-1948 Birweh, Mahmoud Darwish, who was Muhammad's age, went to school with him in Kafar Yaseef. When they were preparing for their graduation exams, Darwish crafted their chemistry formulas into a rhyme, creating an effective mnemonic device for the entire class to learn with.

·   ·   ·   ·   ·

The sense that Israel was not about to disappear was strengthened further by the October war of 1973.[14] Egypt and Syria, Israel's most powerful enemies, launched a coordinated surprise attack in circumstances that, from a military standpoint, were disastrous for Israel. Israel, however, managed to regroup, ending the war with IDF positions nearer to Damascus and Cairo than they had ever been before.

Books and museums in the Arab world, particularly in Egypt, tend to commemorate the first week of the 1973 war. Israel prefers to remember its final stages. In the eyes of many Arabs, however, including many Palestinians inside Israel, the IDF's ability to sustain its defense against the military pressure exerted on it in the early days of that war was even more impressive than its victory in 1967. The 1973 war also left the Palestinians with even less hope than before that their cause might be assisted by the Arab states. Within Israel, Palestinian citizens let go of any doubts they may have harbored regarding the durability of the state.

This new realization had profound political implications for the Palestinian citizens of Israel. Members of the first generation of Palestinians born as Israeli citizens, those whom Muhammad Ali Taha addressed as "children of our neighborhood," were about to transform their view of their relationship with the Jewish majority and with the state at large. Having internalized the fact that Israel was here to stay, this generation, while intensely preoccupied with building bridges to the Arab world, now began channeling more energy than ever before to the struggle for genuine equality and integration inside Israel.

.   .   .   .   .

Dan spent the 1973 war guarding an outdated antiaircraft gun near al-Arish in central Sinai, two hundred kilometers from the front line, where Israel and Egypt were waging some of the biggest campaigns since World War II. Ten of his high school graduating class were killed. A childhood friend was taken prisoner by Egypt; another disappeared in a Syrian prisoner-of-war jail for a year. But the war bred changes too. The widespread protest mounted in its aftermath was a breath of fresh air and a source of hope. At last, the fundamentally conformist Israeli youth dared to express irreverent distrust of the leadership and to question the clichés that had underwritten their own blind obedience for so many years.

Immediately after his discharge from the army, in November 1975, Dan joined the staff at the Tzukei-David Field Study Center run by the Society for the Protection of Nature in Israel near the monastery of Santa Katerina in the granite mountains of South Sinai. In many ways, the years he spent there as a guide and a researcher shaped his professional destiny. The staff at the center led groups of Israeli and foreign tourists on ecological seminars and hiking expeditions, conducted field surveys of hitherto uncharted sections of the vast peninsula, and served as research assistants on projects conducted by professors from various Israeli universities.

The staff members had a unique relationship with the Jebalya Bedouin—an ancient clan whose ancestors were brought from the Balkans in the Byzantine period to serve and to defend the isolated Christian monastery. Jebalya Bedouins and the Israeli staff members at the field center had close personal relationships characterized by mutual learning. The balanced flow of information, the fact that the majority of the staff felt they were only temporary guests in Sinai, and the sense of mutual loathing between them and the IDF personnel stationed at a tiny outpost next door all blurred the colonialist context of the interaction between Bedouin and Israelis. In 1977–1978, the peace initiative started by Begin and Anwar Sadat was finalized into an agreement that involved the Israeli evacuation of the Sinai and the return of the peninsula to Egyptian control. The members of the staff at Tzukei-David, all of them secular, left-leaning Israelis, found themselves supporting a process they knew was going to bring an extraordinary chapter in their lives to a close. In October 1979, after four years in Sinai, Dan packed his bags and left for London, to study for a bachelor of science degree in human environmental studies at King's College.

. . . . .

As suggested before, the sobering effect of Israel's stability as demonstrated in the 1973 war, had a profound effect on its Palestinian citizens. The trajectory they adopted in the last quarter of the twentieth century was evident in the vast expansion of civil society organizations and their infrastructure. New parties joined the contest for positions in Israel's parliament, the Knesset; outfits and alliances seeking to participate in local government became more numerous and diversified; an expanded core of exceedingly professional nongovernmental organizations assumed an increasingly important role in public life within the community as well as in the interface with central government.

The focal point was always Nazareth, where professionals, merchants, businessmen, and students had been politicized for decades under the aegis of the Communist Party. This new political awareness yielded its first significant political results in 1975, when a front led by the Communist Party won the municipal elections by a landslide. The notion that a political formation that adhered to the rules of play of Israeli politics could at the same time challenge some of its fundamentally ethnocentric premises encouraged other groups and individuals to seek political agency. A national council of Arab high school students was soon established, and Palestinian students in Israeli universities began forming representative committees that were independent from the general, Jewish-dominated student unions. The Communist Party, which was instrumental in both initiatives, soon upgraded its core involvement in Israeli politics. It did so by forming the Democratic Front for Peace and Equality (DFPE)—an umbrella organization built around the party that fielded a diverse list of parliamentary candidates. The DFPE became the best representation of the interests and values of Palestinians inside Israel until the middle of the 1990s, possibly beyond.[15]

The DFPE evolved partly as a result of the dramatic transformation of the Israeli Communist Party in the 1960s. Initially based on a small nucleus of Jewish urban voters faithful to Marxist tenets that they had absorbed in prewar eastern Europe, during the 1960s and 1970s the party gradually became identified with the cause of Palestine and Palestinians.[16] Openly critical of many of the basic premises of the state, the DFPE could provide the Palestinian community in Israel, for the first time since 1948, with political expression for their interests and an identity that was not compelled to pay lip service, or otherwise subordinate itself, to the Zionist agenda. The DFPE regularly sponsored cultural activities and community organization and offered opportunities at universities in the Soviet bloc for youngsters seeking professional and academic training. Old patterns of cooptation of local Palestinian functionaries, with bloc voting on the part of Palestinians, rewarded by the state with favors in ways that stifled real representation, were quickly losing currency.[17] A new strain of independent leadership emerged, posing a viable alternative to the *mukhtars* (coopted village headmen) of yesteryear.[18] On March 30, 1976, a huge demonstration took place in Sakhnin, a large Palestinian village in Lower Galilee. Thousands of Palestinians from all over the country came to protest the policy of land closure and expropriation the government embarked upon in the interest of what it called "security and settlement purposes." The real objective of these seizures, the demonstrators knew, was to transfer more land from Palestinian ownership to Israeli control. When Israeli police and border patrol forces appeared, the situation spun out of control. Six Palestinian demonstrators were shot dead in what was immediately labeled "Land Day." The event became a milestone symbolizing a new divestment from the state. It had unprecedented significance and important political and historical repercussions.

Compared to the large-scale land expropriations of the 1950s and 1960s, the amount of land actually seized from Palestinians in 1976 was relatively small.[19] The Palestinian community, however, was no longer the docile and submissive one that had so passively endured the loss of property and livelihood twenty years earlier. The events surrounding Land Day in Sakhnin in 1976, and the rage expressed by Palestinians at the brutality instigated by the state police, became the platform for annual memorials dedicated to the event. These annual gatherings reflected the gradual solidifying of political will and became important elements of a new politicized identity.[20]

The 1970s saw far-reaching changes in the structure of local government within the Palestinian sector, with political control steadily shifting from Zionist parties to the countrywide and local Palestinian outfits. Two related factors precipitated this transformation. One was the gradual loss of interest on the part of Zionist parties in controlling local councils in the Palestinian sector. The other was a growing awareness within the Palestinian community of the municipal arena as an alternative space for political assertion.

The victory of the DFPE in the municipal elections in Nazareth in 1975 triggered a similar process in several other municipal councils. The DFPE, which became a municipal force to be reckoned with in many towns and villages, soon found additional political formations seeking representation and control in this realm. In the late 1970s, Abna al-Balad, a highly ideological movement with strong roots in Nasserite pan-Arabism, gained seats on several village councils. By the early 1980s, the Islamic movement began its own assault on local councils, securing seats and even dominance in a number of key towns.[21] The success enjoyed by these political parties encouraged kin-based alliances to seek influence and power on the local scene. Admittedly deficient in ideology and national political agendas, these parties were nevertheless independent of the Zionist establishment.[22]

On the parliamentary level, the DFPE's consistent success in the 1970s and 1980s encouraged other social forces to emerge as parties, providing Palestinian voters with a more varied spectrum of ideological and political positions than they had known before.[23] In 1984 the advocate Muhammad Mi'ari, together with other veterans of the al-Ard movement, established the Progressive List for Peace (PLP), an outfit whose anti-Zionist platform was bolder and clearer than that of the DFPE. In 1988 yet another party emerged. Labeled the Arab Democratic Party, it was founded by a Labor Party member of Knesset called Abed al-Wahab Darawsha. In 1996, ʿAzmi Bishara, a fiery intellectual and a brilliant speaker who had left the DFPE, joined forces with members of Abna al-Balad and disgruntled former DFPE activists to form the National Democratic Alliance (Balad) and gain a seat in the Knesset. In 1999 Ahmad Tibi, a physician and a close advisor to Yasser Arafat on Israel, established the Movement for Arab Renewal and gained a Knesset seat. Other, less successful groups abounded. By the end of the 1990s, political party activity in Israel's Palestinian sector had the distinctive character of pan-Palestinian mobilization. Reliance upon and the appeal for Jewish-Arab cooperation became a secondary issue.

The 1980s exposed the difficulties of forging solidarity between Palestinians and the Zionist left into a meaningful political alliance. Individuals and coalitions associated with the more leftist segments of Labor and Meretz consistently preferred a mainstream Jewish-Israeli stand to a genuinely socialist position or humanitarian empathy for the suffering of Palestinians. This pushed Palestinian citizens further toward political ghettoization, promoting an exceedingly more assertive agenda. Abna al-Balad, the PLP, and Balad consciously presented themselves as political alternatives to the DFPE, each developing its own version of the demand for collective rights.

Space for cooperation with Jewish Israelis was narrowing. At the end of its first term in the Knesset, the PLP became an independent, all-Palestinian party with no Jewish individuals in any of the leading positions. Parties that formed later made no real attempt to integrate Jewish activists. By the time of the 1999 elections, the DFPE was the only "Palestinian" party that still adhered to the principle of Jewish-Palestinian cooperation. In the parliamentary elections of 2003, it failed to have even one Jewish candidate elected to the Knesset—a situation that had never occurred before.

In the early 1990s, Emil Habibi and Tawfik Ziyad, two prominent leaders of the DFPE whose lives had been devoted to cooperation between Jews and Arabs in the struggle for rights, equality, and peace, became embroiled in contentious debates with a new rebellious cadre of DFPE leaders. This very public argument, fought as it was in boldface on the pages of Israel's Arab-language newspapers, saw young activists questioning whether the Palestinian community in Israel could really afford to trust the Jewish majority and the state.

.   .   .   .   .

Muhammad May and Khawla Abu-Baker had two daughters in less than three years. Khawla, who planned to start her academic training as soon as she found proper day care for the little ones, joined a group of young Palestinian women who, like her, were searching for solutions that would enable them to study and have careers. They ended up establishing the Palestinian Women's Organization for Social Welfare. The first initiative of its kind since 1948, it became a model for dozens of organizations designed to help Palestinian women countrywide to juggle higher education, work, and family life. In fact, it was this endeavor that convinced Khawla to finally abandon her dream of becoming a physician and switch to education and social welfare.

In the summer of 1984, Muhammad, Khawla, and their daughters moved from Acre to Shu'afat, a Palestinian suburb of East Jerusalem. Muhammad began specializing in ophthalmology at St. John's Hospital, while Khawla took up African studies at the Hebrew University of Jerusalem. Naomi Chazan—later a professor at Hebrew University and member of Knesset for the left-of-center Meretz Party, was a young lecturer in the department. Avraham Burg, later a member of Knesset for Labor and the Speaker of the House, was a fellow student.

Khawla lived a mixed life in Jerusalem. The Hebrew University was a definitive Israeli experience. East Jerusalem, however, was a bubbling center of Palestinian life and culture. Her daughters studied in East Jerusalem schools and were exposed to a clear-cut Palestinian political curriculum. In fact, the poems and stories they were taught served as the inspiration for Khawla's master's thesis in education, which dealt with political socialization.

Politically, the mid-1980s was an eventful time in Jerusalem. A militant right-wing Jewish underground organization was exposed after an attempt to assassinate Palestinian mayors in the West Bank. Tension on the Hebrew University campus on Mount Scopus was running high. Khawla took part in demonstrations organized by the Committee of Arab Students headed by ʿAzmi Bishara, ʿAziz Haidar, Nathem Badar, and others, often finding herself in confrontations marked by violence by the extreme right wing.

.   .   .   .   .

Political developments in the Middle East and the world in the last quarter of the twentieth century, particularly the peace accord between Israel and Egypt in 1979 and the transformations of the Soviet bloc through glasnost and perestroika, pushed some Palestinian leaders inside Israel to further seek coexistence. Efforts in this realm increased despite the harsh memory of Land Day in 1976, Israel's invasion of Lebanon in 1982, the Sabra and Shatila massacres of Palestinian refugees in Beirut in September of that same year, and the ongoing insistence of Israel throughout the 1980s to treat the Palestine Liberation Organization (PLO) as a terrorist organization.

Inspired by the peace agreement with Egypt, Israel's Ministry of Education began promoting structured encounters between Jewish youngsters and their Palestinian counterparts from Galilee, the Negev, and the Triangle. This new approach, called coexistence education, featured groups and organizations such as the Van Leer Institute in Jerusalem, the Institute of Peace Research at Givʿat Haviva, and others who supplied related programs and educational packages for wider use within the education system.[24]

Children from both sectors attended meetings held in their schools and in private homes. Some went on joint weekend trips to various sites where, separated from daily routines, more intensive sessions could be held. The overriding assumption was that direct encounters between youngsters would shatter mutual stereotypes, thus narrowing social distance and political alienation between the two communities.

The meetings, while providing many participants with uplifting experiences on a personal level, hardly contributed to greater peace and reconciliation. For the majority of Palestinian participants, the meetings reinforced the cultural and political dominance of Israelis, highlighting their own alienation and marginalization.[25] Palestinian participants became defensive about their culture, and a growing number of meetings were characterized by a mutual lack of understanding, an absence of cultural awareness, and even nationalist-political hostility.[26] Palestinian participants were also frustrated by the absence of a convincing body of alternative information that might contest the hegemonic Jewish perception of reality and present a counternarrative.

During the late 1980s and early 1990s, the Ministry of Education became more actively involved. Programs such as Education for Democracy and Tolerance were prepared for various age groups, and teachers in Palestinian as well as Israeli schools were asked to sponsor open classroom discussions on current events. By this stage, however, many Palestinian teachers no longer had faith in declarations of political equality and ideological openness made by the Jewish captains of the system, and they refused to take part in coexistence programs. Based on past experience with education handled by the British and later by the Israelis, many Palestinian teachers suspected that the coexistence project was a political trap. Few schools chose to participate in it on a permanent basis.

Meanwhile, the state education system was successful in isolating Palestinian schools from processes of political maturation that took place in the greater Palestinian fold. Many schools complied with expectations and directives issued by the system, staging ceremonies for Israel's Independence Day and suppressing sentiments of identification with and support for Palestinian nationalism. Some teachers were convinced—in many cases correctly—that colleagues were appointed to positions in schools and seminaries by the Shabak and were under instructions to report any sign of Palestinian consciousness. Teachers were interrogated, arrested, and sometimes dismissed because of their political convictions. There were even occasions on which students who organized activities in response to current events were questioned by police, reflecting the state's concerted effort to monitor the Palestinians.

Naturally, the tension between the educational exercise to promote "education for coexistence" and Israel's aggressive policies with respect to the Arab world caused internal strife in the Palestinian community. Veteran leaders and other public figures who promoted the activities were often accused of appeasement and surrender to coopting policies. This criticism was undoubtedly related to the realization among Palestinian intellectuals that the Zionist left in Israel was never a genuine partner in the Palestinian struggle against prejudices and discrimination embedded in state institutions. This situation was exacerbated by the fact that many in the Zionist left adopted a self-congratulatory attitude concerning their own support and participation. Showcasing what was merely a willingness to attend events as proof of their "commitment to democracy," they tended to ignore the deeper needs of Palestinian counterparts to articulate alternative narratives, express pain, and seek genuine change in Israel's power structure.

The promotion of coexistence should be evaluated realistically. It did provide opportunities for youngsters and adults on either side to become better acquainted. This probably invalidated a certain portion of the stereotypes inculcated by the media. But claims that such activities, deployed and expanded as they were in Israel in the 1980s, could change political realities are grossly unsubstantiated.[27]

One indication of the expansion and proliferation of civil organizations and activity in Israel's Palestinian community is that by the early 1990s there were some 190 nonprofit associations, organizations, committees, and institutions operating in Palestinian towns and villages. Already representing a huge expansion in comparison to earlier decades, this figure more than tripled by the end of the decade and is still increasing steadily.[28] Nongovernmental organizations are dedicated nowadays to improving services in education, enhancing economic development and welfare, promoting cultural events, and doing political work. And while some of these activities are direct results of organizational endeavors that had been in place before 1948, the great majority of these organizations were established after 1980.[29]

A major development on the national political scene was the formation in the 1980s of the Supreme Follow-Up Committee of the Arabs in Israel, composed of the heads of Palestinian local councils. The committee established subcommittees on land, education, health, and social welfare that began providing blueprints for an institutional infrastructure that would permit greater autonomy for the community.[30]

Despite the impressive pace at which all this was taking place, a major transformation in the overall circumstances of the Palestinian citizens of Israel was looking as remote as ever. The 1980s and 1990s witnessed a number of significant improvements, but civil achievements remained limited in scope. The glass ceiling glazed by Israel's Jewish majority did not easily crack. Palestinian leaders and the community at large were sensing that, whatever gains were made, the structural reality of the Zionist project and its definition of Israel as a Jewish state remained robust. Belief in genuine change began to fade away.

.   .   .   .   .

During Khawla and Muhammad's second year in Jerusalem, Muhammad developed the first symptoms of a serious illness. He was hospitalized several times, sometimes for extended periods. Within a year his situation deteriorated, and the young family had to return to Acre, where the support that both extended families could afford them was more easily available. Khawla began a course of study at Haifa University and also took a job. Before long, however, Muhammad's disease spread aggressively, becoming the dominant factor in the family's daily routine throughout the first half of the 1980s. Muhammad was bedridden most of the time, and taking care of him, raising two young children, studying at the university, keeping her job, and meeting various social and family obligations resulted in a heavy load on Khawla.

In 1985 Muhammad died. Mahmoud Darwish, by then in exile, wrote an article mourning the loss of his boyhood friend. Khawla and her daughters, who were nine and seven when their father passed away, began a slow and painful process of grieving.

Shortly before Muhammad died, Khawla had begun a master's program in education at Haifa University. Interested equally in political sociology and psychology, she chose to write a thesis that examined the emotional and educational influence of children's books on Palestinian youths. Her research involved collecting and analyzing children's books from all over the Arab world and conducting interviews with intellectuals and authors on the West Bank, in Egypt, and in England.

As Khawla was approaching the final stages of her research, the security services were informed of "subversive materials" she ostensibly had in her possession. A police investigation was initiated that lasted a year. The president of the university; her adviser; U.S. officials of the International Association of Poets, Playwrights, Editors, Essayists, and Novelists (PEN); and Jewish writers publicly intervened on her behalf. Palestinian intellectuals, however, were less inclined to make public comments. In private, some of them disparaged her for being critical of Palestinian culture and democracy at a time when the Palestinian national movement was fighting for its life. This kind of self-reflection, some said, must wait until after the revolution.

In late 1987 Dan, his wife, Iros, and their four-month-old daughter, Gal, moved to Natzerat Illit (Upper Nazareth), a predominantly Jewish town built in the 1950s outside the old Palestinian town of Nazareth in Lower Galilee. Dan began anthropological fieldwork in the town as part of a doctoral dissertation at Cambridge University. His project focused on relations in Natzerat Illit between the Israeli majority and the considerable Palestinian minority that had formed in the town since the late 1970s. The project assumed particular significance due to its timing: fieldwork began in December 1987, within days of the eruption of the first Palestinian intifada in Gaza and the West Bank.

Dan's direct contact with a large and varied Palestinian community in Natzerat Illit and Nazareth, and his firsthand exposure to the daily oppression and discrimination they are subject to, was a transformative experience. Close liaison with activists and supporters of the dominant DFPE in Nazareth exposed him to this organization's historic role as a main vehicle for the expression of identity and interests of the Palestinian citizens of Israel. These sensibilities triggered a redefinition of many of the political tenets that hitherto had been part of his worldview, including demarcation lines between legitimacy and deviance, acceptable politicization and extremism, and good and evil.

In early 1989, the weekend magazine in the daily newspaper
Hadashot, to which Dan was a regular freelance contributor, received
word from a junior television reporter who served as an IDF reservist
near Jenin. The reporter described what appeared to be a murderous
punitive action perpetrated by an IDF unit against villagers. The affair
began when a jeep convoy carrying infantry reservists entered the village of Faqu'a and was hit by a barrage of stones. Some soldiers sustained light injuries, forcing the jeeps to hurriedly depart the village,
which left the unit's pride seriously bruised. The commanding officers,
preoccupied primarily with their image in the eyes of their subordi-
nates, determined they should return to the village and restore esprit de
corps by teaching the Palestinian villagers a lesson. As a result, the soldiers went back and destroyed some houses in the village.

Dan went to Faqu'a, only forty kilometers away from Nazareth but
across the Green Line that separates Lower Galilee from the West Bank,
to investigate the incident. He made several visits to the village. On one
of them he heard a vivid account from a twenty-three-year-old electronic technician named Yusuf Abu-Na'im. Yusuf had witnessed from
afar the IDF platoon's destructive tour de force and saw the jeeps
undergoing a fresh barrage of stones from defiant youngsters. But this
was not the last of it. Several days later the soldiers were back once
more, intent on taking further action to repair their wounded pride. By
the time their mission was over, two young Palestinian villagers were
dead. One of them was Yusuf Abu-Na'im. The circumstances of his
death, as relayed to Dan by Yusuf's family and friends in some detail,
entailed a manhunt through an olive orchard and had absolutely no
connection to self-defense on the part of the soldiers. It was more like
an execution than a fight against a dangerous terrorist.

His visit to the isolated village in the mountains of Jenin and the
encounter with Yusuf's bereaved family had a powerful effect on Dan.
Not least, the episode was a vivid reminder of the bond between Palestinians on both sides of the Green Line, and of the disturbing analogy
between the current occupation and the events of 1948.

After the intifada erupted in late 1987, Khawla spent a year working as a
volunteer on weekends at a psychological care center in the Gaza Strip,

training psychologists in play therapy for young victims of the intifada. She took part in a number of activities organized by women's committees and groups and gave lectures to kindergarten teachers. Soon after, she joined Imut, a mixed Palestinian-Israeli group of mental health workers that promoted mutual professional projects between Israelis and Palestinians during the intifada. In 1990 she was appointed chief executive officer of Shutafut (meaning, partnership), an association for coexistence education, based in Haifa. Her term at Shutafut coincided with the Gulf War of 1991, an episode that forced activists to face the complex challenge of promoting peace and reconciliation in times of war. The Israeli Zionist left was panic-stricken by Palestinian positions on Iraq at the time. When Arafat declared his support for Saddam Hussein, who linked the Iraqi occupation of Kuwait to the Israeli occupation of the territories, Meretz leader MK Yossi Sarid was up in arms. When asked on Israeli television in 1991 about the Palestinians and Iraq, he came back with a famously sarcastic line: "If Arafat now wants [to talk to] me, he will have to seek me hard."

.   .   .   .   .

Sarid's remark, a succinct summary of the sentiments of many Israeli liberal leftists, exposed the yawning gap between Palestinian and Israeli understandings of concepts such as peace and coexistence. The Israeli left, strongly resenting the occupation, was clear when it came to the situation of Palestinians in the territories. The empathy with Palestinians there could be formulated as a relatively simple political struggle, easily translatable into idioms such as *peace* and *coexistence*. The situation of the Palestinian citizens of Israel, however, was much more complicated for Israelis on the Zionist left, whose sense of cultural superiority and patronage creates blind spots that are not easy to overcome. Jewish-Israeli society is in many ways a hierarchical arrangement, whereby the dominant ethnic classes often define themselves in terms of the Israeli-Palestinian conflict. Curiously, this further marginalizes the Palestinian citizens, many of whom see themselves as victims of an occupation that began in 1948. This sense of internal occupation is difficult for liberal Israelis to come to terms with.

The intifada that began in 1988 saw new bonds forged between the Palestinian citizens of Israel and their brethren in the Occupied Territories. Palestinians from Israel made more of their purchases of food and household hardware in the West Bank and Gaza. This strategy was suitable for the modest income levels of Palestinian citizens compared to other Israelis, and it served to boost the economy of producers and merchants in the Occupied Territories. Likewise, across the Green Line, links between Palestinian women's organizations, political movements, academics, physicians, and mental health workers augmented these groups' loose sense of solidarity and unity.

This notwithstanding, the first intifada also exposed the absence of a shared political goal for Palestinians on either side of the Green Line. Whereas Palestinians in the territories easily united around the struggle for an independent Palestinian state, Palestinian citizens of Israel were waging their own battle for equal rights within the Jewish-dominated state. If there was political interaction between the two communities beyond economic assistance, it was short-lived and ineffective.

·　　·　　·　　·　　·

Muhammad Abu-Baker's two younger brothers Walid and Sa'id lived and worked in Kuwait starting in the 1970s and were there in 1991 when the first Gulf War erupted. They sold whatever they could, gathered their families and some belongings in two cars, and headed west to Jordan. Sa'id found work and settled with his family in Amman.[31] With Muhammad's assistance, Walid applied to the Israeli authorities for permission to return to his mother's home in Ya'abad, where he now lives with his family.

In 1991, Khawla was offered a place in a doctoral program in sociology at the University of London. She deferred acceptance of the offer, preferring to wait until her eldest daughter graduated from high school in Haifa. At the end of 1994, she joined a doctoral program at Nova

Southeastern University in Florida. In the United States she was accompanied by her new partner, Marwan Dwairy, a psychologist from Nazareth she had met at an Imut meeting a few years earlier.

The political strife of the Middle East followed Khawla to the United States. She chose to write her doctoral thesis on families of Arab immigrants in the United States. To gain the confidence of her informants, she had to prove to a suspicious Palestinian community in Florida that her Israeli citizenship was compatible with being a legitimate Palestinian rather than an Israeli in disguise. Fortunately, some Palestinian immigrants originating in al-Bira near Ramallah knew her uncle Mahmoud, who had been living there with his family since the 1970s. The suspicion faded; the research went ahead and was soon completed, forming the basis of her dissertation and doctoral degree.

In mid-1989, Dan, Iros, and Gal moved to Cambridge, England, for the writing period of Dan's anthropological thesis. Dan's father, Lenny, died in March 1990. In September of that year, soon after the Iraqi invasion of Kuwait that would become the casus belli for the first Gulf War, which erupted in early 1991, Dan submitted his dissertation and the family returned to Tel Aviv. Dan was offered a tenure-track position at the Department of Sociology and Anthropology at Hebrew University in Jerusalem, and Iros began building her private practice as a psychotherapist and later as a psychoanalyst. During the 1990s Dan became a regular contributor to the op-ed page of *Haaretz*, in which he writes on political and environmental issues. In 2001 he accepted an offer to join the faculty at Tel Aviv University and left Hebrew University.

.   .   .   .   .

The first intifada, in which the Palestinians carefully avoided using firearms against Israeli soldiers, was registered locally and internationally as a genuine popular uprising against the occupation. This, together with the results of the Gulf War of 1991, triggered a spiral of negotiations and agreements. The Madrid Peace Conference of 1991 reconvened after

Rabin's victory in the 1992 elections, and undertook direct negotiations between Israel and the PLO in what became known as the Oslo process. This culminated in mutual recognition of Israel and the PLO, which was sealed by the historic signing in September 1993 of an agreement that established the Palestinian Authority (PA), which began governing parts of Gaza and the West Bank. The return of Yasser Arafat to Palestine in early 1994, accompanied by thousands who had been employed as PLO officials and security personnel in exile, convinced many that the PA was in fact a Palestinian protostate, and that events in this blood-soaked region were finally, irrevocably, turning positive.

But the extraordinary symbolism associated with these early signs of Palestinian self-determination were not matched with genuine advancement toward statehood and nation building. In fact, the mid-1990s saw the consolidation of the PA under Arafat at the expense of many of the fine achievements made by Palestinian civil society in the Occupied Territories in the late 1980s, in particular during the intifada. Arafat's regime, which in many ways reflected the particular interests of those PLO operatives who returned with him from exile, systematically eroded the initiatives developed by local civil institutions. Israeli and U.S. patronage of the PA gradually became a means to subdue the Palestinians in the West Bank and in Gaza, subjecting them to a stifling and corrupt apparatus of control. The Palestinian Authority became a subcontractor for Israeli security—a no-win situation that gradually made the political process hostage to militant extremists on both sides. "Regional stability" in the Middle East became a euphemism for American ambitions, personified by George H. W. Bush and subsequently his son George W. Bush, to keep Persian Gulf oil flowing.

Meanwhile in Israel, a dual-balloting system was adopted in 1996 that enabled voters to cast one ballot for prime minister and another for a party seeking Knesset seats.[32] The new arrangement gave sectarian parties, including those seeking to represent the Palestinians, a considerable boost: people could now vote for a relatively small party in the parliamentary election and back a contender associated with a bigger mainstream party who stood a realistic chance of election as prime minister. In fact the campaigns of 1996 and 1999 saw many Palestinians splitting their vote between "Palestinian" parties seeking Knesset seats and Labor candidates (Shimon Peres in 1996, Ehud Barak in 1999) for the position of prime minister. Not surprisingly, the campaigns of 1996 and 1999 installed as many as twelve Palestinian individuals in the Knesset—an unprecedented number that came nearer than ever before to the proportion of Palestinians in the overall population.

While obviously encouraging, this considerable success also cast into stark relief the insurmountable obstacles that face Palestinians seeking real representation and actual power in the Israeli system. The dozen Palestinian members in the Knesset—10 percent of the entire house— hardly effected any change. For example, none of the "Palestinian" parties was ever invited by a mainstream power to join a ruling coalition. The only (partial) exception to this rule took place following Yitzhak Rabin's victory in the elections of 1992. When Rabin was forming his coalition government, the DFPE and the Arab Democratic Party (MADA) agreed to support his cabinet in Knesset elections without actually being offered seats in it.[33] This arrangement helped Rabin's Labor-Meretz government stay in power even when the third component in their coalition—the ultraorthodox *mizrahi* (oriental, sephardi) party Shas—quit the cabinet and threatened to topple it in no-confidence votes in the Knesset. In exchange, the DFPE and MADA had Rabin's commitment—which he honored to the letter—to direct a substantially larger share of the national budget to the Palestinian sector, boosting education, housing, infrastructure, and light industrialization.

The agreement with Rabin's coalition, while anything but trivial, stopped short of having Palestinians assuming executive positions in government, and it maintained the separation between parliamentary representation of Palestinians and real influence. Salient issues such as policies governing land and water allocation, budgets for local councils, criteria for regional subsides and tax relief, resources and reforms in education system, and the discourse that determines the state's core values all remained largely beyond the reach of Palestinian representatives.

Palestinian Knesset members habitually engage in energetic parliamentary activity, competing with each other to unleash the most vitriolic rhetorical attacks against the Zionist establishment. This tends to push them even further from the Israeli mainstream, ever narrowing their chances to gain access to real influence. It also had a profound effect on relations with the Zionist left. By the late 1990s most Palestinian leaders no longer believed in cooperation with parties such as Labor or Meretz and were determined to wage their main political campaigns alone. This tendency would later make it easier for the Israeli right wing to stigmatize the Palestinian community by claiming that it was dangerously subversive and had a separatist agenda.

Frustration with the lack of influence and with the failure to bring genuine change reached a high point during Ehud Barak's brief term as prime minister from June 1999 to February 2001. No Israeli politician has ever had the level of support that Barak got from the Palestinian community during the election of 1999. The turnout of Palestinians reached an impressive 75 percent. A total of 321,444 Palestinians voted for Barak,[34] a number representing well over 90 percent of the valid ballots.

This extraordinary result, which represented the highest level of support Barak enjoyed in any sector of the Israeli population, clearly failed to impress the former general. After taking office in the summer of 1999, he hardly referred to the Palestinian sector. The new prime minister's most loyal constituency received no official visits from him, nor were its representatives invited to his office. Palestinian Knesset members, who between them represented almost 10 percent of the entire house, were not even invited to the first round of preliminary meetings held by the prime minister and his advisors in preparation for forming the ruling coalition. The Palestinian community felt neglected, used, betrayed.

In contrast to Rabin's and Peres's administration between 1992 and 1996, Barak's government did not initiate any change in allocation of resources to the Palestinian sector. Barak made no attempt to revise the geographical—hence ethnic—distribution of areas earmarked for accelerated development, where residents and investors are eligible for tax breaks and other economic incentives. Barak's administration did not even acknowledge the fact that Benjamin Netanyahu, his predecessor as prime minister, modified Rabin's progressive map of development areas, thus seriously injuring the Palestinian sector. Fifteen months in fact elapsed between the time Barak took office and the first official meeting that he initiated with delegates of the Supreme Follow-Up Committee, the representative body of the Palestinian citizens of Israel. This belated meeting, incidentally, took place in the first week of October 2000, when six young Palestinian demonstrators had already been killed by Israeli police fire.

At the outset of the new millennium, the Palestinian community in Israel plunged to a new nadir of despair. The intermediate generation, the one that tried to lead a transformation by means of parliamentary and civil action, became the Worn-Out Generation.

Chapter Four

The eruption in late September 2000 of Intifadat al-Aqsa was an event of historic proportion. Unlike the outbreak of the first intifada in December 1987, which came on the backdrop of a prolonged stalemate, Intifadat al-Aqsa was a reaction to concrete initiatives and processes. Essentially, it was the Palestinian response to the fundamental flaws of the political developments known as the Oslo process that had shaped their lives since the beginning of the 1990s.

Conventional wisdom in Israel and the United States suggests that the Oslo process, complete with the phased withdrawals of Israel from parts of the territories, was a positive peace plan woefully subverted by irrational, primordial ethnic hatred and religious extremism. This rendering of the 1990s as a decade of hope flanked by bloody upheavals is, in our view, erroneous. Rather, the tragic violence that began in 2000 is better understood as the inevitable result of a decade of misguided, sometimes malicious, choices. Many of these mistakes were made by local actors caught up in the asymmetric web of U.S. power and the ignorance that so often characterizes the U.S. State Department and the White House when it comes to the Middle East.

The Oslo process, which was sealed with a number of agreements and protocols in 1993 and 1994, created a regime in which the newly formed Palestinian Authority became a subcontractor for Israeli security—a formula that blatantly conflicted with the sentiments and interests of Palestinian nation and state building.[1] This was compounded by the norms that defined Arafat's protostate in Palestine: the abuse of power, the manipulative tenor of the inefficient bureaucracy, the opaque and undemocratic nature of the political process, and the corrupt administrative domains established and controlled by security chiefs and political figures to milk the vast resources offered to the Palestinian people through the European Union–funded People-to-People Program, all under the watchful eyes of Israel and the United States.

The Oslo process was disastrous also because of a more insidious and less visible aspect of the regime that it created: the launching, under the umbrella of a "peace process," of Israel's real military occupation of the Palestinian territories. Between 1967 and 1994, Israel's military control of the West Bank and Gaza was rather loose. The IDF, which was deployed primarily on the outer perimeter of the territories, facing outward to Jordan and to Egypt, was deliberately kept disengaged from the civilian Palestinian population. A civilian Israeli administration provided an approximation of governmental services like education, health care, planning, and policing. Military presence was, to use Franz Fanon's suggestive image, assumed rather than experienced—a cardboard facade that represented a readily available but otherwise invisible and distant force. For the IDF, the territories were less a military frontier and more an administrative chore.

All this changed after 1994. Israel's handover of major towns in the West Bank and Gaza to Palestinian control included a relatively smooth transfer of administrative responsibilities to various departments and civilian bureaus established as part of the Palestinian authority. The IDF

now had to redefine its role, which it did by adopting an increasingly suspicious attitude toward the Palestinian Authority. The old mission statement formulated by Moshe Dayan in 1968, designed to keep the IDF at a
healthy distance from Palestinian civilians and let daily life take its normal course, was out. Instead, the IDF now looked at every bit of territory
handed over to the Palestinians, particularly in and around the bigger
Palestinian towns, as a potential military threat and acted accordingly.
IDF redeployments following each withdrawal included systematic
encirclement of Palestinian towns with new roads, strategically placed
roadblocks, bases, depots, and observation points. Physical infrastructure was supplemented by contingency plans for the rapid intervention
of heavy machinery and troops in the event of future Palestinian hostility. A vicious self-fulfilling prophecy was set in motion that would come
full circle in the fall of 2000.

The negotiations held in July 2000 at Camp David under the auspices
of U.S. President Bill Clinton between an Israeli delegation headed by
Prime Minister Ehud Barak and a Palestinian delegation headed by Chairman Yasser Arafat exposed a number of seemingly unsolvable issues. One
was the territorial contiguity of the future Palestinian state; another was
the question of Jerusalem; a third was the fate of Palestinian refugees. Settling these differences, many agree, was the sine qua non of any solution
to the conflict.[2] But at Camp David, a conference that Arafat did not really
want in the first place, none of these seminal issues was resolved. Instead,
the Palestinians were frustrated and insulted by the patronizing attitudes
of both Barak and Clinton, and the conference ended in complete failure.

The crisis was exacerbated on September 28, when Ariel Sharon, then
opposition leader, made his famous visit to the Temple Mountain compound in Jerusalem. Sharon's motivation for the trip may have derived
from internal power struggles in his Likud Party, where former Prime
Minister Benjamin Netanyahu strove to position himself as the genuine
hard-line leader of right-wing Zionism. Whatever motivated Sharon, his
visit to the site, under heavy police escort, was viewed across the Arab
and Islamic worlds as direct provocation.

The show of Israeli military presence that accompanied Sharon at Temple Mountain, the spontaneous rage of thousands of Palestinians, and a

counterdemonstration staged the next day in the compound of Temple Mountain left seven Palestinians killed by Israeli riot police and threw the Occupied Territories into an unprecedented wave of violent protest. On Saturday September 30, thousands of Palestinian youths confronted Israeli troops throughout the West Bank and the Gaza Strip with barrages of stones. The following days, weeks, and months were marred by incessant clashes.[3] By the end of 2000, more than three hundred Palestinians had been killed and many thousands had sustained injuries. Further escalation throughout 2001 and 2002 brought the death toll to over eighteen hundred Palestinians and more than seven hundred Israelis. By mid-2004 the death figures had almost doubled, with tens of thousands injured.

On Saturday, September 30, 2000, Muhammad al-Dura, an eleven-year-old Palestinian boy, was shot dead in his father's arms at the Netzarim Junction on the Gaza Strip. The hopeless attempts of the thirty-seven-year-old father, a man who had spent most of his life under Israeli occupation, to protect his son from a senseless shooting by the occupation forces was captured by the cameras of a French television crew. Within hours the excruciating image became a universally recognized symbol and a powerful personification of the Palestinian struggle for personal and national freedom. The Arab world was instantly united in moral support for the Palestinians. Sympathy for the Palestinians throughout the world grew dramatically.

Fiercer Palestinian demonstrations drew more Israeli fire, and the violence in the territories became comprehensive, at times spiraling out of control. Israeli public discourse resurrected dormant idioms. People were suddenly talking about "the situation" (*hamatzav*) and the "events" (*ha'eru'im*)—terms coined decades earlier, when Israel still perceived itself as a weak and vulnerable entity threatened by powerful Arab opposition. An even more archaic term, *hameo'ra'ot*—a pre-1948 idiom roughly meaning "the unusual events," coined specifically to denote the victimization of Jews during the Palestinian revolts of 1929 and 1936–1939—also made a brief return to Israeli parlance.

Within days of the outbreak of violence in the Occupied Territories, it became clear that this time around the Palestinian citizens of Israel were ready to support their brethren in the territories, even at the cost of clashing with the Israeli authorities. A spontaneous sense of unity and solidarity swept Galilee, the Triangle, the Negev, and, to a lesser extent, mixed towns inside Israel.

The Supreme Follow-Up Committee, the most senior forum of Palestinian leaders of the Palestinian citizens of Israel, convened on the night of Saturday, September 30. Under normal conditions, its decision would probably have been to declare a one-day strike and assign two or three towns as sites for organized regional protest rallies. That night, however, was anything but normal. Tension ran high. Rage was everywhere. Time was running out. Sunday was the second day of the Jewish New Year, which meant businesses and factories would be shut anyway. The committee made a decision by default: it declared a strike day but could not put plans in place for any organized rallies. The implication was that the masses in every town and village were left without clear guidance or concrete plans for regulated action. Local councils had virtually no control over what was about to happen and had no means to shape the gathering storm.

Not surprisingly, in many towns the protest on Sunday, October 1, went out of control. The police—ill equipped, ill trained, unprepared, and prone to execute summary justice at short notice when facing Palestinians—failed to keep its distance, entered Palestinian towns in force, and sometimes opened fire in a trigger-happy fashion. Two young men—one in Jat in the Triangle, the other one in Um al-Fahim—were shot dead. Many were wounded, including Sheikh Ra'ed Salah, the Islamic leader and then-mayor of Um al-Fahim, who was scratched by splinters from a police officer's rubber bullet while trying to dissuade youngsters from exacerbating a confrontation near the entrance to the town. The next day, the protest and violence spread even further, with more fatalities and damage.

The intensity of the demonstrations held in Palestinian communities in Galilee, the Triangle, and the Negev took the participants themselves, the Palestinian leadership, the Israeli establishment, and the public by complete surprise. The death toll and number of injured rose quickly, provoking greater indignation, igniting a chain reaction, and escalating the protests. Demonstrators blocked roads, including intercity thoroughfares, sometimes for hours and even days. Palestinian towns, including Nazareth, Um al-Fahim, Kafar Manda, Kafar Kana, and Sakhnin, saw the burning of Israeli banks, post offices, gas stations, and other premises associated with the state. A number of mixed towns saw spontaneous Jewish retaliation. For example, a Jewish crowd vandalized stores owned by Palestinians in Acre.

.   .   .   .   .

When Intifadat al-Aqsa began in October 2000, the writing of this book was already under way. Dan and Khawla's writing sessions were enveloped by the rapidly evolving new reality. As information trickled in from Galilee, and as casualty lists from the Triangle were compiled in the first days of October, Khawla recognized names of children of people she knew. Khawla and Dan felt deep anxiety and had a sense of national calamity approaching. Palestinian families they knew who lived in mixed building complexes in Acre, Nahariya, Haifa, and Natzerat Illit feared for their lives. Violent demonstrations and counterdemonstrations in Jaffa made Palestinian residents reluctant to go to work in Jewish-dominated areas of Tel Aviv, including even, for a few days, the university. Most Israelis refused to set foot in Jaffa, not to mention Palestinian neighborhoods, villages, and towns further afield.

A young relative of Khawla's walking in his own neighborhood in Acre was beaten by an Israeli youth. The young Palestinian lost some teeth and sustained a broken jaw that required medical attention for the better part of a year. When his parents filed a complaint at the Acre police station, it turned out that the assailant was the son of a policeman. The officers tried to dodge filing the complaint. The family was suddenly faced with a deep, disturbing sense of insecurity that characterized the daily experience of many Palestinians.

For Khawla, Dan, and many of their friends, every time the phone rang that October, it prompted new fears.

.   .   .   .   .

On the eve of Yom Kippur, October 8, hundreds of Jewish residents from Natzerat Illit, the predominantly Jewish town established next to Palestinian Nazareth in 1957, began marching west toward the road that separated the two towns.[4] Seeking retaliation for demonstrations staged by Palestinians in downtown Nazareth the previous days, the marchers were thirsty for fresh violence. The border police, which had prior warning of the march, deployed a platoon in the area that included sharpshooters, but the police did not prevent the crowd from heading west toward the eastern neighborhoods of Nazareth. The platoon's rifles were pointed westward.[5]

The advancing crowd—eyewitness reports suggest that many of them spoke Russian—became more agitated as they approached the road separating Natzerat Illit from Nazareth. Once they reached it, they began hurling rocks across it westward, hitting cars and houses on the Palestinian side. Some crossed the road, causing more damage from closer range. Palestinian residents who heard the noise came out of their homes to see what was happening and to protect their property. Word of the assault spread quickly via telephone. Soon a few hundred Palestinians, among them several public figures, arrived at the scene and lined up, looking eastward.

Skirmishes developed. At some point, police opened fire. Several Palestinian demonstrators were struck. Wisam Yazbek, who stood next to a number of Palestinian dignitaries, was hit in the head and died on the spot. It later transpired that the bullet entered through the upper part of the back of his head: he had his back turned to the policeman who shot and killed him. Another young Palestinian, 'Omar 'Akawi, who stood nearby, was shot dead too. Many were wounded.

By mid-October, thirteen Palestinians, twelve of them citizens of Israel, had been killed by police fire. Hundreds more were injured.

Official government responses to the violent events of October 2000 in the Occupied Territories as well as inside Israel is best characterized as confused urgency. Eighteen months after he took office, partly the result of almost half a million Palestinian votes, Ehud Barak at last agreed to meet with the leaders of the Palestinian community in Israel. A series of hurried telephone conversations and meetings with mayors, members of

Knesset, and deputies ensued, some including Barak, others with the minister for internal security, Shlomo Ben-Ami, whose ministry was in charge of the police. It was an uphill climb: with little in the way of personal acquaintance or common work experience between the prime minister and the Palestinian leaders, and with the number of Palestinians hit by police fire growing daily, trust was wearing thin. Agreement was proving difficult to reach.

The central and destructive role that the police played in the crisis reflected a lack of reconciliatory contingency plans for an event of widespread discontent among the Palestinian citizens. This was one aspect of a more general failure to provide long-term policies that could improve conditions in the Palestinian sector and normalize its relationship with the state.

Many factors contributed to this lacuna. One was the monochromatic tenor of advice that Israeli politicians had been getting for decades when it came to Palestinians generally and the Palestinian citizens of Israel in particular. The reliance on "experts on Arab affairs"—in other words, men with military and secret-service training and experience—created a stagnant, cyclic style of thought that regularly stifled change. Most such "experts" are in fact part of a closed circuit of men who move between research departments inside the security establishment, senior positions in government, research institutes in universities, and consultant positions in influential private institutes.[6]

The socialization of these experts in the realm of national security encourages many of them to view all Palestinians as a military or demographic threat. Thus, instead of looking for positive solutions, this approach reifies old security concerns, perpetuating a hegemonic policy of majority control of the majority.[7] This further alienates the Palestinians, triggering further indignation and the practices and statements that result from it, which the "experts" can then present as vindication of their earlier forecasts. This of course boosts their professional prestige and brings them more currency and import for their security-oriented approach.

Significantly, experts on Arab affairs, and specifically the control of Arabs, do not necessarily hold extremist political views. Many are sophisticated, well-polished liberals genuinely convinced their role is honorable and useful. Trained in the best military tradition to prepare for worst-case scenarios, they are trapped by their own limitations. In October 2000, by the time the cabinet realized that procedures suitable for battlefield were counterproductive for stability and coexistence, the body count was already too high.

·   ·   ·   ·   ·

With radio and television broadcasts suspended on Yom Kippur, the disturbing news of the events in Nazareth first trickled in by phone. Many felt that events were spinning out of control. Having been involved in activism for equality, dialogue, and understanding for decades, Dan and Khawla felt that previous efforts were going up in smoke. The Nazareth pogrom, with large-scale Jewish provocation against Palestinians, was more disturbing than most events that had been taking place elsewhere in Galilee during the previous days. It brought back fears of the ultimate nightmare—an all-out violent and potential murderous confrontation between Jewish and Palestinian crowds inside Israel.[8]

A marathon of urgent phone calls ensued during the afternoon and evening of Yom Kippur, with Dan's home serving as the hub. The callers were a growing circle of academics who felt that standing back and waiting would be morally wrong. By late evening they decided to form a working group of academics who specialize in minorities issues generally, and the Palestinian minority in Israel in particular, and to jointly put together an emergency report that would be presented to Prime Minister Barak. The contents: new ideas for government policy concerning the Palestinian citizens of Israel. Each section of the report, it was agreed, would be prepared by a subteam of experts who would focus on a particular dimension, provide background data, identify the processes that shaped the present situation, and set forth a series of practical recommendations for change.

The next morning fifteen experts were committed to the project. By day four, a team of twenty-six was on board, working in six subteams.

An introduction describing the project and its goals was written and agreed on by all. Drafts were composed, edited, and revised in a flurry of e-mail messages. By late November, the comprehensive, unsolicited report was printed, bound, and submitted to Ehud Barak.[9]

For Dan and Khawla, working on the emergency report was therapeutic—something that combined conviction, expertise, and passion. Troubling and frightening as the crisis was, all contributors hoped that it might also create an opportunity for change. The crisis of governability so clearly visible in statements by government officials and by politicians created space for practical solutions that the Israeli mainstream had never dared to contemplate before.

.   .   .   .   .

All but one of the Palestinian citizens killed by police fire in October 2000 were under thirty. Two were in their late teens. A similar cross section of ages is discernable among the injured, and television images likewise suggest that a vast proportion of participants in the mass demonstrations, where these injuries were sustained, were people in their teens or early twenties. This protest, which had required no inducements and had had none, was clearly led and carried out by a new generation. The Stand-Tall Generation was making its debut in national and regional politics.

In November 2001, the writer Salman Natour spoke at an event in the Tel Aviv Cinematheque, noting the first anniversary of the October 2000 killings. In his address, which he titled "On Death and Heroism," Natour asked:

> How does it come to be that a young person, leaving his home innocently, carrying with him nothing but his conscience, is gunned down by a bullet from a rifle steadied on a boulder, held and aimed by a policeman who squeezes the trigger? A policeman under orders from an officer who condones the loss of life, and who in turn is backed by a government minister who has learned nothing from the history he teaches,[10] and who in turn is backed by a government that controls the space between the boulder and the young man, the one who carried with him nothing but his conscience? The young man becomes a bird hovering in

the air; he is a target in a hunting expedition, not a human being with the right to live.

Do not turn the victims into heroes or symbols in an effort to preserve their humanity. Do not turn death into heroism; death is one thing, heroism is another. The thirteen young men each had a father, a mother, brothers, sisters, friends. Their relatives now live with their absence, but also with their presence. The lost ones still remain with them—children who laugh and cry and play and romp about. These young men did not find their deaths; death found them.

There is no time to speak here about each one of them as an individual. There is not even time enough to cite their names or to address each of their mothers. I did not know them when they lived. But I would have liked to know the stories of their lives. For each, I would have liked to know his childhood, his dreams, his love for others and himself; his anger and his jealousy; and what he liked to eat and drink and wear. I want to hear how each loved his mother and siblings; how he got up in the morning to go to school or work; how he would stay up at night, having fun with friends; how he would be untidy at his home or at school, lose his temper and regain his cool, fall asleep and wake up, stir at all hours of the night and fall asleep during the day, act lazily, industriously, philosophize vulgarities, ignore his mother's advice ("take care of yourself"), ignore his father's protective caution ("stay away from evil out there").

I return to them with the mother who enters the room of her dead son. She opens the door to the room. The mother does not knock. Perhaps she does not want to wake him up; perhaps she does not recognize his right to rule the room: he is part of her, she takes liberties with him, doing things others are not permitted to. He is a part of her, exclusively. And she doesn't knock on the door because she loves to surprise her son, to prove she has control over him. Because he is her son, and only hers.

Now she knows he is not there. She closes her eyes for a second, seeing him in a variety of impossible situations. Sitting and standing at the same time. Speaking while remaining silent. On the bed, behind the desk, on the floor. Turning up the volume on the sound system and lowering it simultaneously. Looking at her impatiently and glancing away disdainfully. Putting on and taking off his shirt. Telling her to leave the room and asking her to come in. Now he is here, now he is no longer, leaving her in tears, his articles strewn all over the room.

The mother who has lost her son looks for the little things that he would do. She peers at doodles in his notebooks, seeks his short letters, his clothes with the smell of perspiration. She takes his shirts, smells them one by one. Perhaps she'll find the one he wore before he went out last. . . .

Mothers do not wash their children's clothes after they die. Mothers do not tidy up their children's rooms after they die. Mothers never fully believe they have gone and will not be back again. Mothers do not fall asleep until their sons return home.

She waits for him as if she thinks he is out for the evening with his friends; she stays up late into the night, rising occasionally, looking out the window, staring into darkness. She imagines his reappearance in the dark; she hears steps, and a door opening; she cranes her neck, frightened and deliriously happy. He comes in, and then does not.

When the memorial services are over, after all the words are spoken, mothers go back to their loneliness, to the quiet weeping, to the sea of tears, to the delirious expectations.

Asil ʿAslah, a high school senior at the Mar Elias College in ʿIblin, was shot by a policeman during the October 2000 demonstrations in ʿArabeh, his home village in Galilee. The bullets were fired at short range. Asil ʿAslah was lying on the ground at the time he was shot; he did not pose the slightest threat to the policeman who killed him.

Asil, who was on the science track at ʿIblin and who specialized in physics, had a lucid political outlook and stood out as a leader from an early age. Coming from a well-read home, he was something of an expert on Palestinian history and knew the biography of every Palestinian leader in rich detail.

Encouraged by his parents and the school, Asil was a leading participant in coexistence meetings held between Palestinian youths, Jewish Israeli youths, and youngsters from the West. He made a special effort to convince his peers at the ʿIblin school to join these encounters. When friends wanted to boycott these meetings in protest against Israeli intransigence, Asil convinced them not to quit. He insisted that such meetings were politically meaningful, that they presented Palestinians with an opportunity to influence Israelis' views on Palestinians, Arabs generally, and the conflict.

Like others of his generation, Asil ʿAslah sharpened his political outlook and beliefs in debates at home as the family watched television. Like his peers, he was exposed to a variety of news and current affairs shows that reflected a wide spectrum of ideological and political outlooks. He watched the news in Arabic and Hebrew on Israeli state television, Hebrew language news on Israel's commercial stations, and, via satellite, news and analyses on many Arabic language stations broadcast from various countries in the Middle East. His family's living room became a theater for arguments over facts, interpretations, and potential implications of political events and process. During his last years at high school, Asil joined the local youth branch of Balad, quickly establishing himself as one of the party's up-and-coming young leaders.

Palestinian students from around the country were stunned by the manner in which Asil was killed—perhaps *murdered* or *executed* is a more accurate term.[11] Local and national Arabic language newspapers vented people's grief and pain. For many, the death of this particular young man became an emblem of collective loss. Poems, letters, and declarations of political resolve were published for months after his death; newborns were named after him.

A solemn ceremony held at Mar Elias College forty days after Asil's death was a major event in the political socialization of youngsters at the institution. Teachers, pupils, and relatives dwelled on the circumstances and meaning of his death. Those participating in the ceremony felt compelled to make some sense, extract some meaning from the tragedy. Many felt the whole event was turning them into better, prouder Palestinians.

For members of an entire generation, the deaths of Asil and the other victims in October 2000 transformed Intifadat al-Aqsa and the Palestinian problem itself into an urgent, highly personal matter. In interviews conducted at the end of 2000, Asil's classmates described the murder as a turning point in their political consciousness. Many related that, prior to Asil's death, they had been hardly aware of the labels they and others were using to describe themselves. They had used labels such as "Palestinians," "Arabs," "Arabs in Israel," "Muslims," "Christians," and others cavalierly, almost at random. This changed after October 2000. Youngsters repeatedly described how the events pushed them to redefine themselves emphatically as Palestinian Arabs. Some added *Muslim* or *Christian* to this label. Among them, allusion to the state of Israel was made only in a technical, descriptive manner, as in "resident of the state of Israel."

Signs of this new awakening had been apparent even before the crisis of October 2000. One vivid illustration came in April 2000, when Palestinian students at Haifa University and later Tel Aviv University and Hebrew University embarked on large-scale protest demonstrations. The wave began at Haifa University, where the Committee of Palestinian Students announced a rally in protest of the death of Shaikha Abu-Saleh, an elderly Palestinian woman from Sakhnin, who died during the annual Land Day demonstration there on March 30.[12]

Adhering to standard procedures at the university, the committee chair, Khulud Badawi, applied to the campus authorities with a formal request to stage a rally. The university administrators, who normally approve such requests on the spot, indicated that in this case they intended to make full use of the seventy-two-hour period that the regulations allow them for reaching a decision and communicating it to the applicants. Badawi and her colleagues in the Committee of Palestinian Students saw the delay as a ploy to deflate their enthusiasm and derail the demonstration, an unfair infringement of their right to express protest at the moment it counted. After some deliberation, they decided not to await authorization. Undeterred by the prospect of clashing with the university administration, right-wing Jewish student groups, and the police, they decided to go ahead and stage the rally.

Right-wing Jewish student organizations were drawn to the event like moths to a flame. Harsh words were quickly supplanted by physical abuse, and the demonstration was soon transformed into a battlefield. The police intervened and made arrests—of Palestinian students only. The following days saw demonstrations and counterdemonstrations organized by Palestinian and Jewish students in other universities. Gradually, the focus of the protests shifted from the controversial death of Shaikha Abu-Saleh to the inherent right of Palestinians to protest. Palestinian Knesset members of all parties, many of whom had begun their own careers a generation earlier as student leaders, showed up on campuses and joined the demonstrations. The high visibility of Palestinian women leaders enticed the Israeli media to give the demonstrations extensive coverage.[13] One photograph became particularly engraved in public memory. It shows Khulud Badawi, surrounded by her Palestinian supporters, sitting on the hood of an automobile, provocatively flashing a finger at right-wing student activists.

Badawi was not the only female Palestinian leader to emerge during the tempestuous spring of 2000. The Palestinian student leadership at the Hebrew University of Jerusalem included, among others, Rinad Haj Yahiyye and Shirin Yunis. 'Arin Hamud, Ruba Hashibon, and Arij Sabaj figured prominently in the leadership of Palestinian students at Tel Aviv University. The interest shown by Hebrew newspapers and television stations grew, creating unprecedented opportunities to spread a message that was becoming ever clearer: Young Palestinian citizens do not see Israel as their state; they have no bond with it and no commitment whatsoever toward it. Their affiliation with it is limited to technicalities. Services rendered to them by virtue of their formal citizenship are irrelevant to their sense of belonging and identity. The affiliation that matters to them in terms of pride, meaning, and fulfillment of identity is the one they have with the Palestinian struggle for national assertion. This is where their politicized ambitions lie. They will never be content with second-class citizenship in their own homeland. These sentiments, and the assertive demand for change that came with them, were expressed in a militant rhetoric that angered the Jewish Israeli mainstream. Not surprisingly, responses on the part of Israeli readers oscillated between disappointment, indignation, and blatant racist incitement.[14]

The Stand-Tall Generation, members of which had been born roughly at the time of Land Day 1976, came of political age in the shadow of two parallel processes. One was the disillusionment of Palestinian citizens with the struggle for civil equality, as described in the previous chapter. The other was the strides made by the Palestinian national movement since the beginning of the 1990s.

The Palestinian national movement took its current shape with the first intifada, which began in 1988, when members of the Stand-Tall Generation were still children. During the 1990s, however, they were old enough to realize the significance of the intifada for Palestinian history and nation building.[15] Admittedly, the pro-Iraqi position held by Yasser Arafat and the PLO during the Gulf War of 1991 threatened to marginalize the Palestinian cause in the West. But as the Madrid Peace Conference took shape later that year, the PLO and Arafat became internationally recognized as the only legitimate representatives of the Palestinians. Paradoxically, it was the insistence of then Prime Minister Yitzhak Shamir and his young deputy Minister of Foreign Affairs Benjamin Netanyahu that the PLO be excluded from Madrid that underscored the indispensable role of the organization. Arafat and his colleagues in exile participated indirectly in the conference, influenced its outcome, and arranged for themselves to be treated as equal partners in the discussions that led to the Oslo process in 1992–1993.

The fundamental flaws of the Madrid negotiation process and its outcomes notwithstanding, this chapter in the history of the Middle East achieved a number of significantly positive results. First, it persuaded Israel to recognize the legitimacy of Palestinian national aspirations and the PLO as its representative organ. Second, it won widespread international support for an independent Palestinian state alongside Israel. Third, it enabled the return of the Palestinian national leadership from exile to the territories. Finally, it established the principle and practice of transfer of territories from Israeli control to Palestinian sovereignty, thus signaling the inevitability of establishing a Palestinian state.

The Palestinian national movement has a long way to go before its goals are genuinely fulfilled. But these achievements, coming at the tail end of a century that saw Palestinian defeat, dispossession, and humiliation, were tangible and irreversible. They turned Palestinian nationalism into a viable option for young Palestinians everywhere; those who happen to be citizens of Israel are no exception. Their sense of national belonging could now cross geographic, class, and religious lines to form a solid anchor for their newly asserted identity.

These achievements of the Palestinian national movement and the pride it generated made the tepid results of the civil struggle within Israel look all the more inadequate. Youngsters became outspoken critics of, for example, Palestinians' focus on gaining membership in the Knesset. They saw it as a Sisyphean struggle, unlikely to yield acceptable solutions to fundamental problems of identity, belonging, or equity in the distribution of resources.

While the actual place of Palestinian citizens of Israel within the Palestinian fold is yet to be determined, nationalistic sentiments clearly became a focal point of their identity at the expense of other options. The political significance of pan-Arabism subsided. Softer versions of this ideology, including those articulated by the Ba'ath movements in Iraq and Syria in the 1980s and the 1990s lost currency when the United States–led coalition during the 1991 Gulf War had Arab expeditionary forces fighting, symbolically at least, alongside Western armies. The weakness of pan-Arab solidarity becomes abundantly apparent whenever Egypt, Jordan, Saudi Arabia, Libya, or other Arab states seek economic or strategic understanding with the United States. Not surprisingly, many Palestinian citizens of Israel are uncomfortable with the pro-Syrian inclinations displayed by some of their leaders, particularly when they are couched in pan-Arabist discourse that has little effect on realpolitik. The aloofness and unhelpful attitude of Damascus toward the Palestinians in recent years exacerbates this disenchantment, as does the hesitancy of most Arab states to go beyond verbal support for the Palestinians even at times when Israeli incursions, the inhumane construction of the separation wall, and the brutal erasure of entire sections of Palestinian towns such as Jenin or Rafah are the order of the day.

The Muslim paradigm, while clearly on the ascent, is likewise limited in its capacity to form a new focus for Palestinian self-perception. As elsewhere, emerging technologies and new transnational communication networks notwithstanding, youngsters seek to articulate identity and solidarity in terms of secular, local and national paradigms. The Islamic movements in the territories and inside Israel do not offer a radical alternative to national identity. Their strength hinges on their promise to provide a more determined and effective pursuit of the nationalist agenda and, in the case of youngsters in the territories, a more empowering way to cope with the humiliation and oppression of daily life under occupation.

Members of the Stand-Tall Generation are well aware of the frustrations associated with the civil struggle for equality and genuine inclusion waged by their parents' generation. This awareness has bred impatient skepticism on their part regarding promises by Israeli politicians and slogans written into preelection manifestos of most Zionist parties. They know discrimination when they see it, and they are enraged by the routine elements of marginalization that their parents may have swallowed. Their very political identity is rooted in a cultural exchange that often turns to struggle—struggle with the state, with the Jewish majority, between ideological generations, between classes and religions, between modes of cultural expression, over tradition and its meanings, for gender equality, and more.

The disappearance of Palestinian urban life and culture from what became the state of Israel in 1948 has severely limited the possible arenas in which productive exchanges might have taken place. Palestinian towns in Galilee and the Triangle, many of which are no more than overgrown villages with limited economic capacity and politicocultural freedom of the kind that typifies most modern cities, hardly provide conducive contexts for such dynamics to be played out productively. Mixed towns, perhaps with the recent exception of Haifa, are unsuitable due to the overwhelmingly Jewish Israeli character they have and the limited sociocultural space they offer Palestinians.

.   .   .   .   .

In 2000, during her last year in law school, Khawla's younger daughter, Nidaa, became engaged to Bilal Abu-Hashem, a young computer expert from Tarshiha, a town some twenty miles northeast of Acre. As a student, Nidaa had been working part-time for the Israeli cell phone company Cellcom at their offices in Haifa, and the couple initially contemplated living there after the wedding. Nidaa was confident she would find a suitable law firm in Haifa for her internship and possibly for further employment. Soon, however, Bilal was offered an excellent job at Yiskar, one of the world's biggest and most technologically advanced producers of industrial steel blades, and one of Israel's most successful corporations. He was to be employed at the main plant in Tefen, near his home town of Tarshiha. Because of the distance, Haifa was no longer an attractive option, and the couple had to reconsider where to settle. Tarshiha, where Bilal's family had property and a leading social position, was of course an option, but Nidaa was not persuaded. Village life did not generally appeal to her, particularly if she was going to be the external party to a large, wealthy, and closely knit family. The couple also knew that living in Tarshiha would greatly reduce Nidaa's professional opportunities as a lawyer. In August 2000, after they were married, they rented an apartment in Nahariya—a predominantly Jewish town next to the Lebanese border on the Mediterranean, ten miles from Tarshiha. Nidaa got an internship in a law firm; Bilal commuted up the hill every day to Tefen.

Then came the October upheaval. Their Jewish neighbors turned nasty. Although they had a two-year lease, by late November they felt so vulnerable, isolated, and even threatened that they pulled out and took an apartment in Acre, on the same street as Nidaa's grandparents Nada and Muhammad. Nidaa found employment in a local law firm, where she worked until she had her first baby, A'dan, a girl, in May 2003.

·   ·   ·   ·   ·

The restrictions on location of residence and on employment that members of the Stand-Tall Generation are subject to leave Israeli universities as a singularly meaningful arena for the quests and challenges that define their place within the Palestinian fold and Israel at large. This is partly why we chose the dilemmas and experiences of university students and, not least, a profile of their leaders, as a primary locus of inquiry into the social and political realities of Palestinians in Israel today.

For the majority of Palestinian youths, enrollment in a university or regional college presents a first opportunity to maintain normal daily contact with Israelis. For those who take up residence on campus or near it, living in a predominantly Jewish town becomes a first encounter with Israeli society and culture. A major issue that emerges for Palestinian youths as a result of this encounter is the extent to which national consciousness, patriotism, and tradition should play in their individual lives and collective experience.

Israeli university campuses make very few provisions for Palestinian students and do not earnestly attempt to integrate them. They treat them mechanistically, reluctantly, like a host begrudgingly extending hospitality to an uninvited guest. This often deepens the conviction among Palestinian students that life for members of minorities who seek proximity with individuals identified as the majority, and with institutions associated with them, is a perpetual struggle.

The different generations of Palestinians inside Israel have varying experiences of university education. The few who attended university in the 1950s and 1960s were loath to complain, viewing whatever obstacles they faced as personal, not communal or political, matters.[16] In subsequent decades Palestinian students became considerably more numerous and grew ever more critical of the system that marginalized them. Their tendency to question and improve their situation led to their initiative in the early 1970s to form independent representative committees outside the general Israeli-dominated student unions. The predominantly male cohort of Palestinian student leaders of that period drew a parallel between the struggle against individual discrimination, the quest for equitable collective status for Palestinian students, and the general struggle for equality in Israel. These leaders, incidentally, constitute the backbone of the cohort of members of Knesset currently representing the DFPE, MADA, and Balad.

Some of the issues that troubled the student leaders of the 1970s and 1980s still vex their counterparts today. Khulud Badawi, who in 2001 was chosen as head of the Committee of Arab Students countrywide, talked in late 2000 of the exclusion that Palestinian students attending Israeli universities experience:

> Everything is strange at first. Your very arrival at the university is overshadowed by a struggle to come to grips with a different, and in many ways quite threatening, environment. You don't know how to put together a course schedule, read a syllabus. You know the language, but it is foreign. Having grown up in an Arab town, I hardly ever heard spoken Hebrew in normal daily life; everything I knew about that language

came from school. Then during study, I find myself thinking in Arabic while the language of instruction is Hebrew. . . .

The feeling of not quite belonging, of being a foreigner, gets worse as time wears on, as does the sense of alienation. This applies to all Palestinian students; but the pressure on the women students is even stronger. They are supposed to "preserve themselves," in line with Arab tradition—a duty Arab men are quite exempt from.

. . . . . .

Dan and Khawla conducted their work sessions on this book mostly in Hebrew. Khawla, who is keenly sensitive to language and fluent in Hebrew, nevertheless made some intriguing slips. Describing her family's departure from Haifa port in 1948, for example, she described the Palestinians gathering on the pier—the Hebrew word for pier is *mezah*—as being huddled on the *mizbeah*. Phonetically similar to *mezah, mizbeah* is nevertheless a radically different word meaning a sacrificial altar. The quay from which her family was sent away from their old hometown was thus transformed into a sacrificial site where victims get sent out of this world to be ritually and sometimes physically consumed.

On another occasion, when Khawla spoke about her family's forced transformation into homeless refugees, she created the neologic Hebrew verb *paltu*—a nonexistent permutation of the noun *palit* (refugee), which resembles the Arabic verb denoting "were made refugees." This irregularity reflects a significant philological fact: unlike Arabic, modern Hebrew (and, for that matter, English) has no verb to describe the process whereby an individual becomes a refugee. In modern Hebrew, being a refugee is construed as a condition that just happens, without definable, preceding action worthy of a verb. Seeing it as a bland occurrence with no real perpetrators, Hebrew allows the assumption that being a refugee might even be a state that develops as the victim's own fault.

Some of the long telephone conversations between Khawla and Dan were conducted in Arabic. Asked the customary question "How are you?" *(Kif halak?)*, Dan sometimes gave the somewhat irregular Arabic

reply "*mdabrin halna*," meaning "Managing ourselves." The first time
Khawla heard this, she thought Dan in fact said "*mdamrin halna*," which
means "Destroying ourselves." Every reference between them to
"*mdabrin halna*" since that time evokes the possibility that the speaker in
fact means that we are all part of collective effort at self destruction.

There is a gap between Dan's colloquial Bedouin Arabic and the high
style that Khawla uses and expects to hear in conversation between
educated people. Dan's Bedouin-Egyptian dialect amuses and surprises
Khawla. His inferior command of what is a third language for him,
compounded by their mutual insistence on speaking Arabic whenever
possible, partially compensates for the asymmetry characterizing their
joint project—a book originally commissioned for an Israeli publisher
and written in Hebrew, and which focuses on Khawla's people as its
object of inquiry.

.   .   .   .   .

Lina Qasem, a medical student who led the Committee of Palestinian Students at Tel Aviv University in 2000–2001 and who, like Khulud Badawi,
is a prominent member of the young cadre of activists in the DFPE, agrees
that the initial encounter with Israeli academia is painful. In 2001 Lina
talked of the need "to justify ourselves at all times":

> The Jewish-Arab struggle is everywhere. First there is the dominant sta-
> tus of Hebrew, a language we do not fully master, particularly at the ini-
> tial stages at the university. Then there is discrimination concerning
> scholarships, loans, and access to dormitories, and of course the long-
> standing refusal of the universities to grant the Committee of Palestinian
> Students formal recognition. There are deep political and emotional rea-
> sons for the growing sense of alienation that all of us experience.

Khulud Badawi believes that Palestinian students in Israeli universities today are more capable and willing to defend their rights than their
predecessors were. From their first moment on campus, she says, they
learn that the only way to attain anything is through a political struggle

along national lines. Shirin Yunis, a member of the Committee of Palestinian Students at Hebrew University in 2001 and a member of the leadership committee of Balad, shares this conviction. She recalls that, upon her arrival at the university, she requested a room in the student dormitories and was turned down. She quickly recognized the rejection as symptomatic of a wider housing problem facing Palestinian students, whom apartment owners in the Jewish parts of town are loath to have as tenants. Yunis immediately embarked on a campaign, initiating meetings, organizing rallies, placing posters, and distributing leaflets. She even brought before a Knesset committee the housing problems that Palestinian students face. Within a month she became one of the better-known female activists on campus.

"Political activity on campus is a natural extension of political work on a national level," says Lina Qasem. "The link between the two is self-explanatory. The Palestinians have been engaged in struggle since 1948, and our generation learned a lot by studying past political experiences. The most important lesson is not to keep quiet. Particularly when the situation is as dire as that of the Palestinians citizens of Israel today."

The link between personal experience and the wider political predicament may be natural and self-explanatory for Palestinian youngsters, but it is a challenge for the Israeli mainstream, university authorities being no exception. Lina Qasem repeatedly encountered attempts by university administrators to squelch political activity on campus. As leader of the Palestinian student body at Haifa, Khulud Badawi too has had to contend with attempts by university authorities to restrain her work, not least by scrutinizing posters and flyers published by the committee. Many such texts are in fact translated from Arabic to Hebrew for inspection. The translations often invoke interpretations that are not intended in the Arabic original, pushing the administration to ban texts under the pretext that Jewish students' feelings might be hurt.

Intifadat al-Aqsa erupted a few weeks before the start of the 2000–2001 academic year. Recalling the tumultuous events of the previous spring and fearing another round of violent clashes on campuses, university administrators countrywide collectively issued a sweeping ban on demonstrations and other political events on campus. The frustration of

Palestinian students knew no bounds. Nihad Buqaʿi, then chairman of the Committee of Palestinian Students at Hebrew University, believes that students must be allowed to express themselves and to respond to whatever happens in society, and that the "awakening" of the Palestinian students in April 2000 was a precursor to the widespread willingness of Palestinians countrywide to stage the demonstrations that October. As he put it to us in 2001, "The universal outcry of all Palestinians in October 2000 addressed the same objective our demonstrators had promoted back in April. Had Ehud Barak done something then to grant us equal rights and to narrow inequalities, he could have given the Palestinian citizens of Israel some hope of being heard."

Politicization is sometimes frowned upon even within the Palestinian camp. Some Palestinian students are critical of deliberate attempts on the part of their own parents to dissuade them from political engagement. A student leader at Tel Aviv University had this to say about her own parents and the trajectory they represent: "Our parents have been too busy preaching avoidance of political activity. They say that politics is for those who have spare time after classes, and that our time should be devoted to real work, one that creates income. It is not the implied refusal to support us economically that bothers me. I am more troubled by the failure to acknowledge that in our circumstances everything and everybody is politicized."

Very few parents are supportive when their children choose politics as a vocation. Some of the youngsters believe this reticence stems from old fears of heavy-handed sanction by the state. One student explains: "The attempts of our parents to stop us [from political activity] is an eerie reification of the long reach of the military government they grew up with in the 1950s and 1960s. The goals of the Israeli establishment, the same establishment that deployed aggressive means to stop them and their parents from legitimate political activity, are achieved today through their deep-seated fears for our well-being."

Parents displayed their lingering fears when they mounted intense efforts to stop their children from participating in the widespread demonstrations and protests in October 2000. For the most part their appeals were unsuccessful. The overwhelming majority of the tens of thousands that gathered on the streets during those fateful days were men and women in their late teens and early twenties. Their rage was partly a belated reaction to the submission and humiliation of the generation shattered by the war of 1948. The suspicion that depoliticized acquiescence may have preceded the expulsion, and that it was perhaps a contributing factor to the defeat of 1948 as much as its result, is not easily discussed in Palestinian circles, because it challenges the notion of uniform, uninterrupted national resilience. Off the record, however, many young Palestinians say they believe this was the case.

A different type of intergenerational tension is apparent in the delicate choreography that takes place between student activists and leaders of parties they are personally affiliated with. Lina Qasem stresses that political parties who represent the Palestinian sector take student activities and organizations very seriously, genuinely recognizing that work within the universities is an important asset. Rinad Haj Yahiyye is more critical. Palestinian leaders, she feels, including Knesset members who all belong to her parents' generation, tend to patronize student activists. "They hear me and my peers," she says, "and then continue treating us like babies. They want us to partake in demonstrations that they stage, but do not really go along with our opinions."

Gender presents young Palestinian men and women with a number of perplexing dilemmas, many of which become particularly relevant once they arrive at an Israeli university. One is the tension between values of gender equality and individual freedom on the one hand and deeply embedded male-centered cultural norms on the other. Young women are especially preoccupied with the extent to which they can adopt norms that prevail in Israeli daily life on campus without compromising themselves and being shunned in their more conservative communities of origin. Unlike male students, they are expected to refrain from trends and lifestyles associated with the West, particularly in terms of attire, dating, and sexual behavior. Many Palestinian women students in fact prefer to "play it safe" and confine themselves to the unofficial, self-proclaimed Palestinian "ghettos" on the various campuses, keeping contact with Israelis to a minimum. Remarks such as "We must remember at all times that we are Palestinian women, and that our values differ from those of Israelis" are commonplace among women students and their families, to the extent that they sometimes sound like compulsive mantras.

The issue is not confined to individual conduct. It has collective aspects, and Palestinian students sometimes articulate these in terms of politico-cultural responsibility: to safely filter the influences of modernization, globalization, and other signatures of Western values so that change, when it finally takes place, is not forced on them. Likewise, young women who on a personal level may insist on higher education, a career, freedom to choose a partner, control over the timing of their own marriage, and the right to lead a life away from rigid supervision by kinsfolk may at the same time declare heartfelt commitment to traditional Palestinian values.

"We must be different from our parent's generation," one male student said of gender relations. "It would be wrong if all we did was complete our studies, take our diplomas, and just go home. We have to change the way we think." Some of his female colleagues wondered whether his statement in support of gender equality was genuine, or whether it was just a bon ton utterance, a Stand-Tall-Generation version of political correctness.

Palestinian women have been trying to put gender issues on the public agenda for over fifty years.[17] Success, however, has been elusive. The few who managed to liberate themselves know full well that the majority of women are still subject to traditional male control. Moreover, they are cognizant of the frustrating choice many Arab women face between active feminism and normative incorporation in their communities and families.

Thirty years ago the number of Palestinian women enrolled in Israeli universities was so small that it was possible for one to know most of them by name.[18] Those days are long gone. The Israeli Central Bureau of Statistics indicates that, by the late 1990s, 51 percent of Palestinian undergraduates at Israeli universities and colleges were women. This increase did not come easy. Palestinian women who seek academic training when they graduate from high school must have a strong self-image, a proven record of academic achievement, and parents who support their desire to realize their potential.

What remains unclear is the extent to which increased female enroll-ment in undergraduate programs expands women's influence and status in their communities and in the public sphere.[19] A clearer picture emerges when it comes to postgraduate degrees.[20] The evidence suggests that more women than ever before now pursue higher degrees, many of them persisting after they become engaged and married and even after they have children. The old reluctance to delay marriage has obviously dimin-ished. Women students we interviewed expressed their confidence that, even if unmarried by their late twenties, they will nevertheless find the right partner if and when he comes along.[21]

Most Palestinian students in Israel, including many women, now live in or near the campuses at which they study. Some finance their studies themselves. A select few find attractive, well-paid jobs—becoming, for example, parliamentary assistants or managers in nongovernmental organizations—and are likely to join the growing ranks of Palestinian women who play leading roles in professional institutions or find ways to become involved in industry and commerce. Unwilling to be stereo-typical Arab women, this vanguard is at the same time reluctant to be assimilated into Western culture and its values.

The Palestinian student body on Israeli campuses is a microcosm rep-resenting future trends in the Palestinian community. It supports women's struggle for gender equality but, at the same time, is still a cul-tural-normative collage of fragmentary and contradictory views. It is home to an incoherent assortment of ideas eclectically drawn from Arab tradition and Western sources, where young, innovative reformers rub shoulders with conservative traditionalists. Not surprisingly, its mem-bers and leadership are often caught up in fierce debates about equality, democracy, and the obstacles that still prevent the realization of these ideals.

.   .   .   .   .

After Nidaa and Bilal set a date for their wedding, the groom's family was invited to Khawla's home in Acre to discuss the preparations for the engagement party. Bilal's affluent family graciously offered to take over

Nidaa's tuition fees for the balance of her legal training, purchase the wedding dress, and provide the furniture for the couple's new apartment. Khawla declined to allow this, indicating that Nidaa's education had been and would always be her responsibility. She also insisted on paying an equal share of the expenses associated with the marriage. Nidaa used her next visit with her elder sister, Taymaa, in Montreal, to purchase the clothes she needed for the wedding ceremonies.

A fortnight or so before the wedding, the groom's family invited Khawla to their home, this time to finalize the *kitab,* the marriage contract between the partners and, by extension, between their families. The *kitab* typically includes the sum agreed upon as bride-price, a sum agreed upon as future compensation in case of subsequent divorce, specification of the couple's place of residence, and so on. Bilal's father, an imam, is also a professional *m'azun* (religious clerk), and was going to write the *kitab* himself. In preparation for the meeting, he made a telephone call to Khawla, requesting the presence of her father and her two brothers. Since Nidaa's father, Khawla's first husband, Muhammad May, had died when Nidaa was a toddler, requesting the presence of the bride's grandfather and uncles was understandable.

When the meeting began, Khawla noticed that the groom's father was addressing her father, whom he appropriately called *kbirna* (our eldest). Khawla's father, fully aware that his presence in the meeting was mainly ceremonial, looked at Khawla, expecting her to take the lead in a talk that concerned her own daughter. He was right. Khawla respectfully allowed the two elders to complete their mutual salutations, then made her own speech.

Beginning with a statement to the effect that her daughters had been raised laboriously, and that she, a single mother, had made a considerable effort to give them everything they needed at whatever cost, Khawla then firmly requested that the *kitab* not specify a sum as brideprice. "My girl," she said, "is an independent person, and specifying a price tag for her will be degrading." The *m'azun* politely mentioned that a price is required in Islam, to which Khawla replied by inquiring what would be the minimal symbolic sum that met this religious stipulation. The answer was that twenty shekels—the sum required to purchase

official contract stamps to make the formal document a binding one—
would do, and so it was agreed.

With bride-price out of the way, the next hurdle was the *mu'akhar*—
the potential compensation the bride would be entitled to should the
marriage run aground. Once again, Khawla refused to discuss a sum.
The *qadi* (Muslim Shari'a judge) of Acre, a friend of the family who was
with them, suggested the *mu'akhar* could be written down as the
amount "appropriate to a young woman of her standing." Next they
turned to what the *kitab* might specify as the couple's future place of
residence. The groom's father, who wanted his only son to live near his
family, insisted on Tarshiha. Khawla argued that the place of residence
should remain undecided, and that the couple should make their own
decision later. A genuine argument ensued, at the end of which Khawla
got her way again. The place of residence was written as "where the
couple decides." The *kitab* was finally ready, and Khawla signed it on
behalf of Nidaa's side—an unusual step that she repeated a year later,
when the time came to sign the *kitab* of Taymaa, her older daughter.
Khawla is probably one of very few Muslim mothers who have negoti-
ated their daughters' betrothals in such fashion.

·   ·   ·   ·   ·

Female Palestinian activists had participated in student committees
before. In April 2000, however, many women in leadership positions in
the student body found themselves in the media spotlight. As is often the
case, visibility was partly the result of novelty: young Palestinian women
are seldom in militant leadership positions, and journalists always appreciate an interesting change. More important, however, was the women
leaders' own agency with respect to the media. From an early stage that
spring, they consciously refused to play a decorative role, consistently
cultivating their images as professional, efficient, and reliable leaders. For
many Israelis, the appearance of this type of leadership offered insight
into the work and lives of Palestinian women the likes of which had not
been seen before.

Some male Palestinian student leaders claim that their female peers had not been particularly active on the campuses before April 2000. In their view, had male student leaders not been arrested at the early stages of the protest, the role of women students would have remained obscure. This argument, which may reflect the sequence of events as they developed, is only partially relevant. By taking charge of the situation, women leaders proved beyond any doubt that, given proper opportunity, they could demonstrate their merit, and that rigid demarcations between gender roles can be successfully eroded even in a society where tradition, stability, and continuity are at a premium.

As indicated, the Israeli media was quick to recognize the significance of the emerging female leaders. The leaders themselves, however, could never relax their battle against stereotypical clichés and orientalizing gazes that some journalists and editors were tempted to employ. Some articles and broadcasts were premised on simplistic dichotomies between the archaic image of Arab women as submissive, inarticulate, and tame, on the one hand, and the image of these contemporary, charismatic, and dynamic students on the other. A year after this stream of media images first appeared, the young women depicted in them were still unwilling to forgive sloppy, decontextualized remarks and quotes and the distortions they produced. Some of them indicated that Jewish women journalists were often as bad as their male colleagues, because they focused on the private lives of activists as Arab women, disregarding their political achievements.

Khulud Badawi's picture, seated on the hood of a car flashing a finger defiantly at right-wing demonstrators in Haifa University in April 2000, appeared in a popular Israeli newspaper the following day and was reproduced a number of times afterward. Does the bold finger flash carry sexual connotation or not? If it does, was it intended? Badawi, who had successfully imposed her leadership on large crowds where men were in a majority, inspired Palestinian youngsters up and down the country and gained personal prestige in the process. Her hope was to use the publicity she got to raise the issue of the right of Palestinians, particularly women, to free speech. She soon found out, however, that her image sparked a different discussion, one she hardly wanted to be part of.

Rather than turning into a serious debate of the political agenda she was devoted to, discussions concerning her tended to focus on her image as "a provocative woman."

Khulud was under scrutiny in both the Israeli and the Palestinian public spheres. In the Palestinian camp, she was subjected to a classic attempt at the social control of women. In discussions between students, male leaders questioned the leadership image she projected. Such discussions were ostensibly framed in terms of political efficacy, but the subtext was quite different and had more to do with the extent to which a woman should be allowed to lead national events. Clearly, the potential hidden in this option threatened Badawi's male contemporaries in ways that went beyond mere jealousy of individual roles. A deeper sociocultural dynamic was at play.

Criticism of Badawi in the Israeli public sphere was different. Here the tendency was to depict her as politically extreme, a recalcitrant figure that had taken beyond the pale the liberties afforded her both by her own community and by the state. The debate thus assumed ethnonational proportions, making crafty use of cultural differences between Israeli and Palestinian norms of acceptable public behavior. In both cases, the debate provoked by Khulud Badawi's defiant photograph muffled her actual political agenda. In the following months she invested considerable effort in reconstituting her credentials as a political leader valued for her convictions, personality, and talent.

.   .   .   .   .

After Nidaa had her baby girl, A'dan, in May 2003, she took almost a year off work, looking after the little one at home. Khawla was there a few times a week, combining visits to her daughter and granddaughter with calls upon her parents next door. At the end of ten months, Nidaa, who was ready to go back to work, decided to start her own law practice. Khawla enthusiastically encouraged the move and, initially, helped out with the rent of an office in downtown Acre. Khawla also took time off work and looked after A'dan, thus affording Nidaa more free time.

Khawla often took the baby over to her own mother, Nada, A'dan's great-grandmother. When Nada's older women friends saw Khawla's car parked on the street, they sometimes came over, bringing with them official documents or letters they wanted Khawla's help with.

As Nidaa's practice grew, she became more willing to live in Tarshiha, where Bilal's parents had set aside a handsome plot for their youngest child and only son to build a home on. A house much larger and luxurious than they could ever dream of in Acre, Nahariya, or Haifa was indeed being built for them on the plot in 2004, and the couple planned to move there in early 2005. Nidaa made plans to commute to her law offices in Acre five days a week.

.   .   .   .   .

Leaders of the Palestinian student body in Israeli universities are well-known figures. Some combine their studies with employment in the service of senior politicians. Their names are often in the Arab-language newspapers, at times making the Hebrew press as well. They publish articles and occasionally appear on Israeli television news.

Surprisingly, many of them come from depoliticized homes, their link to politics having been formed elsewhere. One obvious avenue is the cultural and community activities organized over the years by the Communist Party and more recently by other political movements. Another path is through meetings with Israeli youths that are organized by schools as part of programs promoting coexistence.

Mu'ayad Mea'ari, a native of Sakhnin in Galilee, whom we interviewed in 2001, became politically motivated by other means. When he was a child, his family moved from Galilee to East Jerusalem, where he grew up surrounded by Jerusalemite Palestinians. His peers saw Mu'ayad and his family, with their Israeli citizenship and identification cards, as outsiders. They called him "the Israeli kid," causing him to feel like an outsider. His inner desire to prove that his national conviction and his loyalty were equal to that of all his friends, he says, later fueled a deep infatuation with Palestinian history and politics.

Ironically, when Muʿayad Meaʿari applied to Tel Aviv University and presented his matriculation record from the excellent East Jerusalem high school that he attended, he was treated as a foreigner. However, he was determined to study law in Israel, and so he refused to quit. He fought for a place in the law school, was offered one, and later became the chair of the Committee of Palestinian Students at the university. His tenacity originated partly in his desire to have professional credentials in Israeli law and to enjoy the opportunities that come with such credentials. At the same time, having lived outside Israeli life in East Jerusalem since childhood, he was fascinated with Israeli culture and wanted to know as much as possible about it. And while Israeli students had difficulty accepting him, a Palestinian resident of East Jerusalem, he insists that their exclusionary attitude only strengthened him. "I refuse to accept their sense of superiority" he says. "I will not let them treat me as though they're doing me a favor."

For Palestinian youths, student life on the fringe of Israeli cities and in the Palestinian enclaves that emerge in them can aggravate their sense of alienation from Israel and Israelis. Despite appearances as bustling, liberal, and open arenas, Israeli cities remain, in essence, spaces designed for Israeli Jews. Unable to penetrate them—Haifa, again, is the exception—and no longer attracted to their rural communities of origin, young Palestinian urban immigrants remain liminal.

But Israeli universities are, of course, more than merely homogeneous normative expressions of Zionist hegemony against which Palestinian youths must struggle to define themselves as members of a national minority. Academic training remains a central avenue for personal growth, and the university is a site where individuals gain vital resources and qualifications that they bring back to their communities—without which the communities stand even less chance of gaining parity.

Like their Israeli peers, and indeed like youngsters who enroll in higher education institutions anywhere, young Palestinians are strongly committed to professionalism. With economic development in their home communities remaining slow, most employment opportunities lie in Israeli cities. These young people are aware that, like their parents and their older siblings, they are unlikely to be offered challenging profes-

sional positions in cities at the expense of Israelis with compatible qualifications. The only sector relevant for them that has seen significant
development in recent decades is the voluntary sector, where non-
government organizations (NGOs), many of them funded from abroad,
fill in the vacuum left by state neglect in an attempt to strengthen education, welfare, and social services for Palestinian communities. Alongside
service-providing NGOs, there are also those designed to review goals,
policies, performance, and results of state agencies that provide services
to Palestinian individuals and communities.

With time, professionals and experts who serve in such watchdog
institutions became authoritative figures in their own right; their advice
is keenly sought, and some of them are invited to spearhead new
attempts to improve and restructure services. This growth may provide
a temporary solution to the rhetorical question, *Hakmak zalmak tishki
hamak lamin?* (When the one who rules you is also he who abuses you,
where can you carry your complaint?). When the one who rules is the one
who persecutes, people voice their pain to NGOs run by expert Palestinian professionals and funded by Western foundations and organizations.

Many young Palestinians see a future for themselves in organizations
and institutions such as ʿAdallah, which addresses legal questions; Itijah,
Musawah, and Jmaʿiyat al-Jalil, which do applied social and economic
research; Huquq al-Insan (the Center for Human Rights); Iʿalam, which
deals with coverage of Palestinians inside Israel in the Israeli and international media; Mada, which provides up-to-date surveys and social studies of various aspects of minorities in Israel; and many more. Hopes placed
with such organizations are premised on the belief that genuine change
requires expert, professional specialization applied with dedication in
well-defined fields; that the third sector will continue to play a critical role
in the struggle for progress and equality; and that responsible individuals
who become active will help expand existing institutions and establish
new ones and are bound to motivate the state to do its share as well.

The trust that Palestinian citizens of Israel place in NGOs reflects their
dwindling faith in governmental agencies as well as disillusionment
with formal parliamentary politics. The fact the Knesset has some Palestinian members may provide an opportunity to occasionally speak truth

in the face of power. This notwithstanding, many point at the miserable failure of Palestinian Knesset members to effect any real change in the condition of those they represent. Many Palestinians realize that campaigns ostensibly mounted to serve the interests of the community are often marred by ugly, inner power struggles and sometimes lead to self-defeat. Some Knesset members, they know, end up exerting less influence on processes of social change than do activists in humbler civil institutions. Shirin Yunis referred to this duality in an interview with us:

> I was born to a political reality in which the state of Israel is a solid entity, not an ephemeral episode. The Palestinian citizens had realized that Israel had taken root, and that their task now was to stage a struggle aimed at changing their positions in it. My own plan is accordingly to persist in this struggle through my activity in politics. True, I am a party person, a member of Balad's central committee. But I view NGOs and formal activity in the Knesset as divergent options that ultimately contribute to the same objective. I believe that even for those individuals who do become members of the Knesset, parliamentary activity is no more than one stage in life.

Like Shirin, Khulud Badawi is not convinced that student leaders should necessarily view Knesset membership as the supreme goal of their careers. In fact she believes that the social needs of Palestinians in Israel are better served by leaders involved with popular organizations, and that members of her generation will soon lead such groups.[22]

Practical considerations thus lead many Palestinian students to seek involvement with NGOs rather than with parties. At the same time, and like many of their Israeli counterparts, many want to graduate, conclude their stint as activists, and then use whatever professional expertise they possess to gain economic security. A survey conducted in 1994 looked at the relative importance that Palestinian citizens of Israel assign to eighteen parameters of personal and community progress. Given top priority was the ability to provide one's children with a good education so as to positively influence their future. Adequate municipal services came second. Purchasing or building a home, attaining a challenging job in a field of professional expertise, and making connections "with the right people" also ranked high.[23]

.   .   .   .   .

When A'dan, Nidaa's baby, was a few months old, Nidaa began to plan her own return to work. As one option, she could have filled a vacancy for a police prosecutor just announced at the Acre police department. Nidaa, who had the qualifications required, and who lived literally across the street from the police station and the courthouse, was very clear in her decision not to apply. As a Palestinian, she found the idea of wearing a police uniform and representing the state so soon after the October shootings to be simply untenable, especially since a substantial proportion of the cases the Acre precinct brought to court were against Palestinian individuals. Joining the civil service, attractive as it may have been in terms of work hours and the possibility of reconciling it with raising a young family, was not really an option for Nidaa.

In May 2004 Khawla was approached by a personal aid to Limor Livnat, Israel's minister of education, who offered her an appointment as an adviser to the minister in the Palestinian sector. This type of opportunity seldom arises for independent Palestinian intellectuals in Israel—a chance to make a difference at the highest level. On the other hand, it might have been a meaningless appointment designed mainly to function as another feather in the cap of hard-line right-winger Livnat, a shrewd operator and an avowed protagonist of women's empowerment. Khawla inquired for further details. The aid explained that she would be working as part of an advisory committee and suggested that they send her some forms so the appointment process could get under way. Forms did indeed arrive, but they had no further information whatsoever on the context and actual influence of the position. Khawla did not fill them in or return them. A few weeks later a secretary called to inquire. Khawla explained that she needed a comprehensive job description as well as strong assurances that her time and energy would not be wasted. Her Jewish colleagues at Yezrael College urged her to accept the appointment. Their argument was that, if she let this opportunity pass her by, it would be offered to someone less likely to bring positive change. Khawla was not convinced, and awaited further clarification and assurances.

·   ·   ·   ·   ·

Many mainstream Israelis, in particular those within the liberal left known as the "peace camp," would dearly like to believe that the collective strife of Palestinian citizens will be resolved by incremental improvement in the lives of individuals. However, Palestinians, like many members of minorities elsewhere, know that ideologies stressing equality of individuals tend to overlook matters like identity, historical justice, and collective rights. Many Israeli liberals who champion equal individual rights consistently refuse to recognize the Palestinian citizens of Israel as holders of collective rights analogous to rights that Jewish Israelis have in, among many other laws, the Law of Return and the Law of Israel Lands, which effectively bar Palestinians from access to and ownership of state-owned land.

In fact, groups belonging to the left wing of Zionism such as Mapam, Hakibbutz Ha'artzi, and others have played significant roles in seizure and expropriation of Palestinian property during and immediately after the war of 1948.[24] There is a direct connection between the Zionist Left's insensitivity to this element of the Palestinian predicament and its persistent failure to effect change. Liberalism, which puts a premium on individuals as the chief social actors and minimizes the import of groups and their collective interests, plays into the hands of those who hold more power. Alternative subaltern histories that have no representation in mainstream public discourse remain suppressed. Members of hegemonic groups take the representation they produce for granted. Others have to fight to get a hearing. Liberalism is thus incorporated in a larger, more exploitative system camouflaged by the veneer of cleanliness and justice that shapes the liberal package.

The ahistorical approach that stresses individual rights subverts the pursuit of historic justice for collectives. This is one reason why the demand to make Israel "a state of all its citizens," adopted wholesale in the 1990s by most Palestinian citizens of Israel, has lost some of its impetus and is eclipsed by a perspective that takes into account the limitations of civil discourse in Israel. Offering prestigious economic or political appointments for Palestinian individuals, and even remedying gaps in physical or social infrastructure in a particular village, will no longer do.

Leaders of the Stand-Tall Generation seek to obtain their rights from the state while at the same time preserving and developing their natural affiliation with the Palestinian people. Keenly aware of the solid and legitimate status of Jews, including Zionist-inclined Jews, in democratic Western states, they view their own duality as equally valid and proper. They do not seek secession from the state; rather, they seek an arrangement that allows them legitimate expression of solidarity with Palestine and Palestinians within the framework of the state. Young Palestinian citizens of Israel harbor a deep faith—perhaps unrealistically—in the ability of the Palestinian national movement to offer them a clear identity. This sentiment, combined with rage at Israeli policies of discrimination and marginalization, feeds their sober disillusionment with the prospects of genuine civil equality in Israel.

One result of this is a dilemma that recently has preoccupied many Palestinians of the Stand-Tall Generation: namely, whether or not to participate in projects that promote coexistence. The validity and legitimacy of such participation became a pressing issue after the events of October 2000. The killing of civilian demonstrators by police presents some penetrating ethical problems that have no simple answers. Are coexistence activities merely used by the state to cloak continuing oppressive policies? Do such activities allow Israelis to dodge debates of more unsettling issues associated with majority-minority relations? Is the self-congratulatory assumption on the part of Israeli counterparts that they have "done their bit" by taking part in coexistence events an impediment to genuine reconciliation? Do these workshops broadcast a distorted message of "business as usual" when the ground is burning? Are they traps that stop Palestinians from engaging in more meaningful political activity?

As a member of the DFPE committed to promoting cooperation between Jewish Israelis and Palestinians, Khulud Badawi concedes that the protests of April 2000 damaged such efforts, but she thinks that the events of October 2000 were even more significant. They triggered, she says, a widespread process of soul-searching and reevaluation on the part of Palestinian youngsters. Many activists who had regularly participated in coexistence activities were finding them, after 2000, to be less justifiable, less worth the trouble. She herself, Badawi said in early 2001, needed more reflection before she could return to projects and activities she once pursued regularly. Within the DFPE, activists appear to have kept faith in the basic notion of coexistence, but members of other movements are more skeptical. All are less inclined today than they were before to spend time and effort in attempts to "persuade" Israelis. The willingness to view the very cultivation of dialogue with Israelis as a worthy goal in its own right is on the decline.

The events of October 2000 moved many of our interviewees to refute Israel's self-image as a rational, evenhanded, and egalitarian entity that confers equal rights on all its citizens. For our interviewees, the state of Israel has failed, and it is now their turn to put it on probation. Once the state offers genuine equality, including the recognition of collective rights and the rectification of past wrongs, it will be up to them to consider the option of genuine participation. Until then, they see the state as a mere provider of services, not a locus of true affiliation. The confused ambivalence that plagued their parents' generation, a generation that belonged and was excluded at the same time, has vanished. Their point of departure—a clear sense of not belonging—is their first step toward emancipation.

The Stand-Tall Generation is no monolith. No generation is. A significant number of its members have been socialized in the apolitical manner intended by the state and administered through its formal education system. The result is neutral, denoting neither "Israelization" nor Palestinian consciousness. Instead, individuals with a barren sensibility have emerged, fearful of political involvement, merely seeking "to get along" and find safe havens in the middle ground. Shunning public activity, those who subscribe to this trajectory are satisfied with relatively small improvements in living conditions. Their Arabic is replete with Hebrew, and they speak neither to perfection. Some view service with the Israel Defense Forces as a viable employment option; many others shy away from the normative moral debate this option raises.[25] While education levels continuously rise, many Palestinians drop out in junior high school, ending up with no real knowledge of Palestinian history, no vocational qualifications, and hardly any options in the employment marketplace. Some seek residence in Israeli cities in an attempt to blend in and to escape the difficult conundrum of Palestinian identity and fate.

Four years after the tumultuous events of April and October 2000, some are questioning the effect of the Stand-Tall Generation. In an article titled "Where Has the Stand-Tall Generation Disappeared?" (2004), Khulud Badawi converses with some of the individuals we also interviewed for the Hebrew version of this book, published in late 2002. One of them complains that the generation no longer stands tall. "Most of its members," he says, "are immersed in their own personal interests and have lost interest in what is happening around them with their fellow nationals, in their society, in the state. . . . They are led by the media revolution, absorbed in the world of consumerism, and are into 'super star' and 'star academy.'"[26] Others indicate that whatever ideas the members of the Stand-Tall Generation may have had, their influence on reality has been limited, not least due to an atmosphere of fear that has emerged during Intifadat al-Aqsa, following September 11, and as a result of terrorist attacks in Israeli cities and the tight security that was instituted to contain the threat.

Both ideas, we feel, are true. Yes, the Stand-Tall Generation does represent a quantum leap in its political awareness and its ability to communicate its sensibilities to the Israeli public; and yes, reality has not become transformed by it. For the Palestinians in and outside Israel, life has become much harsher in recent years. But the Mannheimian test of generations is first and foremost their sense of unified experience, common awareness, and sameness of interpretation of reality as it unfolds around them, not necessarily their ability to shape it, as Generation X of the 1980s amply illustrated.

Ideas and ideologies affect reality in surreptitious ways. One manifestation of a trend that characterizes the Stand-Tall Generation—namely, the tendency to disengage from Israeli parliamentary politics—came in the prime ministerial elections held in February 2001 following the resignation of Ehud Barak, when Palestinian voters decided to boycott the elections. Out of 520,000 eligible voters in what is officially classified the minority sector (including Druze), less than 100,000 (a mere 18 percent), came to cast their ballots. Compared with his performance in 1999, Ehud Barak lost over 320,000 votes in this sector, in a campaign in which the winner, Ariel Sharon, had a total of just over a million votes.[27]

Some view the Palestinian boycott of 2001 as a luxury: the elections did not involve Knesset seats, and there was no Palestinian candidate for the premiership. Moreover, all surveys indicated that Ehud Barak was going to lose even if the entire Palestinian population turned up to vote for him. But the dynamic that produced this boycott, in which members of the Stand-Tall Generation, families of victims of October 2000, and various NGOs played a major role, was most significant. For the first time ever, the Palestinian citizens of Israel decisively turned away from the Zionist left, signaling that they have had enough of settling for lesser evils, indicating they can no longer be expected to vote only so as to stop a right-wing candidate. From now on, they will insist on hard political currency in exchange for their support.

The Stand-Tall Generation and the consciousness that it engenders is likely to play a role in years to come as well. Raja Zaʿatrah, former president of the countrywide Committee of Palestinian Students, is convinced that the reeducation of Palestinian students and their transformation into a viable political force can happen only if their numbers increase. Quantitative expansion of academically trained individuals, he argues, will strengthen their qualitative influence. To help stimulate this growth, he seeks to create a forum for Palestinians with academic credentials. "A people that wants to be treated with respect must establish institutions that serve its needs," he told us in 2001. "And that can happen only if the status and influence of those with academic training is enhanced."

In 2001, Muʿayad Meaʿari made the following forecast: "In fifteen years, the generation currently enrolled in universities will spearhead parliamentary activity. If we go on like our fathers and grandparents, we are doomed to fail and might arrest change rather than enhance it. The Palestinians must refuse to live on the margins of Israeli society. Palestinian students must learn from historical examples elsewhere in which students inspired changes in regimes."

Chapter Five

In March 2000 a panel of Supreme Court judges headed by Chief Justice
Aharon Barak delivered a precedent-setting ruling. The case in point
involved a young Palestinian family named Qaʿdan. The family, a couple
and their three young children, applied in 1995 to buy a plot of land and
build their home in Katzir, a suburban settlement established by the Jewish Agency a few years earlier in Wadi Aʿara, near Um al-Fahim.

The Qaʿdans were not the first Palestinian family to seek residence in
Katzir. A dozen or so Palestinian families already lived there as tenants
or homeowners. The Qaʿdans were different, though: they wanted to buy
and build on Western Hill, a relatively new section of Katzir designed to
become the settlement's most exclusive and attractive project. In fact, the
Jewish Agency, the driving force behind the planning and implementation of all new settlements in Israel, had taken measures to ensure that

the residents of Western Hill were ethnically and socioeconomically select. It registered a cooperative association to run the new project, complete with bylaws that required all prospective residents to be vetted by a screening committee. Such screening processes are by no means unique. Kibbutzim, moshavim, and other community settlements in Israel have depended on such things for decades. The Qaʿdans applied and were flatly rejected. The new community, they were told verbally in response to their inquiry, was designed for Jewish Israelis only.

Israel has no constitution. Instead it has a number of basic laws that define, for example, major institutions of the state such as the Knesset, the office of prime minister, the presidency, and the court system. In 1992 the Knesset passed a new basic law titled the Law of Human Dignity and Freedom. It stresses that equality is paramount, and that when the allocation of state resources is at stake, individuals can neither be excluded nor enjoy preferential treatment. The Qaʿdans, who had in their possession documents exposing a sordid sequence of institutional manipulation the sole aim of which was to exclude them because they were Palestinians, contacted the Association for Civil Rights in Israel. The association quickly realized that refusal on the part of the Cooperative Association of Katzir to let the Qaʿdans buy land and build their home was a flagrant infringement of the Law of Human Dignity and Freedom and, on behalf of the family, appealed to the High Court of Justice. The defendants named were the Cooperative Association of Katzir, the Jewish Agency, and the Israel Land Administration.

The early stages of the case revealed the Supreme Court's difficult position. On the one hand, it could not condone such an obvious violation of a basic right. On the other hand, the justices realized that a ruling in favor of Qaʿdan and against Katzir, the Jewish Agency, and the Israel Land Administration would have far-reaching historic and political consequences. Chief Justice Aharon Barak himself remarked more than once that the (Jewish) population of Israel was not yet prepared for a ruling on this case. He and his colleagues, in fact, did all they could to avoid or at least delay a ruling. They urged the parties to settle out of court, cajoled them to negotiate, and offered them repeated extensions to facilitate agreement. In March 2000, five years after the initial appeal, when it finally became apparent that reconciliation was impossible, the court reluctantly ruled in favor of the Qaʿdans.

Compared with earlier rulings by Israeli courts on land issues, the decision was indeed groundbreaking. It explicitly barred Israeli institutions from allocating land in a discriminatory fashion. It upheld the right of individuals to settle wherever they wish, thus challenging practices that had been routine for almost a century. In doing so the ruling established itself as one of the most emphatic manifestations of the principal of equality ever to be expressed in an Israeli court. Society, the verdict stated, must not and can not tolerate inequality. People who suffer exclusion and discrimination grow bitter and jealous and might become irrational. This might erode their willingness to cooperate, thus putting the very foundations of society in peril.

But this emphasis on individual equality left two salient issues unresolved. First, despite its lucid emphasis on principles, the court shied away from dictating a practical solution. It did order the Jewish Agency and the Cooperative Association of Katzir to offer an empty plot to the Qaʿdans, but it left tentative and fuzzy the actual procedure by which the family would gain property rights, build a home, and take residence. Nor did it specify a timetable for enforcement.[1] Moreover, worded as a recommendation rather than a decree, the verdict in fact allowed the Jewish Agency and the Cooperative Association of Katzir a number of escape hatches, which they diligently utilized for almost four years. In 2003 the Qaʿdans appealed again, requesting the court to hold the defendants in contempt. The court upheld the appeal. In mid-2004, however, the Qaʿdans still had not legally secured their right to the plot that had been set aside for them.

A second weakness in the ruling was its wording, deliberately designed to avoid retroactive reform. In the famous Mabu case, an Australian court ordered the state to compensate the current members of an aboriginal tribe for property their ancestors lost to European settlers generations back, thus creating a "jurisprudence of regret." Unlike the Mabu case, the Qaʿdan ruling explicitly avoided wording that might be used to reexamine past injustices. The result was a relatively narrow reading of liberalism. Forcefully condemning the current discrimination against Palestinians, it refrained from acknowledging the historic fact that Palestinians have been subject to similar practices for decades. By insisting on keeping history out of the courtroom, and by limiting its scope to stopping future wrongs, the court consciously undermined a comprehensive retroactive reform.

"Ethnic cleansing" is an idiom most Israelis abhor. They associate it with dramatic, extreme steps in which the military expels mass civilian populations at gunpoint. Such scenes, most Israelis fondly believe, do not occur among them. They happen elsewhere, in other eras, other places.

Michael Mann suggests that the term does not pertain exclusively to sordid episodes in which whole communities are deported in the dark of night.[2] It may and often does include a wide spectrum of measures and scenarios, from relatively "soft" ones to the most murderous. Beginning from the softer pole, Mann identifies mechanisms that exclude minorities from fora and arenas where core values and political arrangements are determined.

In some cases, exclusion has been more practical in nature. Minorities have sometimes been barred from certain projects and professions. Sometimes they have been stripped of the right to be elected or even to vote. Exclusion has involved freedom of movement: prohibitions on building or residing in certain areas, or denied or restricted presence in particular locations at particular times. States have been known to curtail reproduction by some, justify administrative detention as preemptive action, encourage emigration, initiate intimidation, and embark on expulsion campaigns. In some cases, leaders of politicized minorities have been jailed, and in others they have simply disappeared. Ethnic cleansing has sometimes entailed selective murder by state agents and, of course, mass murder of members of a target ethnic group. Some genocidal campaigns have played out in a chaotic, popular manner, such as in Rwanda in early 1994. Others have come about in a more centralized fashion, as was the case of genocidal actions by Serb military personnel in Bosnia. Still others have taken place on a massive scale, in a highly organized and systematic manner, as happened in the Armenian genocide in Turkey and the Jewish Holocaust perpetrated by Nazi Germany and its accomplices in Europe.

Practices located on this continuum of ethnic cleansing have a common thread: in all of them, dominant majorities self-proclaimed their authority to rob subordinate minorities of their fundamental rights and privileges. In states governed by the rule of law—or a semblance thereof—such moves are sometimes even sanctioned by a democratically elected parliament, ostensibly reflecting "the will of the people," which is, inevitably, some approximation of the will of the majority.

A second element in Mann's argument is that acts of ethnic cleansing have not been confined only to the dark, barbarous ages of the past or the totalitarian, tyrannical regimes of the present. On the contrary, many of these practices and, not less important, their rationalizations surfaced in the nineteenth and twentieth centuries, the age of modern nations. Some in fact emerged at times and places that celebrated modern democracy and the rule of law.

Paradoxically, the root cause of acts of ethnic cleansing could be the modernistic democratic notion of the demos—the people—as the supreme source of political legitimacy. Premodern monarchical regimes were generally indifferent to the ethnic composition of their subjects. Political legitimacy was linked to ideologies of holy lineages and their divine rights, often consolidated, and the blessing of the appropriate religious establishment. But when the notion of "the people" emerged as the new source of political legitimacy, the issue of who actually belongs took center stage. A new preoccupation with ethnic minorities and the contradictions they pose for the ideational apparatus that underwrites the state became an increasingly tense locus of political contention.

Ethnic minorities, whether large or small, assimilated or jealous of self-determination, have always been present within or at the margins of ostensibly homogenous nations. External to the dominant majority that rules the state, they are repeatedly condemned to be excluded from the national ethos and the state, to be constructed and controlled by the majority. Unlike dominant majorities, ethnic minorities tend to resist the metanarrative that sees society, culture, history, and territorial integrity as being bound together in a natural and perfect fit. Their very presence, and the particular historic narratives they nurture, subverts the majority's desire to represent itself as a homogenous, unitary territorial nation.[3] This often becomes the pretext for xenophobic distrust, racist attitudes, and discriminatory practices on the part of dominant majorities, liberals being no exception.

●　　●　　●　　●　　●

In June 2001, Khawla and her husband, Marwan, returned to Israel after attending a conference in India. In the Mumbai airport they stumbled on Abie Nathan, the veteran Israeli peace activist, now in a wheelchair and suffering an illness that badly hampers his speech.[4] Khawla and Marwan introduced themselves. Nathan nodded his head, tried to smile, and struggled to utter an audible sentence.

A few moments later, at the El-Al passenger counter, Khawla and Marwan were questioned in depth, in Hebrew, by an Israeli preflight security officer. The experience was not new to them—dozens of flights had seasoned them to this infuriating and discriminatory ritual. But the unusual location, combined with the intense emotions they had experienced since October 2000 and the chance encounter with Abie Nathan— a man whose name is still a source of inspiration for many of those involved in peace and coexistence efforts—triggered in them a response unlike anything they had experienced before.

The security officer asked about the places they had visited. They answered. The officer pressed on. She wanted them to produce a list of the hotels they stayed in, and she inquired about the nature and objectives of the conference. Astonishingly, their answers created a demand for more specific details. What was the topic Khawla had lectured on? What was her main argument? Did she project any slides? Were they available for inspection?

When the young woman demanded that Khawla open her suitcase and produce her lecture notes, Khawla lost her patience. "What does any of this have to do with aircraft security?" she yelled at the officer. "Is this relevant to state security? You are a racist. If I were Jewish, you wouldn't dream of asking anything about my lecture. Do not deceive yourself. You are not here just because you happened to see a classified advertisement announcing 'interesting work abroad.' If you were not a racist, you'd have answered other ads. I know: you looked for a job that would be 'challenging and exciting.' Am I your challenge? Is this your excitement?" The officer said Khawla's remarks were humiliating. "That's good," Khawla said; "now you know how I feel in these situations."

Khawla's idiomatic Hebrew and assertiveness was not lost on El-Al's personnel. Seeking to somehow ease the tension, they murmured that the security inspection was routine, not personal, and brought the couple chairs and cups of coffee. Khawla was adamant that everything was personal. The suspicion was directed at them as persons, simply because they were Palestinians. The director of the EL-Al branch arrived, admitted that Khawla's complaints were justified and ushered the couple to the VIP lounge.

Waiting in the lounge before boarding, Khawla and Marwan developed a theory: airports everywhere, and Israeli security officers in particular, bring out the worst in people. In the case of Khawla and Marwan, it was the demon dwelling within, the raging Palestinian that was unleashed. In their moment of infuriated humiliation, when they realized that every bit of information they provided triggered more unreasonable demands to authenticate verbal detail with receipts and printed documents, the demon overcame the voice of reason. "Enough," it said; "I'm not having any of this any longer. I am about to scream, tell them what I think, show my frustration, confront them head-on. Let them bring their chief investigators, their commanding officers and managers. I'll miss my flight. I'll stay right here. Let them jail me. I do not care. I have had enough."

Israeli security officers are unaccustomed to encounters of the kind they had with Khawla and Marwan They are more comfortable with suspicious and potentially dangerous Arabs, or, at the opposite end, as occurs much more frequently, with docile, passive, and subservient ones.

To dissipate their anger and humiliation, Khawla and Marwan tried to analyze the training that Israeli security officials get and the effect it has on them. A trained psychologist and a therapeutic social worker, they sat there in the Mumbai airport, passing professional judgment on the conduct of the Israeli officers. Did the tall one keep track of the body language displayed by that woman he was questioning? Did the plump one understand the double meaning of what the youngster in the T-shirt just said? Occasionally, unable to restrain themselves, they intervened, offering the officers professional tips based on their personal experiences as people who had been on both ends of the questioning process. "Ask the question this way," they said. "It's simpler that way." "You should avoid posing a question so similar to one you've already asked—the interviewee may notice the similarity."

Khawla wondered about the extent to which her identity had, despite everything, an Israeli component. Perhaps, she thought, her response to terror attacks against Israelis was an indication? She was horrified by Palestinian suicide bombers. Her revulsion, sense of loss, and sorrow at the waste of human life was genuinely heartfelt. But she had noticed that her feelings when Israelis were killed in such attacks were more acute and personal than those invoked in her by similar reports of terror strikes elsewhere in the world. And the blind compulsion that pushed Israel to escalate its vengeance against Palestinians after each suicide attack, including those in civilian communities, only aggravated her pain and sadness.

.   .   .   .   .

> Write down: I am an Arab.
> Fifty thousand is my ID number.
> Eight children.
> The ninth will come next summer.
> Angry? Write down. I am an Arab!
>
> Mahmoud Darwish, 1964

In 2000, the Interdisciplinary Center of Herzliya held a series of policy-oriented workshops under the title "Israel's Balance of Political and Military Strength." The project, which has since become consolidated as an annual event known as the Herzliya Conference, was organized as a yearlong series of workshops that culminated in a well-publicized and well-attended gathering in December with twenty-five speakers. The all-male list included two former prime ministers (Benjamin Netanyahu and Shimon Peres), one soon-to-be prime minister (Ariel Sharon), the IDF chief of general staff and soon-to-be defense minister Shaul Mofaz, two former defense ministers, two former heads of the Mosad (Israel's counterintelligence agency), and fifteen IDF generals who were either retired or in active service. Prime Minister Ehud Barak, whose name appeared in the program preceded by his military rank (like the names of most participants), apologized at the last moment for canceling his speech due to an overburdened schedule.

The summary report of the Herzliya Conference, which we refer to as the Herzliya Report, was published a few months after the concluding conference.[5] It includes a chapter on the Palestinian citizens of Israel that opens with a solemn prediction: "The current demographic trends inside and around Israel, which have implications for its character and identity as a Jewish state belonging to the Jewish people, amount to a severe threat against it. The demographic threat against the continuation of Israel's existence is the nearest and most probable.[6] This threat is developing at breakneck speed. Work on national policy to counter it is almost at a standstill."[7]

Having described the presence and growth of the Palestinian citizens of Israel as an existential problem, the report goes on to advocate a solution: more stringent control of the Palestinian minority:

> The Arab minority is, of course, entitled to all the cultural, economic, legal, and social rights normally granted to minorities. However, these rights will be realized in full only when this group fulfills its citizenship obligations, and when a new regional reality emerges in which the right of Israel to exist as a Jewish state is no longer contested throughout the Arab world. We must not overlook the general context of the ethnic, ideological, and political links between the Arabs inside Israel and the Palestinian people and the Arab world at large. These links justify distinctions between the situation of this particular minority and that of most minorities elsewhere. Normalization of the political situation of the Arab minority in Israel is thus linked to the political normalization of Israel in the region, and is a matter that can be resolved only in the longer term.[8]

This statement encapsulates the theory and practice of ethnic control. The key phrase, which sets the rhetorical flavor of the passage is, of course, "of course." Ostensibly liberal and lenient, the passage soon reveals itself to be a thin veneer for less progressive sensibilities. Syntactically, it stands the stated ideology of tolerance on its head with an unmistakable message: Palestinian citizens are entitled to a very limited set of cultural, economic, legal, and social rights. Other prerogatives that genuine democracies take for granted such as equality, freedom of political expression, and unmitigated access to state resources are not mentioned in the text at all.

The Herzliya Report implies that even the limited rights that Palestinian citizens theoretically qualify for will be conferred on them only when they meet a number of conditions. Some of these conditions are too harsh to be realistically met. Others are vague, and still others are both. Fulfilling "one's citizenship obligations," for example, is a term often used by right-wing Israeli politicians as a gloss for doing military service. With Israeli security forces routinely policing, killing, and oppressing Palestinians in the Occupied Territories, and with Palestinians inside Israel alienated from even the most benign of state agencies, the likelihood of them joining the military or even undertaking other types of national service is slim.

Likewise, the condition involving the emergence of a new regional reality "in which the right of Israel to exist as a Jewish state is no longer contested throughout the Arab world" is ambiguous to the point of being hollow. What exactly is "contested"? What does "throughout the Arab world" mean? Is linking equality for Palestinian citizens to a normalization of Israel's position in the Middle East not like inscribing a commitment on a block of melting ice?

The conventional formula that describes Israel as "a Jewish state" places it on a slippery slope that could easily let it slide toward various forms of ethnic cleansing. The process is in fact well under way already, as indicated by the plethora of formal and informal patterns of exclusion of Palestinian citizens that we have already presented.

The Jewish majority in Israel thus faces a simple but fundamental dilemma: is the state seeking to become a total expression of Zionism, an ethnonational project perpetuating exclusive control of all important instruments of power by the dominant majority? Or should the state that was initially created to save Jewish lives and offer the Jewish collective a political expression finally become an inclusive project, genuinely open to others too?

We of course subscribe to the latter vision. We do it knowing full well that it requires Israel to jettison ethnicity at large and Jewishness in particular as the main prerequisite for inclusion and to replace it with new tenets of identity and affiliation. For Palestinian citizens to enjoy the full equality and rights that Israel consistently claims it wants them to enjoy, the ideational core of Israel—not just its policies—will have to be transformed.

The opening statement of the chapter in the Herzliya Report quoted above reflects a wider Israeli sentiment: the fear that a rapid increase in the number of Palestinian citizens might threaten the stability and even the existence of Israel. The authors of the report go on to substantiate their concern by introducing a demographic projection for the 2020s in which the proportion of Jewish Israelis to Palestinian citizens of Israel will be "three to one."[9] Linking this alarmist projection to the call for more stringent control of the Palestinian minority—a call so popular with many in the Israeli mainstream—is effortless.

Significantly, the share of Palestinian citizens in Israel's overall population has remained constant since the end of the 1948 war. In the population census of 1949, Palestinian citizens represented 17.8 percent of Israel's population. Figures for 2000 indicate that the proportion of Palestinian citizens was 16.6 percent, a number that grows to 18.7 percent if we include the two hundred thousand Palestinian residents of East Jerusalem, as the Herzliya Report and the *Statistical Yearbook* for Israel do.[10] A projection that begins with Palestinians representing 16.56 percent of the population and assumes that future population growth rates of both Israelis and Palestinian citizens of Israel will be consistent with those recorded in the late 1990s suggests that the Palestinian citizens are not likely to represent 25 percent of Israel's population before 2062.[11]

·   ·   ·   ·   ·

After her graduation from high school in 1993, Taymaa, the eldest of Khawla's two daughters, joined a schoolmate and her sister and went to Berlin to study medicine. The two sisters stayed only a year before returning to Galilee, but Taymaa was determined to finish her studies abroad. Khawla and her second husband, Marwan, were in Florida at that time, where Khawla was completing her doctorate. At first Taymaa contemplated joining them in Florida. But since Khawla and Marwan were going to stay there for only another year or so, it was decided that Taymaa would be better off looking for a school that suited her, rather than fitting her plans to her mother's. She had a number of offers from U.S. universities, but she finally decided on McGill University in Montreal. Canada, she said, was a better place for foreigners.

Canada was indeed good for her. She studied well, earned good grades, and had an excellent choice of hospitals in which to study her specialty. In Montreal she met ʿAli, a documentary filmmaker from Morocco who had studied in Paris before moving on to Quebec. The two were married in Morocco in 2001. In 2004 Taymaa decided to take an internship in gynecological surgery at an excellent university hospital in Toronto. In spite of the language shift that ʿAli would have to undertake, from French to English, he was supportive of the move to Toronto, an important city in the film world.

When Taymaa had left Acre for Berlin in 1994, Israel and Palestine were on a course that many felt was promising and hopeful. The passing years, however, made her ever more critical of Israel's responsibility for the deteriorating situation in the region and of the racist tendencies she saw in Israel's treatment of its Palestinian citizens. ʿAli's work, which focused on human rights, oppression, and discrimination, no doubt contributed to Taymaa's awareness. When she arrived at Tel Aviv's Ben-Gurion Airport and was subjected to the suspicious, condescending, and often humiliating treatment reserved for Palestinians, she told her mother that she could not understand how she and other Palestinians who go through this regularly are able to endure it.

Taymaa's growing distance from and distaste for Israel, her career elsewhere, and the fact that ʿAli is not likely to ever want to live and work in Israel or be eligible for citizenship, convinced Khawla that her eldest daughter's residency in Canada is anything but temporary. Taymaa's life is elsewhere, and Khawla realizes that spending time with both her daughters, their husbands, and their children will be extremely complicated. The best she can realistically hope for is one week a year with all of them together, and at a cost. Otherwise, she will have the company of only bits and pieces of the family at a time, for special events. When it comes to her own family, she feels, she pays a heavy price for the political impasse in which she lives, as well as for instilling in her daughters the conviction that they can have their own professional careers, pursue their happiness, and be independent. Sometimes she feels frustrated: spending so much of her time and energy counseling others on how to maintain proper connections with their families, she herself has difficulty doing it with her own flesh and blood. It is painful for her: critical as she is of her society, she nevertheless belongs in it, sharing many of its family-oriented values—at least those that do not entail control of family members by others.

In the latter part of 2003, Dan spent six months in the United States on a Fulbright grant, teaching graduate and undergraduate courses at New York University and Princeton. In October his eldest daughter, Gal, who was sixteen, came to spend a fortnight with him, staying with him in Greenwich Village. Gal was infatuated with New York City. One day when Dan had to commute to Princeton to lecture, she walked up and down the village, then found her way back to Yafa, the garden café on St. Mark's Place where she and her father had had a meal the previous day. Established in the 1950s by a former Israeli, and operating twenty-four hours a day, seven days a week, Yafa routinely employs young Israeli students among its waiters and waitresses. By the time Dan returned from Princeton, Gal was ready with a plan, which she presented to her father with the single-minded determination that people her age have in abundance: "In four years time, as soon as I have finished school and done away with one or two other duties," she said, "I am coming back here. I'll study film, and it is all arranged. They are saving me a position as a waitress at Yafa. I hear the East Village has great studio apartments. Reasonable rent too." Then, before Dan had a chance to recover, the great-granddaughter of Asher Bodankin, the starry-eyed Zionist who left Kiev for Haifa with zealous resolve, clinched the moment by saying to her father: "Don't even think of suggesting Jersey. Manhattan is the only place to be."

·   ·   ·   ·   ·

The exaggerated demographic projection adopted by the Herzliya Report does not discourage its authors from advocating more stringent state control of Palestinian citizens. There seem to be two assumptions behind this tendency: that the larger the minority, the more difficult it is for the majority to maintain its hegemonic control; and that the more alienated, indignant, and humiliated the minority, the more it will attempt to find empowerment in numbers. The outcome, a resolve to apply a heavier hand on the expanding minority, is a recipe for apartheid-style discrimination and oppression. This trajectory, which has chilling moral implications, is also premised on a paradox. Those who predict a rapid growth in the relative size of an ethnic minority should be the ones advocating more fair and democratic integration. Instead they are the ones who advocate tighter control.

Israel's insistence on embracing ethnicity as the supreme criterion for inclusion and participation in the national project contradicts basic moral principles. Rather than buttressing a liberal democracy, it turns the state into a patron—and a haven—of the Jewish majority alone. This may be enough for those prepared to settle for a minimal, nominal democracy, where periodic elections take place and power is vested in those who are part of the ethnic majority. A genuine liberal democracy, however, must offer minority rights, equal access to resources, full accountability in economic and political processes, and various other means to curtail the tyranny of the majority under the rule of law.

The demographic issue, ostensibly associated with concrete numbers and solid population facts, is in fact a highly symbolic arena. It is, in many ways, an extension of the notion of collectively experienced time, so central to ethnonational projects.[12] One of the most striking achievements of the modernist project is that, as subjects of modern states, people have internalized the notion that they are born into preexisting, self-evident megapopulations: the nation, the state, the ethnic group. The ideologies that underwrite such amalgams successfully produce solidarity, identification, and a sense of belonging. They buttress the belief that group boundaries are predetermined, durable, and rigid, rendering the option of crossing over to another megapopulation a complicated undertaking.

But collective consciousness is not limited to imagining a unified past and an affiliation with a viable collective in the present. Sociopolitical unity and solidarity must also nurture imagery of a collective future. In a world where dramatic technological leaps and rapid social fragmentation defy most people's comprehension—let alone control—of things to come, the inventory of idioms that could depict the future continuously shrinks. Populations, and the notions that people have concerning their future fluctuations, remain singularly concrete idioms for the imagination of collective futures.

Populations have no tangible existence outside conceptual representations. But the numeric nature of such representations, collected by the prestigious tools and methods known collectively as demography, renders them convincing and robust. Easily accessible to virtually anyone able to count, population sizes make remarkably tangible constructions. Like money, public opinion polls, and diachronic data of temperatures and rainfall, projected population sizes form unshakable components of "reality." Like investment options, political projections, and fears of global warming, they can extend experiences from the present to the future. This extension of the collective social self offers the most vivid and emotionally powerful locus of identification.

Preoccupation with numerical aspects of the nation is accentuated in some historical and political circumstances and fades away in others. Contested ethnoterritorial arenas such as Israel/Palestine, where estimates of future population sizes are part of the effort to convince oneself that the nationalizing effort is sustainable, clearly belong to the former. The tendency of Israel to turn Palestinian citizens into objects and targets of "bio-power," and the appropriation of the same discourse by Palestinian citizens of Israel who view reproduction as a legitimate form of resistance, is part of this symbolic struggle.[13]

The timing of Israel's switch from a policy of control to more inclusive policies, and the circumstances in which this transformation will take place, is crucial. A forced transition accompanied by violent crisis will inevitably entail casualties, suffering, and pain. In contrast, a transition ushered in voluntarily and gradually stands a greater chance of being accomplished safely. The Stand-Tall Generation, which in spite of its growing politicization stands to lose much from conflict and polarization, could contribute to a more peaceful transformation.

In 2001–2003, the dilemmas associated with the status of the Palestinian citizens of Israel emerged dramatically in the work of a state commission of inquiry appointed by the cabinet in December 2000. The commission was headed by the Supreme Court justice Theodor Orr; its other two members were Professor Shimon Shamir, a scholar of Middle Eastern history at Tel Aviv University and former ambassador to Egypt and Jordan, and the district court judge Hashim Khatib of Galilee. Its task was to conduct a formal inquiry into the violent clashes that had taken place two months earlier between police and Palestinian demonstrators, which resulted in thirteen dead and hundreds wounded.

State commissions of inquiry seldom frame their fields of inquiry in explicitly political terms. Their tendency, rather, is to look at executive policies, regulations, and the performance of those responsible for implementing them. The general framework they work with is legal; the conceptual tools employed are often borrowed from business management and public administration.[14] They look at levels of compliance with administrative norms, forecasts, and planning; at gaps between planning and implementation; and at the extent to which past lessons had been internalized and applied.

In many ways, however, the Orr Commission became a welcome exception to the usual patterns of investigation. Formed against a background of anger, frustration, and deep shock in the Palestinian community, the commission at first was marked by uncertainty as to the type of inquiry it would conduct and the terms of reference it would use.[15] These initial indeterminacies naturally fed Palestinians' fears of a whitewash. The commission, however, soon displayed a refreshing willingness to liberally interpret its terms of reference, employ a more historical perspective, and cast its net much wider than the localized, particular events. Since it was the state's only major attempt to produce an authoritative review of the situation of the Palestinian citizens of Israel before and after October 2000, this was a positive development.

The commission placed considerable emphasis on transparency. All sessions were held at the Supreme Court building in Jerusalem and were open to the public. Print and electronic media outlets in Hebrew, Arabic, and foreign languages covered the proceedings regularly. A formal call went out to the public to approach the commission with relevant information, which yielded a significant amount of material. Protocols of the hearings were published on the Ministry of Justice's Website at the end of each day the commission was in session.

The decision that the process would be open to the public proved a crucial one. The hall in the Supreme Court building in Jerusalem where the commission convened offered a unique opportunity for the families of victims to watch the men responsible for their sons' deaths give evidence and answer queries posed by the commission. Names and roles that had become well known in the Israeli and the Palestinian media suddenly assumed faces.

This loaded encounter saw some emotional and sometimes violent incidents. Some of the parents erupted during hearings, accusing policemen on the witness stand of being cold-blooded murderers. Pulsing with anger, despair, and fury, these encounters at times ignored the rigid rules of procedure around which panels of this sort are structured. Likewise, the commission's decision to leave the courthouse and travel up and down the country to see and understand the locations where victims had been killed indicated that its members were not satisfied with conventional representations that could be brought before them in camera.

The first commission of inquiry ever to look into policies and strategies dealing with the Palestinian citizens of Israel thus became a major public event. This, combined with the fact that hundreds of witnesses and experts were summoned and then questioned in a systematic and rigorous manner on a wide spectrum of issues, made it a bit more credible in the eyes of an otherwise skeptical Palestinian public.[16] A prominent Palestinian member of Knesset who attended a number of the commission's hearings told an Israeli colleague how impressed he was by commission members' knowledge of minute details surrounding the events.[17]

Expectations about the Orr Commission were varied. Many in the Jewish Israeli mainstream viewed its convening as an unnecessary step taken simply to "appease the Arabs." Less interested in the substantive import of the findings, those of this persuasion were mainly attuned to the political gossip it was likely to produce: which politicians would be damaged by the findings; which ones would triumph.

On the Palestinian side, victims' families soon emerged as a distinct, assertive voice. Their primary preoccupation was that the commission should expose the evidence pertaining to the killings, and that this evidence would lead to criminal charges against the officers responsible.[18] Other Palestinians mainly wanted public figures responsible for the calamity—including Prime Minister Ehud Barak, members of his cabinet, and police top brass—to be reprimanded and publicly humiliated. Not least, they wanted the commission to exonerate leaders of the Palestinian community, who had been accused by the police of inciting the Palestinian masses. Others still were hoping the commission would produce a penetrating historical analysis of the predicament of Palestinian citizens of Israel and of the long-term processes that had enabled seeds of alienation to take root.

In spring 2002, after some fifteen months of intensive work, the commission issued official warning letters to fourteen men who, in light of the evidence it had reviewed, might have their public record tarnished by the final report or even face criminal charges. The fourteen included two top politicians (Ehud Barak, by then the former prime minister, and Shlomo Ben-Ami, who had been Barak's minister of internal security); Yehouda Vilk, the chief of police; Alik Ron, the chief of police, northern command; Yaacov Borovski, one of Ron's regional officers; and seven more police officers and noncommissioned officers. Significantly, the list of those receiving warnings included three Palestinian leaders: 'Azmi Bishara and Abed al-Malik Dahamsha, members of Knesset; and Ra'ed Salah, mayor of Um al-Fahim and chairman of the rescue committee of the al-Aqsa mosque. Bearing in mind that commissions of inquiry are established to exert checks and balances on the executive and ensure the lawful and efficient fulfilment of their responsibilities, the decision to warn Dahamsha, Bishara, and Salah was remarkable. While the three were democratically elected by their own communities, they were not part of the state executive branch and had no formal authority or responsibility in the realm of law and order. This notwithstanding, they were officially warned, no doubt due to the commission's conviction that they were guilty of incitement or, at least, of not using their moral authority to restrain the violent tendencies of demonstrators.

The procedure of issuing warnings at the halfway point of the commission's work was put in place in the 1980s. It was initiated following the Kahan Commission of inquiry into the massacres in Sabra and Shatila in 1982, which issued harsh recommendations against Ariel Sharon, then minister of defense. The procedure allows warned parties to initiate further appearances in front of the commission, to have legal council, to summon expert witnesses, and to cross-examine other warned parties. In the case of the Orr Commission, the procedure took place in the summer of 2002. Fifteen months later, in September 2003, the commission submitted its final report to the government and had it published.[19]

The fifty-page introduction to the report is remarkable. Its narrative and content set a number of precedents in minority-majority relations in Israel. The opening sentence states the commission's understanding of its mission and its scope: "The object of this chapter is to identify issues and problems that have appeared over the years in the lives of the Arab citizens of Israel and in their relationships with the Jews and with state institutions, [issues and problems] which fed fermentation among them that connects, directly or indirectly, with the outbreak of the events of October 2000."[20]

The next paragraph, which explains the commission's choice of the term *Arab citizens of Israel,* is heterodoxic inasmuch as it acknowledges other labels, including *Palestinian citizens of Israel,* as options. It is immediately followed by a paragraph headed "The Basic Problematique":

Majority-minority relations are problematic everywhere, particularly in a state that defines itself according to the nationality of the majority. Dilemmas that arise in such a state do not in fact have perfect solutions, and some even say that an essential contradiction exists between the principles of a majoritarian nation-state and the principles of liberal democracy. In any event, the establishment of a reasonable harmony in majority-minority relations is a difficult task assigned to all sectors of society. This task requires special effort from state institutions that manifest the hegemony of the majority, so as to balance the structural inferior-ity of the minority, numerically as well as in regard to influence. Avoiding such efforts, or making them inadequately, breeds feelings of discrimination among the minority and fosters, over time, a growing reality of discrimination.[21]

A closer look at this text reveals a number of ideas that had never featured in official versions of the story that Israelis tell themselves about the Palestinian minority's rights status. To begin with, the text admits that ethnonational states are inherently problematic. Second, it empathizes with ethnic minorities because of the double bind they endure. Third, it states that harmony in ethnic states is not automatic but instead requires a conscious and persistent effort by the majority group and the state. This is important because it implicitly negates the tendency of many Israelis to blame the victim by placing the onus for normalization on Palestinians. Finally, it argues that failure in the effort to create harmony could exacerbate the situation.

Next the report alludes to the particular predicament of the Palestinian citizens of Israel:

> These characteristics are relevant also for the situation of the Arab minority in Israel, which in many respects is discriminated against. Moreover, in the case of the Arab citizens of Israel, there are a number of unique factors that accentuate the problematic nature of their sociopolitical status. In general, the indigenous character of a minority strengthens its self-awareness. It also buttresses the validity of the claims it makes, particularly when compared to claims made by immigrant minorities who join more affluent societies so as to improve their economic situation. . . . Comparing the lot of the indigenous minority to that of an "immigrant" minority allows the potential for mounting tension.[22]

The indication in this segment that the Palestinian citizens of Israel are an indigenous minority seems, in first glance, a trivial acknowledgment of an undisputed historical fact. However, official Israeli texts, if they mention the Palestinian ("Arab") minority at all, never used such terms before. Instead, their narrative usually highlights a Jewish democratic state that affords full rights and privileges to an Arab minority, the history of which remains unmentioned.

Looking at the situation from the point of view of the minority, the report asserts that Palestinians see themselves as an indigenous minority subordinated to the hegemony of a non-native majority. This, it indicates, is further exacerbated by the fact that the Palestinian minority is in fact an incarnation of a majority group. While avoiding specific reference to 1948, the text is nevertheless revealing:

> The establishment of the state of Israel, which the Jewish people cele-
> brate as the fulfillment of the dream of the generations, is associated in
> the historic memory [of Palestinians] with the most difficult collective
> trauma of their chronology—the "Naqbah" [sic]. Even if nowadays they
> do not cite it day and night, the conception and birth of the state are
> inextricably linked to a polarized confrontation between two national
> movements that produced a protracted, bloody conflict. The content and
> symbols of the state, which are anchored in law and glorify the [Israeli]
> victories in this conflict, commemorate for the members of the Arab
> minority their own defeat. As such, it is doubtful whether they have a
> way to genuinely identify with it. Time may heal their pain, but the
> more their national awareness strengthens, the more they will judge the
> very establishment of the state as problematic.

These opening statements of the report are significant because they suggest an explanatory mechanism for the resentment and alienation of the Palestinian citizens of Israel that stresses universal regularities—elements to be expected in any ethnonational context. This is in marked contrast to explanations previously suggested by Israeli scholars and administrators, who tended to explain hostility against Israel by noting the backward nature of Palestinian culture, the primordial Arab hatred of Jews, or incitement on the part of Arab leaders of spineless, passive Arab masses.

Next the report acknowledges and legitimizes the identification of the Palestinian citizens of Israel with the struggle to create a sovereign Palestinian state.[23] It criticizes the systems of surveillance and control applied by the state against the Palestinian citizens during the military governorate period between 1948 and 1966 and even after it.[24] And it argues that, whereas Israel inherently affords its Jewish citizens a series of collective rights, it systematically denies Palestinian citizens such rights. Comparing the situation to what prevails in other states that have ethnic

minorities, the report says: "Unlike states whose constitutional arrangements assign collective rights to minorities within them, Israel has never
granted such rights to the Arab minority."[25] This, it suggests, has far
reaching consequences:

> These feelings [of vulnerability and discrimination on the part of the Pal-
> estinian citizens of Israel] were fed by the obvious existence of collective
> rights for the Jewish collective. These rights found expression in the Law
> of Return and in the Laws of Citizenship; in the normative definitions of
> the educational, media, and judiciary systems; and in institutions unique
> to Jewish society, such as the Jewish Agency and the Jewish National
> Fund. They were also expressed in the very legal definition of the state
> as a Jewish state, in a manner that enables the majority to impose the
> implications of this definition on the minority through legislation.[26]

The same paragraph in fact cites an earlier decision of the Supreme
Court of Justice that explicitly distinguished between individual rights,
extended to the Palestinian citizens as a matter of course, and collective
rights that are clearly not. The report refrains from commenting on
whether the earlier verdict should present a normative statement or a
mere description of the situation. The implication, however, is that the
principle of equality should not stop at individual rights, but must apply
to collective rights as well. Granted, the commission does not reveal
whether the collective rights that it advocates are to be understood in the
early Kymlickan sense—that is, as means to protect individuals from the
exigencies of being part of a minority that has limited access to its own
language, literature, media, high culture, and other elements required for
identity formation.[27] Nor does it reveal whether it sees collective rights
as being inherent in the collective, thus constituting a bundle of rights
with political implications, including the right to share power. This
notwithstanding, no other document ever produced by an official Israeli
body has come closer to acknowledging the existence of collective rights.
By implication, it opens the way to imagining Israel as something other
than the state of Jews alone.

The introduction to the report is followed by some eight hundred
pages of findings and comments—a blow-by-blow account of how the

police and other state agencies were or were not prepared for what happened in October 2000, followed by detailed accounts of planning procedures and performance on the ground. The conclusion, which includes personal recommendations regarding the fourteen men warned at the halfway point, is a list of required managerial, administrative, and operational improvements that pertains both to routine relations between the state and the Palestinian minority and to police conduct in emergency situations. Significantly, the three Palestinian leaders who had been warned are lumped with the state executives. The report stresses their moral responsibility for public order and for the safety of young demonstrators, reprimands them for their unwillingness and inability to restrain the rolling wave of unrest, and upholds the view that they had been involved in incitement in the months leading up to the outburst.

The particular recommendations of the report regarding the Palestinian leaders is nevertheless inconclusive. The three are criticized—Ra'ed Salah more harshly than Bishara and Dahamsha—but the language used does not imply criminal intent or direct causal responsibility. The main casualty of the report is Minister Shlomo Ben-Ami, whom the commission finds unworthy of serving as minister of internal security again.[28] Ehud Barak, who had already lost the position of prime minister to Ariel Sharon in 2001, came out of the report largely unscathed. The top police officers were severely criticized, as were those in the middle and low ranks.

The report's conclusion makes some general remarks on the structural dimensions of the predicament of the Palestinian citizens of Israel. On the whole, however, the conclusion is a faint shadow of the sweeping and refreshing impetus apparent in the introduction. It is as if, before composing the conclusion, the commission reread its own introduction, panicked at the implications, and decided to shrink the scope of its recommendations to a level more acceptable to mainstream Israel.

Conceptually, the Orr Report makes a number of significant and welcome changes. It presents a powerful, contextualized analyses of inequality, discrimination, and deprivation. And it identifies the inextricable connection between these practices and alienation, bitterness, and rage on the part of Palestinian citizens. This is a major departure from earlier Israeli tendencies to blame the victim. The report allocates responsibility for the crisis in an asymmetric fashion, placing most of it with the state, not the minority. And it sets a precedent by recognizing the legitimacy of Palestinians' demand for collective rights.

When it comes to practical recommendations, however, the commission failed to incorporate these useful tenets into a workable plan of action, thus missing a golden opportunity to instigate reform. Commissions of inquiry are not only about streamlining and improving the executive. They also have a role in educating those in power and the public at large. People seem to notice and respect practical decisions better than they analyze ideas. When the Orr Report was published in September 2003, it made headline news in every Israeli newspaper for the better part of a week. A closer look at the texts produced about it in the media, however, reveals an obsessive preoccupation with "the coliseum syndrome": which actors survive the criticism, which ones go down, who is left to the mercy of the rapturous crowd. Hardly any attention was paid to the commission's general analyses and normative judgments.

The discrepancy between the commission's willingness to talk the talk, and its obvious reluctance to walk the walk, lends itself to a number of interpretations. An optimistic reading might stress the fact that the primary role of the commission, like that of progressive judiciary panels everywhere, was to provide moral authority, shape the hegemonic discourse, and set the standards for public policy. As such, it had to tread gingerly, seeking incremental rather than dramatic change. Any attempt at revolutionary steps on its part might have been seen as partisan and could have alienated important segments of the population and eroded the public's confidence in the commission. Its strategy—to lay the conceptual and normative foundations for such change but to let other branches of government do their part at a politically opportune time—is justifiable.

A reactionary interpretation of the duality apparent in the commission's report might depict its liberal tenor as unrealistic and detached from the exigencies of life in Israel. These liberal tenets, this argument would go, are irrelevant anyway, and if ignored will soon fade away. The more fortunate elements of the report, according to this view, are the attention to managerial and technical detail and the personal conclusions concerning inefficient or even negligent officeholders. These elements, this logic would assert, should be the bases used for necessary modifications to the system.

Finally, a critical approach would stress that the report, including its progressive introduction, is a deception. Designed to create the illusion of liberal progress while at the same time perpetuating current inequalities, the argument would go, the report obfuscates an unacceptable reality by creating a veneer of progressive legalistic change. As such it is yet another manifestation of the narcissistic, self-congratulatory face of liberalism that can only make matters worse.

Various follow-up initiatives associated with the Orr Commission that are currently at play reflect, in their own ways, these various perspectives. A ministerial committee established by Sharon's cabinet upon formally receiving the report in late 2003, which tabled its conclusions in June 2004,[29] reflects a technical and managerial outlook that seeks gradual reform. The criminal investigation started by the Ministry of Justice against officers implicated in the October 2000 killing and maiming of Palestinian demonstrators reflects the view that wrongdoers should be held personally responsible for their actions. Attempts by NGOs to push the government toward more radical policy changes reflect a view of the commission as a conceptual-normative platform capable of instigating subsequent attempts at real reform.[30]

.   .   .   .   .

On a sunny Saturday in March 2004, Dan took his eleven-year-old son, Tomer, to an event organized by Zochrot, an Israeli organization dedicated to maintaining the memory of Palestinian villages destroyed in 1948.[31] The event took place near the ruins of the last existing house of Jelil, a Palestinian village that stood just south of Herzliya. Approximately one hundred people attended the event, in which displaced village elders, now living elsewhere in Israel, shared their childhood memories of their old village, of the events that led to its destruction, and of their case for reparations and return. The little hill where the event was held overlooks, to the east, agricultural plots now owned and cultivated by kibbutz Glil Yam and other Israeli farmers. To the west it overlooks the newly built Cinema City, Israel's largest cinema complex. The testimonies given at the event were followed by an account of the place's history delivered by an Israeli researcher, and by a rendition by three Palestinian rappers of their version of memory and politics.

A few months later, Tomer remembered:

> When we went to that place near Cinema City, they told us all about the old village. How the Israeli army came there and chased the Arabs away from their homes. And I was thinking: what if a nation with an army stronger than ours came and chased me away from my home? What would have happened to me? That is why I am thinking of starting an organization that will prevent this from ever happening again to anyone. But it will be an organization that will also help those who have already been victims of this in the past. For example, it will fix them up with new houses and help them with many things they need. How exactly to do this I am not so sure. I am only a child, remember?

Tomer fails to link his sentiments about injustice done to Palestinians in the past and his own prospective role as a future conscript in the IDF. He does not think about the army much, he says, although he has heard that it is "fun," and that it is good to be there. He does know, however, that he does not want to be *kravi* (combative, meaning in a frontline fighting unit)."Because I do not want to kill innocent people and blow them apart," he says. "I prefer to work with computers, and do things that do not harm Arabs." No, he does not talk about this with his friends. And he is unsure what their reaction would be if he were to talk about it openly with them. And no, he does not detest his older cousins, three of whom have served or are currently serving in crack units, for being *kravi*. "I just think that they did not do the right thing," he says.

"Arabs," for Tomer, are part of the largely detached, highly politicized wider context of his life—elements of the realm to which he is exposed through television news and the morning paper. He takes a while to register the son of a colleague of his father's, whose house near

Be'er Sheva they visited a while back, as an "Arab." The Bedouin and Egyptian men the family repeatedly meets on trips to Sinai, some of whom have become permanent features of the family lore, are also difficult for him to recognize as "Arab." Hares, who joins the family at the orchard in the granite mountains of Santa Katerina for a few days every summer, Tomer thinks, is by far the best chef he has ever met and the funniest man to boot. He remembers diving with Hares along the coral reef of Nuweiba on the eastern coast of the peninsula and sliding down the dunes together. "Yes," he says, "come to think of it, Hares is an Arab too."

Tomer is unsure about the chances of having peace in the Middle East. "In the end it will come," he says, "but first we have to give some of the country to the Arabs. Many of my friends, though, say that this is why it will never work. We will give something to the Arabs, they will start another war, we will need to give them more, and so on until we are left with nothing but Tel Aviv. This is why my friends are right wing. But I remain a leftist."

Chapter Six

The debate regarding Palestinian citizens no longer involves political extremes. It takes place in the mainstream, invoking concepts and configurations that often confuse and conflate the Zionist "left" and "right." Moderate right-wingers in Israel are sometimes more committed to liberal policies than are the Zionist left, the latter's image as the voice of reason and enlightenment notwithstanding. During his first months in office as prime minister, the Likud leader Ariel Sharon, born and raised in a moshav associated with the right flank of the Labor movement, met with Palestinian leaders more frequently and more attentively than did Ehud Barak—who comes from a kibbutz associated with the left of Labor—in his entire term as prime minister. In debates about the meaning of liberal democracy in Israel, right-wing spokespersons sometimes articulate views that are more flexible than those espoused by Labor politicians.[1]

One obstacle to a normative turnabout that might facilitate genuine integration of the Palestinian citizens into the project of the state is common to both Labor and Likud: the self-righteous attitude that has colored public discourse in Israel since October 2000. Self-righteousness—the feeling that one side has a monopoly on justice—is a vice under most clement circumstances. At times of crisis and conflict it becomes particularly vicious. Convinced that only his or her own view of reality is true, a self-righteous person easily loses touch with opposing narratives. Failing to identify and legitimize the basic needs and interests of others, refusing to admit any shade of doubt, and absolving themselves of blame, self-righteous collectives are prone to adopting simplistic views of their opponents as the incarnation of all evil.[2] When this disposition is compounded with disproportionate power, the danger that the situation could flare into violence becomes acute.

To a large extent, the righteousness that gripped Israel after the eruption of Intifadat al-Aqsa stems from Ehud Barak's ability to convince the Israeli mainstream that the failure of the Camp David summit in July 2000 was entirely the fault of the Palestinians. Barak has an extraordinary talent for defining the basic categories of a debate in terms that narrow the range of plausible conclusions to fit his own convictions. In the autumn of 2000, after the failure of the Camp David peace talks, his main discursive effort was to reassure the local and international public that Israel was being led by responsible, rational, peace-loving statesmen. The problem, he argued, speaking with the devastating conviction reserved for narcissistic, charismatic leaders, was that Israel now has no Palestinian partner for its honorable intentions. When it comes to peace, Barak said, the Palestinians are not only hard to strike a deal with: they are also disingenuous. Their participation through the 1990s in the Oslo process, he claimed, was nothing but a duplicitous bluff: a mask of willingness that came off at the moment of truth, as he put it, when, during the Camp David summit in July 2000, he exposed what he described as the bloodthirsty and dishonest nature of the Palestinians.

Ironically, Barak's sanctimonious insistence that, in July 2000, the Palestinians had rejected what he described as the most generous proposals an Israeli politician is ever likely to make them, sowed the seeds of his political demise. In the elections forced on him in February 2001, his opponent, Ariel Sharon, based his winning campaign on Barak's own argument that the Palestinian intransigence at Camp David reflected irrationality, dishonesty, and inherent violence. The voters were easily persuaded by his logic: if this indeed is the essence and style of Israel's chief enemy, who better than the seasoned, hard-line veteran warrior Sharon to lead it into battle? Not surprisingly, after Sharon's election victory, this narrative became the self-evident justification for Israel's consistent refusal to accept proposals for political settlement, a refusal that contributed to the ever-increasing bloodbath.[3]

Tragically, Israel's intransigence intensified when Palestinians started using firearms against IDF soldiers and settlers in the territories, and it was solidified even further when suicide bombers began exploding in Israeli cities within the Green Line, killing civilians by the dozen and wounding hundreds. The refusal of the Palestinian leadership during the early stages of the intifada to address the Israeli public in a direct attempt to acquaint it with the Palestinian perspective further aggravated the already complicated situation.

As the intifada progressed, the Israeli media became more prone to decontextualized descriptions of Israeli casualties, including soldiers and settlers, as innocent victims assaulted for no reason other than for being Jewish.[4] Meanwhile, the suffering endured by Palestinians was systematically minimized, depicted as the fate of agents punished for the violent events in which they were entangled.[5] Whatever the context, Israeli media outlets always seemed to find a convincing, security-related "event" that provided an explanation for Palestinian casualties.

When Barak was prime minister, his team produced a spin on events that shaped the Israeli media's depiction of the intifada's violent incidents as "exchanges of gunfire," in which Israel retaliated for "disturbances of public order." After Sharon took power, the rhetoric changed to include key idioms like "Palestinian violence," "terror," and later even "war." This manipulation of language in the media is not random. It engenders an inner logic of cause and effect that enables Israelis to conduct their ordinary lives largely unalarmed, consistently ignoring the hunger, suffering, isolation, and daily ruin that takes place less than thirty miles east or south of where they live. The ostensible lack of information most Israelis experience regarding the situation in the Occupied Territories is an essential ingredient of the social production of self-righteousness.[6] The result is not limited to harsh declarations on the part of ultranationalist politicians or vitriolic chatter in marketplaces, football stands, or classrooms. Buttressed by the paradoxical sense of victimization Israelis harbor in spite of being a regional power, this outlook, which used to be so basic to Israel's self-image in its early decades as a state, seems to have returned as a central feature of identity.

·   ·   ·   ·   ·

The erosion that Intifadat al-Aqsa created in the attitude of mainstream Israelis was apparent even within relatively solid strongholds of rational political thought. Dan, who was recruited by Tel Aviv University and who moved there from Hebrew University in 2001, was surprised to find among his new colleagues in the social science faculty some hard-line opinions that he thought had largely been phased out since the Oslo process. Even more disconcerting for him was a gradual transformation discernable in 2001 and 2002 at the top echelon of *Haaretz,* the daily paper he had read since childhood and had contributed to regularly since the 1980s. The chief editor, Hanoch Marmari, and his deputy, Yoel Esteron, who had been colleagues and acquaintances for decades, became much less sympathetic to Dan's political outlook. Amira Haas's and Gideon Levy's reports of the suffering of Palestinians in the territories, accompanied by Akiva Eldar's analysis of the politics behind it, they indicated, was more than enough for the liberal readership of *Haaretz*. In 2002 and 2003 Dan had more op-ed pieces shelved by *Haaretz*'s editors than in the twenty years he had been associated with the paper altogether. In the eighteen months prior to Marmari's and Esteron's replacement by David Landau as editor and the new deputy editor Tamar Litani, his op-ed pieces were restricted to his secondary field of expertise and interest—environmental issues, particularly those pertaining to social justice and globalization.

Dan's sabbatical in New York City in late 2003 was another sobering experience of the machinations of the liberal press at times of war. That period, immediately after the U.S. invasion of Iraq but prior to the relative disillusionment of many Americans with George Bush's "War on Terror" in 2004, was characterized by a patriotic wave that swept through U.S. academic institutions and, even more dramatically, through the electronic and the print media. Space for critical thought and effective challenges to the clatter of consensual thought was painfully small. Deliberations that Dan had with U.S. media editors who were acquainted with his op-ed pieces and his academic writing were astonishing. They indicated that articles he published in *Haaretz* expressing criticism of Israel and empathy with the Palestinians were too radical to see the light of day in mainstream media outlets in the United States. During public lectures Dan gave in universities up and down the East Coast and in the Midwest, the vocal opposition of individuals identified with Zionist circles was further indication of the strong reactions triggered by attempts to question the assumptions behind the formal policies of the United States and Israel.

. . . . .

Some of the dynamics of Israeli self-righteousness intensified following September 11. *Terror,* which became a global buzzword, had a familiar ring to Israelis. Many of them believe the term simply denotes attacks against civilians and are thus convinced that their country merely had been responding to terror for the past decades. Locked in a mental trap shaped by simplistic, stereotypical analyses of terrorism of the type espoused by Benjamin Netanyahu's facile edited volume—in which he interprets terror as a culture clash: the West against the rest[7]—Israelis gleefully identified bin Laden, the Palestinian Authority, Hamas, Islamic jihad, Hezbollah, and others as one and the same. This rhetoric buttressed a cosmology that sees Christianity and Judaism as representing benevolent humanity, isolating Islam and Arabs as incarnations of cruelty, despotism, and irrational violence.

In sum, these sensibilities inspired a rigorous reinvention of the old image of Israel as a supremely rational and peaceful society that faces the Arab harbingers of death, and as a vanguard leading the West in a new phase of world history. Many Israelis succumbed to the comfortable belief that imminent dangers inherent in this struggle would unite the West behind it. Not surprisingly, the wave of demonstrations in mid-February 2003 against the looming U.S. invasion of Iraq, in which more than 10 million marched in hundreds of cities across the globe, was hardly noted in Israel. With polls consistently indicating levels of support for the invasion of Iraq running above 90 percent, it is little wonder that only a handful marched in the streets of Tel Aviv that weekend to protest against the war.

· · · · ·

In December 2003, Khawla's father, Muhammad, passed away. His kin in Galilee, the Occupied Territories, and elsewhere were immediately notified. His brother Mahmoud, aged seventy-six, now living in Ramallah, and his paternal half brother, Walid, aged forty-seven, who lives in their ancestral village, Ya'abad, near Jenin, wanted to attend his funeral in Acre. As residents of the West Bank, however, they were not only without citizenship or a passport but also subject to one of the worst phases of the regime of closures and encirclement ever administered by the Israeli occupation forces. Mahmoud walked up to the roadblock near Ramallah equipped with a fax he got from Khawla in Acre. He had hoped the soldiers would let him through into Jerusalem, where he could take a bus or be met by a relative to go to Acre. He was sent back unceremoniously. Walid did not even try. Instead he opened a *diwan* (reception tent) in his backyard, where he received condolence visits. In Acre, not fifty miles away as the crow flies, his brother's kin were sitting in their own *diwan*.

Following the phone call from Mahmoud that told her of his failed attempt to cross the roadblock near Ramallah, Khawla sadly contemplated her uncle's predicament. Having spent many decades of his life away from his paternal relatives, first in the Gulf and then in Ramallah, now he was isolated from them by the political impasse in Israeli-Palestinian relations. His daughter, Lina, who married a French psychiatrist, now lives in Paris. His son, 'Issam, is married to a Spanish woman and lives in Chicago. None of them are likely ever to willingly return to their war-torn, occupied patria. If you die, Uncle Mahmoud, Khawla found herself thinking, who will follow the coffin in your funeral?

. . . . .

It would be a mistake to interpret the quiet that has prevailed in the Palestinian community in Israel since October 2000 as a sign of contentment. It is a forced silence, one that conceals bitter suffering and deep shock. The Palestinian citizens themselves, who were stunned by the intensity of the demonstrations led by the Stand-Tall Generation in October 2000, are frightened of the Israeli iron fist that so brutally crushed their protest. Under the surface, the community is simmering with undercurrents of alienation, hostility, and hate. These feelings are nurtured and exacerbated by worsening economic conditions, by the escalating ruthlessness against the Palestinians in the territories, and by the glaring absence of a genuine policy of reconciliation with the Arab world at large.

In 2001 and 2002, more Palestinian citizens of Israel became involved in support for and, in isolated cases, even perpetration of, terror attacks against Israelis within the Green Line. Actual involvement may be minuscule, but the trend exists. In August 2001, a precedent was set when an Islamic-movement activist from the village of Abu-Snan in Upper Galilee blew himself up at the entrance of the train station in nearby Nahariya, killing four and wounding many more. In 2002 and 2003 a number of suicide bombers from the West Bank were hosted and assisted by friends and relatives inside Israel. While public opinion in the Palestinian sector is firmly and vociferously opposed to suicide bombings, the erosion of mutual trust and escalating despair might push more individuals toward such violent reactions.

Whichever course individuals and organizations within the Palestinian community in Israel decide on, it would be a mistake for the Israeli majority to go on blaming Palestinians for the current crisis. Nothing about the situation is remotely symmetrical. The majority—enjoying an unchallenged demographic, economic, and political hegemony—bears ultimate responsibility for the course that events take. A self-righteous tendency by Israelis to point an angry finger at the Palestinians might further alienate the latter and push them toward an ever growing militancy, augmenting a self-fulfilling prophecy, a blueprint for disaster.

Intifadat al-Aqsa and the events that followed it inside Israel's Green Line may have been led by the Stand-Tall Generation. It has, however, fused together three generations of Palestinians inside Israel. This unity proves that worldviews, moods, and outlooks are not necessarily age-dependent, and that sociological generations do not exist in isolation of each other. In some situations, where members of the middle generation are reluctant to act, and members of the survivors' generation of 1948 are too frightened to do so, men and women of the Stand-Tall Generation are defiant, refusing to stand by. In other circumstances, particularly ones that represent religiocultural pride and existential security, all three generations are mobilized as one.

·   ·   ·   ·   ·

In the summer of 2002, immediately after the Hebrew edition of this book was published in Israel, Israeli Television Channel One did a story on it. Gil Sadan, a veteran television reporter and director, came to Haifa with a team and met with Khawla; Dan; Khawla's mother, Nada; and Dan's mother, Sarah. Sadan's plan was to go with the foursome to a number of locations in Haifa that are relevant to the stories of the families as they were featured in the book. These would have included parts of downtown Haifa where the Abu-Shamlas lived prior to 1948, other parts where Palestinians live today, the seafront, and more.

Soon after the excursion started, however, it ran into difficulty. While Khawla, Dan, and Dan's mother, Sarah, were happy to go on camera, converse with the reporter, argue among themselves, and generally cooperate with the filming project, Khawla's mother, Nada, refused. She consented to be filmed in long shots while walking along the seafront and near some Palestinian houses. But when it came to speaking, she remained resolutely silent. The others took a while to realize that her refusal did not come from camera shyness or a reluctance to perform. Innocent of any knowledge of film or television production processes, she nevertheless sensed that, once the camera rolls, the subject loses control of what the outcome looks and sounds like. "I know," she told Khawla afterward, "that they [meaning the Israelis] always make it look and sound to fit their view. I want no part in this." This, combined with failed attempts to engage Nada in direct conversation with Dan's mother, Sarah—here again Nada was not forthcoming—imbued the day with dense, unresolved unease.

. . . . .

The predicament of the Palestinian citizens of Israel cannot be solved by looking only at the present and the future. Finding a genuine solution will require tackling the injustices of the past. Making substantive change to the land regime, for example, requires an alteration in the basic designation of land in Israel as Jewish land and the adoption of the concept of Israeli land.[8] To do that, the Palestinians must be incorporated into the processes that determine land policies: the Israel Land Administration , the Jewish National Fund, and other institutions that control land and planning must be restructured so as to guarantee Palestinian citizens' representation. Land allocation must be based on population size and its projected needs, not on ethnic affiliation. Wanton expropriation of Palestinian land must be stopped, and all seizure for public use must be subject to transparent processes and clear criteria. Fallow land seized by the state in open areas outside Palestinian villages and towns, as well as property that formerly belonged to Muslim *waqf* (religious endowments) should be returned to the Palestinian community. The state must guarantee that master plans for Palestinian towns and villages include sufficient land reserves for future expansion of residential and industrial areas. Special plans should be drafted for public housing in Palestinian communities, particularly in urban areas.[9]

Laws must be passed that sanction long-term strategic plans to raise levels of state contribution to Palestinian local authorities within a rigid time frame and must be aimed explicitly at reaching the per capita levels provided to Jewish communities.[10] All communities with populations exceeding fifteen thousand persons must be granted town status, complete with budget allocations that suit their growing needs. Infrastructure rehabilitation projects and public housing projects must be put in place in all Palestinian communities, all forms of discrimination in mortgage loan policy must be terminated, and social welfare must be invigorated and significantly strengthened.

The Palestinian community must be given the tools to administer its own educational system as part of an autonomous school system.[11] While formally under the jurisdiction of the Ministry of Education, this system must be allowed to define its own goals, establish curricula, appoint teachers and principals, and handle planning, development, budgetary matters, and administration.[12] The educational objectives in the Palestinian sector must be modified so as to highlight Arab and Palestinian history, culture, and identity. A real effort has to be made to establish and develop schools specializing in technology; and new programs and institutions should be created for students with special needs. Vast changes are required in educational infrastructure and facilities. And long-term plans must be put in place to promote the access of Palestinians—students and faculty alike—to higher education.

Narrowing the structural economic disadvantages that Palestinians are subject to requires that citizenship, not ethnic identity, serves as the chief criterion for the distribution of individual rights and family allowances; for tax deductions and housing credit; and for state assistance with physical infrastructure, education, health, and welfare. Eligibility for such individual and collective benefits and opportunities must be based on transparent criteria that are periodically reviewed, and these must not include military service. Support to low-income regions must reflect genuine economic need, not ethnic preference. Funds must be allocated for industrial and trade development in Palestinian towns and villages. Remuneration should be offered to help narrow the gaps that have resulted from past discriminatory policies, and it should be awarded directly to local councils for allocation according to their perceived priorities and needs.

Judges, state prosecutors, and attorneys should participate in special seminars that address psychological, social, and legal aspects of majority-minority relations in deeply divided societies and states, including the structural discrimination that so often characterizes systems of justice.[13] The judicial system should consider the principles and procedures of "jurisprudence of regret," which was adopted in the 1990s by courts in New Zealand and Australia. This approach acknowledges injustices committed against indigenous populations throughout the history of colonial settlement, and promotes awareness of these injustices in legal procedures and decisions. Likewise, Israel should consider establishing frameworks akin to the Truth and Reconciliation Committees formed in Chile, South Africa, and Rwanda to provide means for coping with traumatic ethnonational histories and their consequences.[14]

Israeli police have yet to internalize the fact that the lives of Palestinian demonstrators count as much as those of Jewish ones. Resources should be allocated immediately for training personnel in crowd control and riot policing and for the purchase of the appropriate equipment. Special emphasis should be placed on making police aware that public demonstrations are a legitimate means of democratic expression. Police use of bullets against citizens must be strictly prohibited. The role of law enforcement in multinational, multicultural democratic societies should be highlighted, and police must be made aware of the perils of stereotyping and prejudice.

Protracted misrecognition on the part of Israelis of the irreconcilable gap between Palestinian sensibilities and the basic categories defining the Israeli project will only aggravate the tension. The state could, for a start, afford formal recognition of the Palestinian Nakbah, thus legitimizing the sense of grief that still engulfs those who lost relatives, livelihood, and property in 1948, and who have endured the deprivation and humiliation of displacement since. This should be done through legislation, a Knesset act that recognizes the Palestinian Nakbah as a national memorial day alongside Israel's day of independence.[15] The state must formally post commemorative signs indicating the sites of more than four hundred Palestinian towns and villages destroyed in 1948, even where the ruined village has since become subsumed by an Israeli settlement. Appropriate measures should be taken to restore and preserve whatever relics remain of pre-1948 structures, including mosques and churches.

Israeli state symbols should be refashioned. Verses of the national anthem could be modified or added. The flag could be designed anew. The government of Israel should issue an official expression of regret for the historic injustice and suffering sustained by Palestinians. Laws that grant remuneration for confiscated and appropriated Palestinian assets should be enacted, along with official acceptance of state responsibility for the health and social welfare for victims of the war of 1948. Israel should revise its immigration laws and policy, premising them on principles of common sense, natural justice, and civil equality.

Recognition of Palestinian collective identity entails incorporation of Palestinian history into school curricula, in Jewish as well as Palestinian schools.[16] The standard of Arabic studies in both communities must be vastly improved, and the prestige of such studies must be rehabilitated. Arabic must appear on every street sign and as part of every official document. Muslim, Christian, and Druze holidays ought to be recognized officially and added to the calendars of all government offices, public services, and institutions. Major changes must be instituted in state-run as well as privately owned organs of mass communication, to ensure that Palestinian and Arabic culture are no longer featured exclusively in negative contexts of war and crisis; Palestinian and Arab culture should be a regular, legitimate element in Israeli media.

Administratively and financially, effecting these primarily symbolic changes will be easy. Emotionally and politically, however, none could be more costly and complicated for the Israeli mainstream.

·   ·   ·   ·   ·

On May 18, 2004, Dan and his youngest son, six-year-old Yonatan, attended the final match of Israel's National Football Association Cup.

Held at the national stadium in Ramat-Gan, the largest sports facility in the land, this particular match was special: for the first time ever, a team from a Palestinian town had reached the finals. Three teams representing Palestinian communities had played in Israel's top professional football division before. None, however, had had any real success. This time, the team Itihad Abna Sakhnin was on the big stage, poised to clinch a national title.[17]

The national cup competition is organized as a knockout tournament. It yields the second-most prestigious football title: only the championship of the national league's top division is a more coveted trophy. The championship is decided by an intricate calculation of league points accumulated against league points still available, and can be decided and declared anytime in the final weeks of the season. Not so the competition for the cup. A meticulously planned affair, the final game is scheduled many months ahead of time, thus enabling the national association to organize it as a state ceremony. An elaborate protocol that has evolved over the years includes attendance by the president, who is the official head of state; by mayors; and by leading cabinet ministers. It entails the singing of the national anthem, a formal presentation ceremony in which the president hands the trophy to the winning captain, and other stately moments.

Yonatan, a football enthusiast, is not a supporter of either Beney Sakhnin or its opponent in the final game, Hapoel Haifa. He only needed to hear, however, that the Palestinian club had never won a trophy, and that it represented a poor town where children had very few playgrounds or other facilities, to become their avid fan. With over thirty thousand Palestinian supporters from Sakhnin, from Galilee at large, from the Triangle, and from the Negev converging on the stadium, Dan and Yonatan could not find tickets in the Beney Sakhnin stands and had to settle for seats in the section reserved for the far less numerous supporters of the opposition. Every time the Palestinian team scored a goal, they clenched each other's hands in secret glee. Minutes from the end, when the Sakhnin lead was too substantial to overturn, Yonatan exclaimed in his father's ear, "Five more minutes and history will be made." The two of them stayed in the stand long after the disappointed fans of Haifa had gone, and watched President Moshe Katzav handing the trophy to Abbas Suwan, the captain of Sakhnin.

The symbolic significance of the Sakhnin victory, which dominated the daily newspapers and television news shows for the rest of the week, cannot be overestimated. State ceremonies in Israel are essentialized renditions of history, morality, and values as seen from the Zionist perspective.[18] Palestinian citizens, by definition, have no role in them, and are not expected to identify with them. Here, however, was a major exception. The fireworks, the confetti in the colors of the winning club shooting out of huge tubes, Freddie Mercury's "We Are the Champions" bellowing out of the official, megadecibel sound system, and the congratulatory proclamation of the announcer were everything but partisan. Orchestrated by the National Football Association, the celebration was, for a brief moment, ethnically blind. Through it, the state, for once, was honoring its most marginal subgroup.

Rank-and-file as well as prominent Palestinian figures, the Israeli and Arabic media, and many Jewish Israelis were all ecstatic with the victory, hailing it as a historic turning point in minority-majority relations. On a more sobering note, there were those who questioned the relevance of this symbolic event to the predicament of Palestinians in Israel. Will the unprecedented event in Ramat-Gan really signal genuine change? Or will it simply be another exercise in cooptation, a semblance of equal opportunity and relative success that enables the government to overlook the structural discrimination and oppression to which the Palestinian citizenry is habitually subjected?

·   ·   ·   ·   ·

Programmatic suggestions for real change in the circumstances and status of the Palestinian citizens of Israel are emotionally and politically acceptable to only a fraction of the Jewish Israeli mainstream. Even among academics and intellectuals, the cadre that seeks transition from axiomatic mobilization along ethnonational lines to an ethnically blind liberal democracy is small, its political efficacy limited. This, however, does not in any way diminish the responsibility this cadre has for voicing the unthinkable and for discussing the unspeakable. The role of critical inquiry is primarily to articulate long-term vision, regardless of its apparent feasibility within particular political circumstances.

In November 2000, when some ideas along these lines appeared in the emergency report cited above, the publication sparked considerable attention and debate. The report was serialized in *Haaretz* over a week, had exposure in other media outlets, and was discussed in a variety of academic and public forums. Within the Jewish Israeli public, it had an especially unsettling effect on a particular subgroup.

Israelis who lived through the events of 1948 as adults are now in their seventies and eighties. For them, dislodging the ethnoterritorial core from the heart of the Israeli project would be nothing short of heresy. The claim that genuine democratization requires a critical review of its most basic ethos, including a reframing of the 1948 war, is a major threat to their cosmology. The notion that the state should move on from declarative intentions to genuine and practical inclusion of its Palestinian citizens is intolerable for them.

This generation of Israelis, the most representative and prominent of whom was Yitzhak Rabin himself, is deeply secular. This notwithstanding, many of them still frame the fateful events that led to the creation of the state in deeply religious terms. Faced with concepts such as the ones mentioned here, which argue for revisions of canonic versions of the past, many of these veterans are thrown off balance. Public occasions in which these notions were debated repeatedly have had one or more of them standing up with trembling, agitated voices, determined to reflect their personal experience of the past as indisputable historic truth. In their world, 1948 will always be connected with the existential Jewish fears that were aroused by the horrors of the Holocaust. For them 1948 can never be anything but a unique historic juncture in which a persecuted minority liberated itself after centuries of helpless vulnerability, finally becoming the master of its own fate.

Blatantly nonreflexive and selective, these men and women can only recollect those aspects of the conflict and the war of 1948 that suit the hegemonic narrative the state has cultivated. They vividly remember every instance of Arab intransigence: the Palestinian leadership's rejection of the British partition plan of 1937 that would have given the Arabs a much larger slice of Palestine than subsequent plans would; the Palestinian refusal to consider the U.N. partition plan of 1947; the aggressive action taken by Palestinian militants immediately following the U.N. resolution; the gleeful belief of most Palestinians in 1947 that the upcoming war would be short and would result in "throwing the Jews back to the sea."

This generation is known in Israel as Dor Tashah.[19] Its members systematically deny the moment, sometime in spring or summer 1948, in which the Israeli military effort ceased to be an attempt to defend the partition plan of the U.N. and became a coordinated military effort to gain control of as much land with as few Palestinians. They stubbornly refuse to distinguish between the Israeli struggle for self-defense and self-determination in the early part of the war, and the deliberate ethnic cleansing that took place during its latter stages. Most of them are still unwilling to accept that the very military prowess of which they were a part, and which they celebrate as just and moral, is the same one that created hundreds of thousands of helpless Palestinian victims. Their cosmology fails to identify the feared "Arabs" of 1948 as the relatives of their fellow citizens in Galilee, the Triangle, and the Negev.

Rethinking the roots of Israel is a formidable, perhaps impossible, task for those unable to look at 1948 as anything but a fully justifiable Jewish struggle for survival against quintessential villains. The illusion that the dark side of 1948 has been kept outside of living memory long enough to be finally eradicated is a cornerstone of the historico-political perspective of this generation.

Members of younger generations of the Israeli mainstream tend to be less rigid in their outlook. A relatively tranquil period in terms of politics, security, and the economy is probably all they need in order to rekindle a more positive attitude toward true equality and genuine democracy. Zionism may remain their orthodoxy, their ideology of choice, but is not as doxic as that of *Dor Tashah*.

Increasing numbers of Israelis, including many in the mainstream, now understand that questions pertaining to the rights and status of the Palestinian citizens can no longer be kept out of public discourse. They appreciate that the crux of the issue is no longer a hackneyed debate of the extent to which the Jewish majority does or does not discriminate against Palestinian citizens, what additional resources ought to be channeled to them, or even how multicultural and tolerant the society will be. The stability, legitimacy, and very future of Israel hangs in the balance here.

．　　．　　．　　．　　．

The final joint work sessions in connection with this book took place in June 2004 in Acre, Tel Aviv, and Haifa. During one of them, which was held on the veranda at Dan's parental home overlooking Haifa Bay, Khawla looked pensively at the open vista and thought of Nazmiyah, her maternal aunt. Nazmiyah, she told Dan, did manage to return to Haifa, and now lives with her husband on the fourth floor of an apartment building in Halisa, a neighborhood spread on a slope just off the eastern edge of downtown Haifa. Her children, who in time purchased the apartments next to hers in the block, now live around her. "I think they are quite happy there," Khawla told Dan. "It is the view of Haifa Bay, so strikingly similar to the one we see from here, that made me think of them. This house and hers look at the same view. But they are worlds apart."

．　　．　　．　　．　　．

The challenge facing Israel is not only to effect change in government priorities but also to transform the values underwriting the very identity of Israelis. It requires vision and political will of the magnitude displayed by Mikhail Gorbachev who, in the late 1980s, rightly or wrongly convinced hundreds of millions that the ideology that had underwritten their lives for seven decades had to be eclipsed.

The practical conclusion of this book is categorically post-Zionist. Zionism, the ideology that saved hundreds of thousands of Jewish families, including the Bodankins and the Veriyers, is also the force that brought excruciating suffering on hundreds of thousands of Palestinians, including the Abu-Shamlas and the Abu-Bakers. If Israel seeks a future of prosperity and peace, sooner or later it will have to replace the ethnoterritorial dictum that engendered Zionism, with an alternative, inclusive approach to history and destiny.

Notes

INTRODUCTION

1. For an explanation of our preference for the term *Palestinian citizens of Israel* to other labels sometimes used to describe the group this inquiry focuses on, see later in the introduction and in chapter 1.

2. A key event in this process is Land Day 1976 (see chapter 3). For an early account, see Matzpen 1976.

3. Alterman 1974.

4. Guri [1949] 1989: 252.

5. The emblematic case here is no doubt Hanoch Levin's groundbreaking satirical play *Malkat Ambatya* (Queen of the Bathroom) (Levin 1987). The play, written and performed originally in 1970, mocks the macabre ritual in which Israeli parents proudly send their sons to certain death. An instant provocation, it was performed only nineteen times before being taken off stage as a result of public scandal, in which claims that the play hurts the feelings of bereaved par-

ents played a major role. The play remains a cornerstone in Israeli cultural history.

6. A clear statement of the mission and prospect of this version of liberal democracy can be found in Waltzer 1983.

7. Habermas 2002.

8. Attempts at comparative work include Gurr 1993 and Green 1994. For examples of theoretical insight, see Svensson 1979; Waltzer 1982; and Asch 1984.

9. Kymlicka 1995.

10. Kymlicka 2001; Kymlicka and Norman 2000. See also Brass 1991; Bennett 1998; Danley 1991; and Bhargava et al. 1999.

11. For studies of this tension, see Oommen 1997; Sheth and Mahajan 1999; and Tomasi 1995.

12. Zureik 1979 is probably the first explicit analysis of Israel as a colonial state. Gershon Shafir, in his 1989 analysis of land and labor within Zionism, highlights the specific circumstances of the Jewish national movement but nevertheless adheres to the colonial paradigm. Similar trajectories are echoed in Michael Shalev's 1992 study of Israel's split economy and Lev Greenberg's 1991 analysis of Israel's Labor movement.

13. See Lustick 1980.

14. Peled's view of Israel as an "ethnic republic" (1992) is supported by works such as Rabinowitz 1997; Ghanem 1998, 2001; and Rouhana 1997.

15. Smooha 1990: 391.

16. Smooha's work on ethnic democracy (1990) has attracted considerable criticism and debate. Ghanem (1998) identifies the inherent contradiction between Israel's pretense to being a Western-style liberal democracy and its rather restrictive practices toward its Palestinian citizens and their collective rights. Yiftachel (1997) applies Donald Horowitz's term *ethnocracy* (1985) to the Israeli case.

17. The total number of Palestinian refugees in 1948 is widely estimated to have been between 720,000 and 740,000. The number of Palestinians who remained within the borders of Israel (the Green Line) is often estimated to have been 160,000. The figure for Jews who lived in Palestine prior to 1948 (the Yishuv) is widely recognized to be 600,000.

18. Ghanem, Abu-Ras, and Rosenhak 2000: 22.

19. Ghanem, Abu-Ras, and Rosenhak 2000. In recent years, the unemployment figure for Israel at large has been fluctuating, from 8 percent in 1999 to 9 percent in 2002 to almost 11 percent in 2004.

20. Ibid., 24. For more details about the welfare policy for Palestinians in Israel, see Abu-Baker 2003b.

21. The rest of the Palestinian population lives in mixed towns.

22. See Ghanem, Abu-Ras, and Rosenhak 2000. With little or no industry and commerce, and with populations that are largely poor, Palestinian communities have a limited potential for income through local taxes. Not surprisingly, the

financial deficits accumulated among Palestinian local councils in 1998 reached a staggering 800 million shekels. Ibid.

23.   See Kretzmer 1990; Kedar 1996.

24.   See Yiftachel, Khamaisi, and Kedar 2000.

25.   Israel has an elaborate system of incentives and subsidies based on geographical zoning. While periodically reviewed, the system only seldom includes Palestinian towns and villages.

26.   For many years, child benefits paid out by the national institute of social security were confined by law to families whose heads had served a full term in the Israel Defense Forces, thus excluding the vast majority of Palestinian families in Israel.

27.   Some of these exclusionary practices go back to the formative period of the military government, imposed on the Palestinians inside Israel from 1948 to 1966. That period saw land confiscation on a massive scale, as well as limitations on manufacturing processes and restrictions on movement and employment— measures that left a long-term legacy of underdevelopment.

28.   The construction industry, which was a major employer of Palestinian laborers and businesses, and which has suffered major stagnation since 1999, has replaced its predominantly Palestinian workforce with laborers from eastern Europe and China. The textile sector, which once employed substantial numbers of Palestinian women, has relocated to production centers abroad, cutting its local workforce by at least 50 percent (see Drori 2000).

29.   For early accounts of the education system in the Palestinian sector, see Mar'i 1978; al-Haj 1996.

30.   Cf. Shavit 1990.

31.   Ratner 1996.

32.   See Rabinowitz, Abu-Baker, Herzog, Mana'a, Peled, Shenhav, and Sliman 2000.

33.   Cf. Rabinowitz 1994.

34.   The Green Line takes its name from the color in which it was marked on maps after 1949.

35.   Mannheim 1940.

36.   For one such formulation, see Ghanem 2001: ch. 9.

37.   For a recent account of the meaning of the border, see Benvenisti 2002.

38.   Shenhav 2001.

39.   For an in-depth attempt to solve this riddle, see Rouhana 1997.

40.   Kimmerling and Migdal 1993.

41.   Bhabha 1990.

42.   Cf. Rosaldo 1988.

43.   Rabinowitz, Ghanem, and Yiftachel 2000.

44.   Arad 2001.

45.   Mann 1999; Rabinowitz, Ghanem, and Yiftachel 2000: 10–11.

46. Significantly, the publication of the Hebrew edition of this book coincided with publications in Israel of other volumes that fuse, in their own ways, the personal with the historical and political. Moti Golani, a military historian from Haifa University, published a book that offers a critical look at Israel's wars since the 1950s, to which he brings his own memories as a child, later as a conscript, then as a young officer, and, more recently, as a reservist during Israel's various campaigns (Golani 2002). Shulamit Volkov, a historian from Tel Aviv University, wrote a history of German Jewry in which she interjects her own childhood memories (2002). And, most famously, Amos Oz's autobiographical account, *A Tale of Love and Darkness*, tells a story in which his family history becomes the pivot of a fascinating rendition of the political and intellectual history of Zionism (2002).

47. For a discussion of the anthropological preoccupation since the 1980s, see Clifford and Marcus 1986; Marcus and Fisher 1986; Ruby and Meyerhoff 1982.

48. De Certeau 1998.

49. Bruno Latour's work on what he calls "truly modern" science (Latour 1993) is another excursion into the realm of intellectual authority, absolutist knowledge, packaged arguments, and reflexive commentary.

50. Jackson 1998: 23–32.

51. Adorno 1991: ch. 1.

52. Benjamin 1969.

53. Jackson 1998: 33.

54. Arendt 1973: 107.

55. Fabian 1983.

56. Ruby and Meyerhoff use this in the final section of their jointly authored introduction to *A Crack in the Mirror* (1982).

57. Haas said things to this effect in a talk on Israel and Palestine that she gave at the Institute for Interregional Studies at Princeton University, November 2003.

CHAPTER ONE

1. Ya'abad, now a town of some twenty thousand in the administrative district of Jenin in the northern portion of the West Bank, was at the time a rather isolated agricultural community of some three thousand. For a detailed account of the area in the 1920s and 1930s, see Sweedenburg 1995.

2. For an account of Haifa in the interwar period, see Seikaly 1995.

3. Palestine in the interwar period was characterized by a slow rate of modernization in mountain towns, as opposed to rapid growth in the coastal plain (see Kimmerling and Migdal 1993: 36–63).

4.   For an account of Palestinians' social and economic situation at that time, see al-Hut 1991. See also Seikaly 1995; De Vries 1998.

5.   The *dabka* is an all-male dance in which a line of men, five or more abreast, with their arms on each other's shoulders, moves rhythmically sideways, backward, and forward, occasionally exclaiming words and syllables.

6.   This pattern of arranged marriage was premised on an agreement between the two families that bride-price would not change hands. Because Maryam's family was richer, the bride-price for daughters from her family would have been higher. This is why two sisters were exchanged for one bride. Such exchange marriages obviously strengthened the ties between the two parental households, but the breaking up of one of the marriages might have brought about the dissolution of the others too.

7.   Al-Jam'iya means "the association."

8.   Nazareth Street, renamed Shderot Ha'atzma'ut (Independence Boulevard, in Hebrew) in 1949, is parallel to the docks of the harbor. Built on land reclaimed from the sea by the British in early 1930, it was, for many years, Haifa's busiest commercial street.

9.   Literally meaning "Jews children of Arabs," the expression usually denotes Jews from Arab countries.

10.   Haifa, where the headquarters of the British Eighth Army was located, saw considerable prosperity as a result of services and goods that it was required to provide to the British army, particularly between 1942 and 1945.

11.   On the Wailing Wall Revolt of 1929, see Monk 2002. On the Arab Revolt of 1936–1939, see Kimmerling and Migdal 1993; Porath 1974.

12.   For examples, see Bernstein 2000; De Vries 1998.

13.   For an account of the dialectical relations between the Palestinian community and successive governments regarding education, see Abu-Baker 1990.

14.   Cf. Tibawi 1956.

15.   Abu-Hanna 1985.

16.   An excellent account of these class tensions can be found in Sayigh 1979. On the anti-British national struggle, see Porath 1974.

17.   For other accounts of this phenomenon, see Totah and al-Rasafi 1921; Tufaha 1947.

18.   Ra'anana was established in 1921 as a semiagricultural settlement (moshava) in the inner coastal plain (the Sharon area), some twenty kilometers northeast of Tel Aviv.

19.   The German Colony is the name of the quarter in downtown Haifa established in the 1860s by the Templars, a German Christian mission that built eleven agricultural colonies throughout Palestine, some in or near existing towns, others in rural parts.

20.   The Anschluss was the consensual annexation of Austria to Germany.

21. On the Bund, see Peled 1989.

22. See Grodzinski 1998.

23. A vivid account of this negotiation process can be found in Shlaim 1990.

24. Ibid., 90–106.

25. Ibid., 110–30.

26. The Arab Rescue Army, commanded by Fauzi al-Qauokji, was an expeditionary force organized and equipped in Syria that was sent to Palestine to fight the IDF alongside the local Palestinians. Relatively organized and well equipped, its units took part in various battles in Galilee until the summer of 1948. See Sayigh 1979: 66–120.

27. For vivid descriptions of one rural and one urban community devastated in 1948, see Diab 1990, 1991.

28. See Cohen 2000: 33–89.

29. Habonim was established in the 1920s by the World Zionist Federation with the aim of having many young Jewish persons from the English-speaking world come to Palestine. To date, it is active in Britain, Australia, New Zealand, South Africa, and Ireland.

30. *Sabra* is the label given to children of Zionist settlers born in Palestine/Israel, ostensibly representing the "new Jew." For an account of the image of the Sabra and its role in Israeli nation building, see Almog 1997.

CHAPTER TWO

1. The early phases of the 1948 war, between November 1947 and May 1948, saw mass flights and deportations of Palestinians from fourteen towns and over four hundred villages. Ten towns had been exclusively Palestinian prior to the war. The smaller and more peripheral among them (Beisan, Bir-Sab'ah, Majdal, and Halsa), each of which had its entire Palestinian community removed, were soon transformed into exclusively Jewish towns. Three larger Palestinian towns located in the heart of pre-1948 Palestine—al-Ramleh, Lid, and Jaffa—had upward of 90 percent of their Palestinian population forced out. These three were transformed after the war into de facto mixed towns overwhelmingly dominated by newly arrived Jewish immigrants from Europe and the Arab world.

The dynamics in the three Palestinian towns of Lower Galilee—Nazareth, Shafa-'Amer, and Acre—were somewhat different. All three had a much smaller proportion of the population displaced. In fact Nazareth and Acre, where many of the prewar population remained intact during the war, experienced a substantial influx of internally displaced Palestinians. The latter fled neighboring villages and eventually settled in the two towns, resulting, in the case of Nazareth, in a remarkable population increase.

Four other towns had been mixed communities before 1948. These are, in descending order of the size of their prewar Palestinian communities, Haifa, West Jerusalem, Safad, and Tiberias. The latter three had virtually their entire Palestinian population removed. In Haifa, on the other hand, some 6 percent of the original Palestinian population—approximately four thousand people—stayed behind (Morris 1991: 134).

2. Cf. Segev 1984.

3. For an account of the term *trapped minority* and its significance for other ethnically divided situations, see Rabinowitz 2001.

4. On the politics of culture via language, cf. Briggs 2002.

5. Rabinowitz 1993.

6. The British Emergency Regulations, were enacted as the King's Word to His Council, 1945.

7. For accounts of this legal revolution, see Kretzmer 1990; Kedar 1996; Yiftachel and Kedar 2000.

8. For an evocative treatment of the term *present absentees,* see Grossman 1992.

9. Cf. Jiryas 1966: 60–86.

10. See Morris 2000: 149–74.

11. Many Israelis believed that Palestinians hid their jewelry and gold in mattresses and food storage containers. For an account of looting in Haifa and the weak attempts made by public figures to contain it, see Goren 1996: 51–92.

12. King Abdullah of Jordan took control of the West Bank in 1950s as a result of an agreement with the few Palestinian notables who remained in the homeland. For an account of this development, which gave Jordan jurisdiction over the West Bank until it was conquered by Israel in 1967, see Shlaim 1990: 390–404.

13. Ghanem prefers the term *streams* (2001: 31–32).

14. Nasserism was named after Jamal Abdul Nasser, who was president of Egypt between 1953 and 1970. His pan-Arabist Socialist vision became popular throughout the Middle East—including among Palestinians inside Israel—in the 1950s and 1960s and is still supported by many to date. Ghanem omits the Islamic stream from the analysis of the early decades after 1948, indicating correctly that its meaningful entry into the reality of public and political life of the Palestinian citizens of Israel took place only in the 1980s (ibid., 123–37).

15. See Jiryas 1966: 13–59.

16. See ibid., 108–58.

17. See Rabinowitz 1997: 101–11.

18. The Gadna (an abbreviation for Gedudey Noar, meaning "Youth Battalions") was a paramilitary training program in every Israeli high school and was compulsory for boys and girls from ninth through twelfth grade. Training, including rifle-range shooting, marching, running, topography, and camping,

was conducted once or twice a week; additional weeklong sessions took place annually in an IDF camp. Between the 1950s and the 1980s, the Gadna had sports squads and an orchestra of its own.

19.   Lenny was in fact one of four judges appointed to the district court in Haifa in the spring of 1960 to deal specifically with land issues. These appointments followed legislation passed by the Knesset in February 1960 that transferred judicial authority over land disputes from judicial settlement officers to district court judges (Forman 2004: 150–51).

20.   See Rabinowitz 1994.

21.   Peled 1992.

22.   Ziad 1959, our translation.

23.   The couple's youngest child was born in the 1960s, after they had moved to Wolfson, a mixed, Jewish-Palestinian neighborhood in the modern part of Acre, outside the walls.

24.   The modern section of Palestinian Acre, which lay outside the walls, was built in the first part of the twentieth century and had spacious townhouses along a well-designed grid of boulevards and streets. In the 1950s most of these houses were declared "absentees' property" and transferred to Jewish ownership. Many are still used as shops, offices, and banks in Acre's main commercial center. For ethnographic accounts of the history of Acre since 1948, see Cohen 1969, 1971; Torstrick 2001.

CHAPTER THREE

1.   Um-Shiya, literally "mother of Shiya," is modeled after the convention in which adult parents are named after their offspring, normally their eldest son.

2.   In the 1960s, Arabic gradually became the chief language of instruction, and the institution fell under the jurisdiction of Israel's Ministry of Education.

3.   The Labor Party was called Mapay; Prime Minister David Ben-Gurion was its dominant leader.

4.   For a comprehensive account of the role of the *mukhtars,* see Lustick 1980.

5.   The Mandelbaum Crossing in East Jerusalem was the official U.N.-supervised border-crossing between Israel and Jordan between 1948 and 1967.

6.   On Gadna, see chapter 2, n. 18.

7.   This was Kamil Matanes, now owner of a medical equipment import business in Haifa.

8.   The particular families evicted from Kurdani were from a group labeled Ghawarna. For accounts of the Ghawarna and their history, see Khawaldi 1994; Khawaldi and Rabinowitz 2002.

9.   Qasam, who operated mostly near Haifa, was the popular leader of the budding Palestinian revolt against the British. Following a number of deadly

attacks that he staged on British officials, the British hunted him for weeks, until they found him in a hideout next to Ya'abad and killed him on the spot. His name still inspires Palestinian youngsters and is often taken up by guerilla groups, such as the Battalions of 'Az al-Din al-Qasam, who have emerged in the Occupied Territories since the late 1990s as an active fighting force.

10.　Between 1950 and the mid-1990s, schools on the West Bank were part of the Jordanian education system.

11.　Students studying in other schools in Haifa had separate scout troops.

12.　NAHAL (Hebrew acronym for Fighting Pioneering Youth) is a branch of the IDF that offers youth groups—mostly ones organized by the various youth movements—an opportunity to do service that is partly military and partly civilian. The youths use part of their time on active duty to prepare for settling a new kibbutz or joining an older one.

13.　Peled 1992.

14.　For recent accounts of Israel's wars, see Shlaim 1999; Morris 1999.

15.　The DFPE is known in Arabic as al-Jabha (the Front) and in Hebrew as Hahazit. For reviews of the Communist Party in Israel and of the DFPE, see Reiter and Aharoni 1992: 31–40; Rekhes 1993; Ghanem 2001.

16.　Cf. Beinin 1990.

17.　On the stifling of real representation in earlier years, see Jiryas 1966: ch. 4.

18.　Ghanem 2001: 65–75.

19.　For an account of land appropriations in the 1960s, see Forman 2004; Rabinowitz 1999.

20.　For additional accounts of Land Day and its political and symbolic meanings, see Benziman and Mansur 1992: 157–72; Yiftachel 1999.

21.　See Meir 1989.

22.　Muharib 1989.

23.　Knesset elections in the 1970s and 1980s saw the DFPE win between 4 and 7 seats in the 120-strong house.

24.　For a critical account of these initiatives, see Rabinowitz 2000; Ophir 2002.

25.　Rouhana and Fiske 1995; Rouhana and Korper 1997.

26.　See Bargal and Bar 1995, 1990. It should be noted also that, for their part, many Jewish schools displayed only limited enthusiasm for these programs. Schools in certain streams of education, notably the national religious stream, shunned participation altogether. Only very few schools, normally ones with a particularly committed headmaster or headmistress, participated in these programs in a sustained manner.

27.　See Rabinowitz 2000.

28.　Payes suggests that the number of Palestinian NGOs registered in Israel by 2005 is almost 1,000 (Payes 2005:1).

29.　Ghanem 1993; Jaffa Research Center 1991.

30.　For sources dealing with the early stages of these institutions, see the

National Committee of Arab Mayors and Follow-Up Committee on Education 1984, 1987; Follow-Up Committee on Welfare 1987, 1991, 1996; al-Haj 1996; Nakhlah 1990; Marʿi 1978.

31.   Saʿid died of cancer in 2001, on his fortieth birthday. His relatives in Yaʿabad were unable to attend his funeral in Amman because of the Israeli army's closure of their village and the severe limitations imposed on travel.

32.   The dual balloting system prevailed for only seven years. In 2003 the previous unitary system was restored, in which the voter selects a Knesset party only. When the results are known, the leader of a party deemed capable of securing the support of more than half the members of the new Knesset is formally invited by the president to form a government.

33.   MADA is a party incorporating representatives of segments of the Islamic Movement willing to participate in the Israeli parliament. Other activists, paramount among whom are the charismatic hard-liners Sheikh Raʾed Salah (once mayor of Um al-Fahim) and Sheikh Camal Khatib of Kafar Kana in Galilee, consistently decline to stand for Knesset elections. Their argument is that their candidacy would imbue the Israeli system with a legitimacy it does not deserve.

34.   Osetzky-Lazar 2003: E1. Note that this figure includes Druze voters.

CHAPTER FOUR

1.   A similar sentiment is reflected in statements regularly issued by Hamas and by dissenting Arab and Islamist voices in Iraq, Saudi Arabia, and Afghanistan against Arab governments perceived as subordinating national interests to the demands of foreign occupying powers.

2.   For a view of this from a Palestinian angle, see Hammami and Tamari 2001.

3.   For an interesting review of the genealogy of the Palestinian armed struggle in 2000, see Saleh Abd al-Jawad, "The intifada's military lessons," *Palestine Report,* October 25, 2000, www.jmcc.org/media/report/2000/Oct/4.htm# feature (last accessed on December 19, 2004).

4.   For a detailed account of Natzerat Illit and its relationship with Nazareth, see Rabinowitz 1997.

5.   In July 2001, the police commander in charge of the district testified before the Orr Commission of Inquiry, the formal body that had been established by the government of Israel to investigate the violent events that took place in Galilee in October 2000. The officer's testimony, given under oath, included the astonishing admission that he had no knowledge whatsoever of sharpshooters being deployed in the area under his direct command on October 8. Similar versions, mutatis mutandis, were produced by Major General Alik Ron, who was commissioner of police (northern command) at the time; by Israeli chief of police Yehouda

Vilk; by the minister of internal security at the time, Shlomo Ben-Ami; and by then Prime Minister Ehud Barak. The four men told the commission of inquiry that they had no real-time knowledge of the deployment of police marksmen.

6.   Eyal 1993 briefly alludes to this circuit. Eyal 2002 offers a more through critical analysis of the epistemological and political influence it has had on Israeli oriental studies and, by implication, government and history.

7.   See Eyal 2002.

8.   See also Rabinowitz 2004.

9.   The full report, titled *After the Rift: New Directions for Government Policies for the Arab Citizens of Israel* (Rabinowitz, Ghanem, and Yiftachel 2000), has since been translated into other languages. It is currently available in Hebrew, Arabic, English, and German.

10.   This reference is to Shlomo Ben-Ami, cabinet minister for internal security in Ehud Barak's government. Ben-Ami, a specialist on early Spanish history, is a professor of history at Tel Aviv University.

11.   In June 2004, the district attorney in Galilee asked Asil's family's permission to exhume his body as part of the criminal investigation of his death by police fire. The family agreed in principle, but stipulated that the postmortem operation should take place only as a last resort, when every other source of evidence had been exhausted.

12.   Shaikha Abu-Saleh died during a demonstration in which Israeli riot police used teargas bombs to disperse Palestinian protestors. Residents of Sakhnin claimed that the cause of death was inhaled tear gas. Israeli police, backed by medical reports released by the Haifa Medical Center, where Abu-Saleh was treated prior to her death, claimed the elderly woman died of a heart attack.

13.   See for example *Ma'ariv Weekend*, June 2000.

14.   The cover interview with Khulud Badawi, 'Arin Hamud, and Shirin Yunis, published in the weekend magazine of *Ma'ariv* (see previous note), drew particularly harsh reactions. Responding with a mixture of shock and revulsion, members of the Jewish public revealed their fundamental ignorance regarding social dynamics inside Israel's Palestinian community. On July 7, *Ma'ariv* published a sample of eight responses apparently culled from a deluge of uniformly angry replies. All writers expressed a visceral sense of recoil from the contents of the interview. Some expressed dismay with the paper's willingness to provide a public platform for a vision they regarded as the ultimate nightmare. For them, the statements made by the three Palestinian women were a vivid demonstration of what the Israeli right wing had often contended: namely, that "the Arabs always bite the hand so generously extended to them by us Jews."

15.   For accounts of the first intifada and its significance, see Lockman and Beinin 1989; Nassar and Heacock 1990; Hilterman 1991.

16. The Hebrew University in Jerusalem and the Technion in Haifa were the only two universities in Israel until the late 1960s.

17. See Abu-Baker 1998, 2001.

18. In 1957, the number of Palestinian students in the Israeli universities was 46 (.6 percent of the total student body). In 1965 it was 239 (1.6 percent) and in 1971, 607 (1.7 percent). Up until the early 1970s, the number of Palestinian female students among these was negligible. (All figures are from al-Haj 1996: 160, table 8.1.)

19. For the dynamics within Arab families that determine which family members are more likely to get a university education, see Shavit and Pierce 1991.

20. For works that look at the role of higher education in Israel's Palestinian community, see Shavit 1989, 1990.

21. For uneducated women, the age of thirty is often a point of no return, beyond which they could be forced to reconcile themselves to being *'awanis* (spinsters).

22. Paradoxically, Khulud Badawi's outspoken critique of what she calls high politics does not stop many from seeing her as a realistic DFPE candidate for the Knesset in the not so distant future.

23. Ghanem 1996.

24. The groups named are two left-of-center Zionist movements with explicit socialist ideologies that nevertheless established collective settlements on Palestinian land following the 1948 war.

25. On Palestinians' employment in the IDF, see Kanaaneh 2003.

26. Badawi 2004: 4. "Star academy" is the Arabic version of "American superstar."

27. See Nir 2001.

CHAPTER FIVE

1. See Kedar 2001.

2. Mann 1999.

3. Cf. Appadurai 1996.

4. Abie Nathan, a former Royal Air Force pilot of Jewish Indian origins, was the owner in the 1960s and 1970s of a famous restaurant in Tel Aviv called California, which was frequented by artists, thespians, and politicians. Nathan became a household name in Israel when, in February 1966, he flew an old Stearman biplane across the Egyptian border on a self-proclaimed, unannounced peace mission. He landed in Port Said and declared that he wanted to meet the Egyptian president Nasser, but instead was arrested and returned to Israel the next day. He continued his peace activism in the 1970s and 1980s; established a

radio station called the Voice of Peace, which he operated from a vessel off the coast of Tel Aviv; and staged a famous hunger strike in 1991 against the Israeli law banning meetings between Israelis and Palestinians. In the 1990s he became involved with humanitarian relief work, mainly in Africa, persevering as long as his ailing health allowed.

5.   Arad 2001.

6.   The comparison the authors make is between the demographic threat and other threats to Israel that are deliberated elsewhere in the report.

7.   Arad 2001: 4. All translations of Arad in the present volume are ours.

8.   Ibid., 7.

9.   Ibid., 4. A more detailed paper published as part of the Herzliya Conference (Ravid 2001: 18) cites a slightly more conservative estimate for 2020, with Arabs (projected at 1.9 million) constituting only 20.8 percent of the entire citizenry of Israel (projected at 9.1 million).

10.   Central Bureau of Statistics 2003: ch. 2.1: 2; Arad 2001. The status of Palestinian residents of East Jerusalem, who live in a territory that was part of Jordan between 1948 and 1967, is different from that of the Palestinian citizens of Israel and Palestinians in the Occupied Territories. Palestinian residents of East Jerusalem hold blue Israeli identity cards: they are entitled to vote in municipal elections (though they seldom ever do) but not in Knesset elections.

11.   Official figures indicate that annual population growth rates in the late 1990s were approximately 3.4 percent for Palestinian citizens in Israel and 2.4 percent for Jewish Israelis (Central Bureau of Statistics 2000).

12.   See Anderson 1983; Fabian 1983.

13.   For an account of how the Palestinians find solace and resistance to Israeli domination in pronatalism, see Kanaaneh 2002: ch. 1.

14.   See Shenhav and Gabay 2001 for a sociological analysis of commissions of inquiry.

15.   At first the Israeli government was inclined to appoint a semiformal "examination committee." Only when the leaders of the Palestinian community declared that they would not cooperate with it did the government reconsider, eventually appointing a formal state commission of inquiry, in line with the Law of State Commissions of Inquiries.

16.   By the end of the hearings, the commission had seen and heard more than three hundred witnesses, amassing almost twenty thousand pages of typed protocols.

17.   The man refused to go on record with this statement or say it on camera, for fear of being accused by the skeptical Palestinian public of playing into the hands of the government.

18.   In Israeli legal procedure, only the attorney general and the subordinate district attorneys are authorized to bring criminal charges. In many cases, the

police mount an initial criminal investigation and then forward their findings to the attorney general's office for a final decision regarding filing charges. Commissions of inquiry cannot bring charges on their own. Like the police, they are expected to submit to the attorney general's office whatever evidence they have gathered that might be relevant to criminal charges.

19.   The full report, in Hebrew, is available at http://or.barak.net.il/inside_index.htm, last accessed December 19, 2004.

20.   "Orr Commission of Inquiry Report," 2003, sec. 1, ch. 1: 1, http://or.barak.net.il/inside_index.htm; our translations throughout.

21.   Ibid., sec. 1, ch. 1: 2.

22.   Ibid.

23.   Ibid., sec. 1, ch. 1: 4.

24.   Ibid.

25.   Ibid.

26.   Ibid.

27.   See Kymlicka 1989.

28.   In 1984 the Kahan Commission, which inquired into the massacre in Sabra and Shatila, tabled a similar recommendation in the case of Ariel Sharon, stating that he was unfit to serve as minister of defense ever again. This recommendation was upheld in a literal sense: Sharon was never again appointed as minister of defense. However, it did not stop him from serving in a variety of other cabinet positions, culminating, of course, in his election as prime minister in 2001 and 2003.

Shlomo Ben-Ami, a history professor at Tel Aviv University and formerly Israel's ambassador to Spain, had never really wanted to serve as minister of internal security. Absent from the political scene since the failure of the Labor Party in the 2001 elections, he is unlikely to seek this post ever again, even in the unlikely event of his return to politics.

29.   The ministerial committee was chaired by Minister of Justice Yosef (Tomi) Lapid, and it presented its report to the cabinet in early June 2004. The report (in Hebrew) is available at http://patent.justice.gov.il/MOJHeb/Subjects/vaadatLapid.htm.

30.   For example Sikkuy, an NGO dedicated to equal opportunities for Palestinian citizens of Israel, organized a series of conferences and public events in 2004 to promote public debate and put pressure on the government to implement changes according to the spirit of the Orr Report. One of these events, which took place on June 24, 2004, at Bet Sokolov in Tel Aviv, had among its participants Minister Lapid, Professor Shimo'n Shamir (a member of the Orr Commission), officers of NGOs, and academics.

31.   *Zochrot*, a Hebrew word, literally means "to remember," denoting "those who remember" in the female plural sense. Established in 2001, this association

holds excursions to ruined Palestinian villages, in which elderly displaced Palestinians and their descendants give testimony about the pre-1948 village and the
fate that befell them after the village had been ruined. Some of these visits include
makeshift exhibitions of old photographs that the old inhabitants bring with
them, the ceremonial placing of signs attesting to the village's pre-1948 existence,
the audio- and videotaping of testimonies, and so on. The organization's Website
is www.nakbainhebrew.org.

CHAPTER SIX

1.   For instance, in early 2000, during a television program commemorating
the right-wing Zionist leader Ze'ev Jabotinsky, Knesset member Dan Meridor,
then a member of the short-lived Center Party and formerly a member of right-
wing Herut Party, agreed that Jabotinsky's notions of citizenship were not unlike
the concept of "a state of all its citizens," promoted vigorously by Palestinian
Knesset members.

2.   Cf. Dwairy 2001.

3.   A fierce debate that took place in early June 2004 on the pages of *Haaretz*
revealed that the view adopted by Barak and later by Sharon—that "Israel now
has no Palestinian partner"—was backed by a particular analysis of Palestinian
intentions developed by the man who was then head of the IDF's intelligence
department, General Amos Gilad. Gilad's conclusion was that the Palestinians
had never been interested in coexistence with Israel, and that their strategic goal
was to annihilate it. The defining moment, Gilad maintained, was Barak's refusal
at Camp David in July 2000 to grant Palestinian refugees the right of return that
would have ensured Israel's demise. Forsaking the hope of doing away with
Israel through demographic means, he claimed, the Palestinians turned to an all-
out campaign aimed at destroying it through terror. Gilad's view was not the
only analysis that came from the IDF's Intelligence Department. If anything, it
was a heterodoxy. His commanding officer, Amos Malka, the head of Military
Intelligence, believed, for example, that the Palestinians were genuinely striving
for a two-state solution, and that the intifada was a tactic aimed at prompting
other nations to apply pressure on Israel that would force additional concessions
in favor of the Palestinians. Gilad's fundamental assessment, however, was ideo-
logically compatible with the outlook of Barak and later of Sharon. Not surprisingly, it was adopted by the government, the media, and the public at the expense
of his direct superior's version, the very existence of which was systematically
silenced for four fateful years.

4.   Cf. Dor 2001.

5.   See Zahalka 2001.

6. After Michael Herzfeld's *The Social Production of Indifference* (1993).

7. Netanyahu 1987.

8. See Kedar 1996; Yiftachel and Kedar 2000.

9. For a more comprehensive analysis of the current situation and of ways to improve it, see Yiftachel, Khamaisi, and Kedar 2000.

10. See Ghanem, Abu-Ras, and Rosenhak 2000.

11. See al-Haj, Abu-Saʻad, and Yona 2000.

12. See Abu-Baker 2003a,b; Abu-ʻAsba 1997.

13. See Barzilai et al. 2000.

14. For an opinion advocating such an approach, see Rouhana 2001.

15. Israel has seen a precedent for such a move. In January 2000, the Knesset passed a bill recognizing May 9 as a national memorial day honoring Russia's victory over Nazi Germany. This law was primarily designed to bolster Israel's sense of identification with a specific group—elderly immigrants recently arrived from the former Soviet Union, for whom the date May 9 still carries deep emotional significance.

16. For accounts of the significance of educational packages for civil and political socialization, see Hess 1968; Oppenheim and Torney 1974; Ichilov 1984; Abu-Baker 1990.

17. The name is loosely translatable as "Sakhnin United" and, literally, as the "Union of the Sons of Sakhnin."

18. Cf. Handelman and Katz 1993.

19. Dor Tashah, which has become an Israeli cultural convention, literally means "the generation of 5708." *Dor* means "generation." *Tashah,* according to the Jewish calendar, means the 5,708th year since the creation of the world, corresponding to 1948 C.E.

References

Abu-ʿAsba, Khaled. 1997. *The Arab school system in Israel: Status quo and alternative structure* (in Hebrew). Givʿat Haviva: Institute of Peace Research.

Abu-Baker, Khawla. 1990. The political socialization of the Palestinian child through the political children's literature (in Hebrew). Master's thesis, University of Haifa.

———. 1998. *A rocky road: Arab women as political leaders in Israel* (in Hebrew). Raʾanana: Institute for Israeli-Arab Studies.

———. 2001. Arab political women leaders, a phenomena of social change? In *Will you listen to my voice? Representations of women in the Israeli culture* (in Hebrew), ed. Yael Azmon, pp. 345–54. Tel Aviv: Van Leer Jerusalem Institute and Hakibbutz Hameukhad.

———. 2003a. Social and educational welfare policy in the Arab sector in Israel. In *The Israeli Palestinians: An Arab minority in the Jewish state*, ed. A. Bligh, pp. 68–96. London: Frank Cass.

———. 2003b. Research on welfare and well-being in Israel: A Palestinian perspective. In *Traditions and transitions in Israel studies. Books on Israel,* vol. 6, ed. L. Z. Eisenberg, N. Caplan, N. B. Sokoloff, and M. Abu-Nimer, pp. 135–55. Albany: State University of New York Press.

Abu-Baker, Khawla, and Dan Rabinowitz. 2004. *The Stand-Tall Generation.* Ramallah: Madar (in Arabic).

Abu-Hanna, Hanna. 1985. *The Russian seminaries in Palestine* (in Arabic). Master's thesis, University of Haifa.

Adorno, Theodor. 1991. *Notes to literature.* Ed. Rolf Tiedemann, trans. Shierry Weber Nicholson. Vol. 1. New York: Columbia University Press.

Almog, Oz. 1997. *The Sabra: A portrait* (in Hebrew). Tel Aviv: Am Oved.

Alterman, Natan. 1974. *Magash hakesef* (The gold platter). Tel Aviv: Ministry of Defense Publishing House.

Anderson, Benedict. 1983. *Imagined communities.* London: Verso.

Appadurai, Arjun. 1996. Territorializing the nation. In *Geographies of identity,* ed. Patricia Yaeger. Ann-Arbor: University of Michigan Press.

Arad, Uzi, ed. 2001. *The balance of Israel's national security* (in Hebrew). Herzliya: Center of Interdisciplinary Studies.

Arendt, Hanna. 1973. *Men in dark times.* Harmondsworth: Penguin.

Asch, Michael. 1984. *Home and native land: Aboriginal rights and the Canadian constitution.* Toronto: Methuen.

Badawi, Khulud. 2004. Where has the stand-tall generation disappeared? (in Hebrew). *Arab Pictures: A Special Shavuot Supplement of Haaretz,* May 25, pp. 4–5.

Bader, Veit. 1995. Citizenship and exclusion: Radical democracy, community, and justice. *Political Theory* 232: 211–46.

Baker, Judith, ed. 1994. *Group rights.* Toronto: University of Toronto Press.

Bargal, David, and Haviva Bar. 1990. Role problems for trainers in an Arab-Jewish conflict management workshop. *Small Group Research* 21, no. 1: 5–27.

———. 1994. The encounter of social selves: Intergroup workshops for Arab and Jewish youth. *Social Work with Groups* 17, no. 3: 39–59.

———. 1995. *Living with the conflict* (in Hebrew). Jerusalem: Jerusalem Institute for Israel Studies.

Barzilai, Gad, Ronen Shamir, Musa Abu-Ramadan, Menachem Mautner, Amalia Saʿar, Amal Jamal, and Nadera Shalhouv-Kavorkian. 2000. Law, society, and the Arab population of Israel. In *After the rift: New directions for government policy towards the Arab population in Israel. An emergency report by an inter-university research team, submitted to Mr. Ehud Barak, prime minister of Israel, November 2000,* ed. Dan Rabinowitz, Asʿad Ghanem, and Oren Yiftachel. Beʾer-Sheva: self-published by the editors, with the help of the European Commission in Israel and Shatil.

Beinin, J. 1990. *Was the red flag flying there? Marxist politics and the Arab-Israeli conflict in Egypt and Israel, 1948–1965.* Berkeley: University of California Press.

Benjamin, Walter. 1969. *Illuminations*. Ed. and with an introduction by Hannah Arendt, trans. Harry Zohn. New York: Schocken Books.

Bennett, David, ed. 1998. *Multicultural states: Rethinking difference and identity.* New York: Routledge.

Benvenisti, Meiron. 2002. The green line. In *Borderline disorder: Catalogue of the Israeli pavilion, the Eighth International Architecture Exhibition, la Biennale di Venezzia 2002*, ed. Zvi Efrat, pp. 34–35. Jerusalem: Ministry of Science, Culture, and Sport, and Ministry of Foreign Affairs.

Benziman, Uzi, and Attallah Mansur. 1992. *Subtenants: The status of the Arabs of Israel and state policy toward them* (in Hebrew). Jerusalem: Keter.

Bernstein, Deborah. 2000. *Constructing boundaries: Jewish and Arab workers in mandatory Palestine.* Albany: State University of New York Press.

Bhabha, Homi. 1994. *The location of culture.* London: Routledge.

———, ed. 1990. *Nation and narration.* New York: Routledge.

Bhargava, R., Amiya K. Bagchi, and R. Sudarshan, eds. 1999. *Multiculturalism, liberalism, and democracy.* Delhi: Oxford University Press.

Bishara, Azmi. 1990. Arab society in Israel: A different viewpoint (in Hebrew). *Medina, Mimshal Veyahasim Beinleumim* 32: 81–87.

———. 1992. Palestine in the new order. *Middle East Report*, no. 175: 2–8.

———. 1994. On the question of the Palestinian minority in Israel. *Theory and Criticism* (in Hebrew), 3: 1–17.

Brass, Paul. 1991. *Ethnicity and nationalism: Theory and comparison.* Delhi: Sage.

Briggs, Charles. 2002. Linguistic magic bullets in the making of a modernist anthropology. *American Anthropologist* 104, no. 2: 481–98.

Cairns, Alan. 1995. Aboriginal Canadians, citizenship, and constitution. In *Reconfigurations: Canadian citizenship and constitutional change.* Toronto: McClelland and Stewart.

Central Bureau of Statistics (Israel). 1999. *Statistical yearbook, 1998.* Jerusalem: Central Bureau of Statistics.

———. 2000. *Statistical yearbook, 1999.* Jerusalem: Central Bureau of Statistics.

Chacour, E., and D. Hazard. 1984. *Blood brothers: A Palestinian struggles for reconciliation in the Middle East.* Grand Rapids, MI: Chosen Books.

Chacour, E., and M. E. Jensen. 1990. *We belong to the land: The story of a Palestinian Israeli who lives for peace and reconciliation.* San Francisco: HarperSanFrancisco.

Chandhoke, Neera. 1999. *Beyond secularism: The rights of religious minorities.* Delhi: Oxford University Press.

Clifford, James. 1988. *The predicament of culture: Twentieth century ethnography, literature, and art.* Cambridge: Harvard University Press.

Clifford, James, and George Marcus, eds. 1986. *Writing culture: The poetics and politics of ethnography.* Berkeley: University of California Press.

Cohen, Erik. 1969. Mixed marriage in an Israeli town. *Jewish Journal of Sociology* 11, no. 1: 41–50.

———. 1971. Arab boys and tourist girls in a mixed Jewish-Arab community. *International Journal of Comparative Sociology* 12, no. 4: 217–33.

Cohen, Hillel. 2000. *The present absentees: The Palestinian refugees in Israel since 1948*. Jerusalem: Institute for Israeli-Arab Studies.

Danley, John. 1991. Liberalism, aboriginal rights, and cultural minorities. *Philosophy and Public Affairs* 202: 168–85.

de Certeau, Michel. 1988. *The practice of everyday life*. Berkeley: University of California Press.

———. 1998. *Culture in the plural*. Minneapolis: University of Minnesota Press.

De Vries, David. 1998. *Idealism and bureaucracy in 1920s Palestine: The workers of Haifa in the labor movement, 1918–1930* (in Hebrew). Tel Aviv: Ha-Kibbutz Ha-Me'uchad.

Diab, Imtiaz. 1990. *A story of a village: Destroyed Palestinian villages in the Jerusalem area in 1948* (in Arabic). Beirut: *al-Muasasa al-A'rabia Lldirasat W al-Nashr* (Arab Institution of Research and Publication).

———. 1991. *Jaffa: Scent of a city* (in Arabic). Beirut: Dar al-Fata al-Arabi (Home of the Arab child).

Dor, Daniel. 2001. *Newspapers under the influence*. Tel Aviv: Babel.

Drori, Israel. 2000. *The seam line: Arab workers and Jewish managers in Israel's textile industry*. Stanford: Stanford University Press.

Dwairy, Marwan. 2001. A psychology of the oppressor, a psychology of the oppressed. In *Real time: Al-Aqsa intifada and the Israeli left* (in Hebrew), ed. Adi Ophir, pp. 265–74. Tel Aviv: Keter.

Eyal, Gil. 1993. Between East and West: The discourse of the Arab village in Israel. *Theory and Criticism* (in Hebrew), 3: 39–55.

———. 2002. Dangerous liaisons: The relations between military intelligence and oriental studies in Israel. *Theory and Criticism* (in Hebrew), 20: 137–64.

Fabian, Johannes. 1983. *Time and the Other: How anthropology makes its object*. New York: Columbia University Press.

Follow-Up Committee on Welfare. 1987. *Proceedings of the Conference on Social Services for Arabs in Israel* (in Arabic). Shafa'amar: National Committee of Arab Mayors and Follow-Up Committee on Welfare.

———. 1991. *Proceedings of the Second Conference on Social Services for Arabs in Israel* (in Arabic). Nazareth: National Committee of Arab Mayors and Follow-Up Committee on Welfare.

———. 1996. *Proceedings of the Third Conference: Toward a comprehensive program of welfare services in the Arab sector* (in Arabic). Ma'lia: National Committee of Arab Mayors and Follow-Up Committee on Welfare.

Forman, Geremy. 2004. "Israeli settlement of title in Arab areas: The 'Special Land Settlement Operation' in northern Israel (1955–1967)." Ph.D. diss., University of Haifa, Department of Geography.

Ghanem, As'ad. 1993. *Arabs in Israel toward the twenty-first century. A survey of basic infrastructure* (in Hebrew). Giv'at Haviva: Institute of Peace Research.

———. 1996. Political participation amongst Arabs in Israel. Ph.D. diss., Department of Political Science, Haifa University.

———. 1998. State and minority in Israel: The case of the ethnic state and the predicament of its minority. *Ethnic and Racial Studies* 213: 428–47.

———. 2001. *The Palestinian Arab minority in Israel, 1948–2000: A political study.* New York: State University of New York Press.

Ghanem, As'ad, Thabet Abu-Ras, and Zeev Rosenhak. 2000. Local government, community, and welfare. In *After the rift: New directions for government policy towards the Arab population in Israel. An emergency report by an inter-university research team, submitted to Mr. Ehud Barak, prime minister of Israel, November 2000,* ed. Dan Rabinowitz, As'ad Ghanem, and Oren Yiftachel. Be'er-Sheva: self-published by the editors, with the help of the European Commission in Israel and Shatil.

Golani, Moti. 2002. *Wars do not happen on their own: On memory, power, and choice* (in Hebrew). Tel Aviv: Modan.

Goren, Tamir. 1996. *From dependence to integration* (in Hebrew). Haifa: University of Haifa, Jewish-Arab Institute.

Green, Leslie. 1994. International minorities and their rights. In *Group rights,* ed. Judith Baker. Toronto: University of Toronto Press.

Greenberg, Lev. 1991. *Split corporatism in Israel.* Albany: State University of New York Press.

Grodzinski, Yosef. 1998. *Good human material: Jews versus Zionists, 1946–1951* (in Hebrew). Tel Aviv: Hed-Artzi.

Grossman, David. 1992. *Present absentees* (in Hebrew). Tel Aviv: Hakibbutz Hameukhad.

———. 2002. *The yellow wind.* Jerusalem: Keter, 1988 (in Hebrew); reprint, New York: Picador.

Guri, Haim [1949] 1989. Hine mutalot gufoteinu (Here are our bodies laid down). In *Nikhtav betashah: A collection of stories and poems written during the War of Independence,* ed. A. B. Yaffe. Tel Aviv: Reshafim.

Gurr, Ted. 1993. *Minorities at risk: A global view of ethno-political conflict.* Washington, DC: Institute of Peace Press.

Habermas, Jurgen. 2002. *On political participation in multicultural societies.* Open lecture at Tel Aviv University Law Department, June.

al-Haj, Majid. 1986. Adjustment patterns of the Arab internal refugees in Israel. *International Migration* 24, no. 3: 651–75.

———. 1996. *Education among the Arabs in Israel: Control and social change.* Jerusalem: Magnes Press and Hebrew University.

———. 2003. Education in the shadow of conflict: Culture hegemony versus controlled multi-culturalism. In *In the name of security: The sociology of peace and security in an era of change,* ed. M. al-Haj and Uri Ben-Eliezer. Haifa: University of Haifa.

al-Haj, Majid, Ismai-ʿil Abu-Saʿad, and Yossi Yona. 2000. Education and community. In *After the rift: New directions for government policy towards the Arab population in Israel. An emergency report by an inter-university research team, submitted to Mr. Ehud Barak, prime minister of Israel, November 2000,* ed. Dan Rabinowitz, Asʿad Ghanem, and Oren Yiftachel. Beʾer-Sheva: self-published by the editors, with the help of the European Commission in Israel and Shatil.

Hammami, Rema, and Salim Tamari. 2001. The second intifada: End or new beginning? *Journal of Palestine Studies* 30, no. 2: 5–25.

Handelman, Don, and Elihu Katz. 1993. State ceremonies of Israel: Remembrance Day and Independence Day. In *Israeli Judaism,* ed. Shlomo Deshen, Charles Liebman, and Moshe Shoked, pp. 75–85. New Brunswick: Transaction Books.

Hannum, Hurst. 1989. The limits of sovereignty and majority rule: Minorities, indigenous peoples, and right to autonomy. In *New directions in human rights,* ed. Ellen Lutz, Hurst Hannum, and Kathryn Burke. Philadelphia: University of Pennsylvania Press.

Herzfeld, Michael. 1993. *The social production of indifference.* Chicago: University of Chicago Press.

Hess, Robert. 1968. Political socialization in the schools. *Harvard Educational Review* 383: 528–36.

Hilterman, Joost. 1991. *Behind the intifada: Labour and women's movements in the occupied territories.* Princeton, NJ: Princeton University Press.

Horowitz, Donald. 1985. *Ethnic groups in conflict.* Berkeley: University of California Press.

al-Hut, Nuayhed. 1991. *Palestine: The problem, the people, the civilization* (in Arabic). Beirut: Dar al-Istiqlal.

Ichilov, Orit. 1984. *The political life of children and teenagers* (in Hebrew). Tel Aviv: Yachdav.

Jackson, Michael. 1998. *Minima ethnigraphica: Intersubjectivity and the anthropological project.* Chicago: Chicago University Press.

Jaffa Research Center. 1991. *Guide to Arab community associations in Israel, 1990* (in Arabic). Nazareth: Jaffa Research Center.

Jiryas, Sabri. 1966. *Arabs in Israel* (in Arabic). Haifa: al-Itihad.

Kanaaneh, Rhoda Ann. 2002. *Birthing the nation: Strategies of Palestinian women in Israel.* Berkeley: University of California Press.

———. 2003. Embattled identities: Palestinian soldiers in the Israeli military. *Journal of Palestine Studies* 32, no. 3: 5–20.

Kedar, Alexander. 1996. *Israeli law and the redemption of Arab land, 1948–1969.* Cambridge: Harvard Law School.

————. 2001. The legal transformation of ethnic geography: Israeli law and the Palestinian landholder, 1948–1967. *NYU Journal of International Law and Politics* 33, no. 4: 923–1000.

Kemp, Adriana. 2002. Border, space, and national identity in Israel. *Theory and Criticism* (in Hebrew), 16: 13–44.

Khawaldi, Sliman. 1994. *Beduinen in Gelobten Land, Die Stamme der Krad-il-Het, Krad il-Gannama und Krad-il-Baggara, Eine Falstudie zum Struktur Wandel im Zuge der Ses'haftwerdung von 1858 und zur Zwangs-umseidlung seit 1951 im Galilee—Israel.* Hamburg: Dr. Covac.

Khawaldi, Sliman, and Dan Rabinowitz. 2002. Race from the bottom of the tribe that never was: Segmentary narratives amongst the Ghawarna of Galilee. *Journal of Anthropological Research* 58: 225–43.

al-Khuri, Iskandar al-Batjali. 1943. *The versed metaphor for schools* (in Arabic). 2nd ed. Jerusalem: al-Quds.

Kimmerling, Baruch, and Joel Migdal. 1993. *Palestinians: The making of a people.* New York: Free Press.

Kretzmer, David. 1990. *The legal status of the Arabs in Israel.* Boulder: Westview Press.

Kymlicka, Will. 1989. *Liberalism, Community, and Culture.* Oxford: Clarendon Press.

————. 1995. *Multicultural citizenship.* Oxford: Clarendon Press.

————. 2001. *Politics in the vernacular: Nationalism, multiculturalism, and citizenship.* Oxford: Oxford University Press.

Kymlicka, Will, and Wayne Norman, eds. 2000. *Citizenship in diverse societies.* Oxford: Oxford University Press.

Latour, Bruno. 1993. *We have never been modern.* Trans. Catherine Porter. Cambridge: Harvard University Press.

Levin, Hanoch. 1987. *Malkat ambatya* (Queen of the bathroom). In *What does the bird care? Songs, sketches, and satires* (in Hebrew). Tel Aviv: Hakibbutz Hameukhad, Siman Kria Books, Hebrew Book Club.

Levin, Michael, ed. 1993. *Ethnicity and aboriginality: Case studies in ethno-nationalism.* Toronto: University of Toronto Press.

Lockman, Zachary, and Joel Beinin, eds. 1989. *Intifada: The Palestinian uprising against Israeli occupation.* Boston: South End Press.

Lustick, Ian. 1980. *Arabs in the Jewish state.* Austin: University of Texas Press.

Macdonald, Ian. 1989. Group rights. *Philosophical papers,* no. 282: 117–36.

Mahajan, Gurpreet, ed. 1998. *Democracy, difference, and social justice.* Delhi: Oxford University Press.

Mann, Michael. 1999. The dark side of democracy. *New Left Review* 235: 18–45.

Mannheim, K. 1940. Man and society in an age of reconstruction. London: Routledge.

Marcus, George, and Michael Fisher. 1986. *Anthropology as cultural critique*. Chicago: University of Chicago Press.

Marʿi, Sami. 1978. *Arab education in Israel*. Syracuse, NY: Syracuse University Press.

Matzpen, 1976. Land Day. *Workers' Monthly, the Journal of the Israeli sociological Organization* (in Hebrew), 77 (May).

Meir, Thomas. 1989. The Muslim youth in Israel. *New East* (in Hebrew), 22: 10–20.

Monk, Daniel. 2002. *An aesthetic occupation: The immediacy of architecture and the Palestine conflict*. Durham, NC: Duke University Press.

Morris, Benny. 1989. *The birth of the Palestinian refugee problem, 1947–1949*. Cambridge: Cambridge University Press.

———. 1991. *The birth of the Palestinian refugee problem, 1947–1949* (in Hebrew). Tel Aviv: Am Oved.

———. 1999. *Righteous victims*. New York: Knopf.

———. 2000. *Errata. Jewish Arab relations, 1917–1956* (in Hebrew). Tel Aviv: Am Oved.

Muharib, Mahmoud. 1989. *The Israeli Communist Party and the Palestinian problem, 1948–1983: A Critical Study* (in Arabic). Jerusalem: self-published.

Nakhlah, Khalil. 1990. *Our civil institution in Palestine: Toward a social development* (in Arabic). Jerusalem: al-Multaqa al-Fikri al-Arabi and Markiz Ihiaa al-Turath (The Arabic Mind Meeting Center and the Center for Folklore Revival).

Nassar, Jamal R., and Roger Heacock, eds. 1990. *Intifada: Palestine at the crossroads*. New York: Praeger.

National Committee of Arab Mayors' Follow-Up Committee on Education 1987. *Problems of education of Arabs* (in Arabic). Haifa: Dar al-Nahda.

National Committee of Arab Mayors' Follow-Up Committee on Education, and the Society of Directors of Departments of Education in Local Government. 1984. *Arab education in Israel: Problems and demands* (in Arabic). Haifa: Dar al-Nahda.

Netanyahu, Benjamin, ed. 1987. *Terrorism: How the West can win*. New York: Avon.

Nir, Ory. 2001. An electoral declaration of independence by the Arabs in Israel. *Haaretz*, February 7, p. 4

Oommen, T. K. 1997. *Citizenship, nationality, and ethnicity: Reconciling competing identities*. Cambridge: Polity Press.

Ophir, Adi. 2002. Jewish-Arab coexistence: The politics of rationality. *Democratic Culture* 6: 9–36.

Oppenheim, A. N., and J. Torney. 1974. *The measurement of children's civic attitudes in different nations*. Stockholm: Almquist and Wiksell; New York: John Wiley and Sons.

Orr, Teodor, Hashem, Hatib, and Shim'on Shamir. 2003. *Report of the Commission of Inquiry into the events of October 2000 in the Arab sector in Israel.* Jerusalem: Ministry of Justice.

Osetzky-Lazar, Sarah. 2003. Trends in voting among Arab citizens as the elections of January 2003 approach. In *The elections to the sixteenth Knesset among the Arab citizens of Israel* (in Hebrew), ed. Elie Rekhes. Tel-Aviv: Moshe Dayan Center for Middle East and African Studies, and the Konrad Adenauer Fund.

Oz, Amos. 2002. *A tale of love and darkness* (in Hebrew). Jerusalem: Keter.

Payes, Shanny. 2005. *Palestinian NGOs in Israel: The Politics of Civil Society.* London: Tauris.

Peled, Yoav. 1989. *Class and ethnicity in the pale: The political economy of Jewish workers' nationalism in late imperial Russia.* Basingstoke: Macmillan; New York: St. Martin's Press.

———. 1992. Ethnic democracy and the legal construction of citizenship: Arab citizens of the Jewish state. *American Political Science Review* 86, no. 2: 432–43.

Porath, Yehoshua. 1974. *The emergence of the Palestinian national movement, 1918–1929.* London: Frank Cass.

Rabinowitz, Dan. 1993. Oriental nostalgia: How the Palestinians became "Israel's Arabs." *Teorya Uvikoret* (in Hebrew), no. 4: 141–52.

———. 1994. The common memory of loss: Political mobilization amongst Palestinian citizens of Israel. *Journal of Anthropological Research* 50: 27–44.

———. 1997. *Overlooking Nazareth: The ethnography of exclusion in Galilee.* Cambridge: Cambridge University Press.

———. 1999. Uri Davis. In *Fifty to forty-eight: Critical moments in the history of the state of Israel* (in Hebrew), ed. Adi Ophir, pp. 169–179. Tel Aviv: Hakibbutz Hameukhad, and the Jerusalem Van Leer Foundation.

———. 2000. Natives with jackets and degrees: Othering, objectification, and the role of Palestinians in the co-existence field in Israel. *Social Anthropology* 9, no. 1: 65–80.

———. 2001. The Palestinian citizens of Israel, the concept of trapped minority, and the discourse of transnationalism in anthropology. *Ethnic and Racial Studies* 24, no. 1: 53–85.

———. 2002. Oriental othering and national identity: A review of early Israeli anthropological studies of Palestinians. *Identities: Global Studies in Culture and Power* 9: 305–25.

———. 2004. October 2000, revisited. *Haaretz,* October 19, p. B1.

Rabinowitz, Dan, and Khawla Abu-Baker. 2002. *The Stand-Tall Generation* (in Hebrew). Jerusalem: Keter Publishing.

Rabinowitz, Dan, Khawla Abu-Baker, Hanna Herzog, 'Adel Mana'a, Yoav Peled, Yehouda Shenhar, and Ramzi Sliman. 2000. Identity and civic/cultural inclusion. In *After the rift: New directions for government policy towards the Arab population in Israel. An emergency report by an inter-university research team, submitted to Mr. Ehud Barak, prime minister of Israel, November 2000,* ed. Dan Rabinowitz, As'ad Ghanem, and Oren Yiftachel. Be'er-Sheva: self-published by the editors, with the help of the European Commission in Israel and Shatil.

Rabinowitz, Dan, As'ad Ghanem, and Oren Yiftachel, eds. 2000. *After the rift: New directions for government policy towards the Arab population in Israel. An emergency report by an inter-university research team, submitted to Mr. Ehud Barak, prime minister of Israel, November 2000.* Be'er-Sheva: self-published by the editors, with the help of the European Commission in Israel and Shatil.

Ratner, Arye. 1996. *The effect of legal and extra-legal variables on sentencing among Jews and Arab in Israel.* Haifa: University of Haifa.

Ravid, Yitzhak. 2001. *The demographic environment of Israel* (in Hebrew). Herzliya: Interdisciplinary Center.

Reiter, Yitzhak, and Reuven Aharoni. 1992. *The political life of Arabs in Israel.* Beit Bene: Institute for Israeli-Arab Studies.

Rekhes, Elie. 1993. *The Arab Minority in Israel between Communism and Arab nationalism* (in Hebrew). Tel Aviv: Hakibbutz Hameukhad.

Rosaldo, Renato. 1988. Ideology, place, and people without culture. *Cultural Anthropology* 3, no. 1: 77–87.

Rosenthal, Ruvik. 2000. *Kafr Kasim: Myth and history* (in Hebrew). Tel Aviv: Hakibbutz Hameukhad.

Rouhana, Nadim. 1997. *Identities in conflict: Palestinian citizens in an ethnic Jewish state.* New Haven: Yale University Press.

———. 2001. Identity and power in Israeli-Palestinian reconciliation. *Israeli Sociology* 3, no. 2: 277–96.

Rouhana, N., and S. Fiske. 1995. Perception of power, threat, and conflict intensity in asymmetric intergroup conflict. *Journal of Conflict Resolution* 39: 49–81.

Rouhana, N., and S. Korper. 1997. Power asymmetry and goals of unofficial third party intervention in protracted intergroup conflict. *Peace and Conflict: Journal of Peace Psychology* 31: 1–17.

Ruby, Jay, and Barbara Meyerhoff, eds. 1982. *A crack in the mirror: Reflexive perspectives of anthropology.* Philadelphia: University of Pennsylvania Press.

Sayigh, Rosemary. 1979. *From peasants to revolutionaries.* London: Zed Books.

Segev, Tom. 1984. *1949: The first Israelis* (in Hebrew). Jerusalem: Keter.

Seikaly, May. 1995. *Haifa: Transformation of a Palestinian Arab society, 1918–1939.* London: Tauris.

Shafir, Gershon. 1989. *Land, labor, and the origins of the Israeli-Palestinian conflict, 1882–1914.* Cambridge: Cambridge University Press.

Shalev, Michael. 1992. *Labor and the political economy in Israel.* Oxford: Oxford University Press.

Shavit, Yossi. 1989. Tracking and the educational spiral: A comparison of Arab and Jewish educational expansion in Israel. *Comparative Education Review* 33, no. 2: 216–31.

———. 1990. Segregation, tracking, and the educational attainment of minorities: Arabs and oriental Jews in Israel. *American Sociological Review* 55, no. 1: 115–26.

Shavit, Yossi, and Jennifer L. Pierce. 1991. Sibship size and educational attainment in nuclear and extended families: Arabs and Jews in Israel. *American Sociological Review* 56, no. 3: 321–31.

Shenhav, Yehouda. 2001. The red line of the green line. In *Real time: Al-Aqsa Intifada and the Israeli left,* ed. Adi Ophir. Jerusalem: Keter.

Shenhav, Yehouda, and Nadav Gabay. 2001. Managing political conflicts: The sociology of state commissions of inquiry in Israel. *Israel Studies* 6, no. 1: 126–56.

Sheth, D. L., and Gurpereet Mahajan, eds. 1999. *Minority identities and the nation-state.* Delhi: Oxford University Press.

Shlaim, Avi. 1990. *The politics of partition: King Abdullah, the Zionists, and Palestine, 1921–1951.* Oxford: Oxford University Press.

———. 1999. *The iron wall: Israel and the Arab world since 1948.* New York: Norton.

Smooha, Sami. 1990. Minority status in an ethnic democracy: The status of the Arab minority in Israel. *Ethnic and Racial Studies* 13, no. 3: 389–413.

Svensson, F. 1979. Liberal democracy and group rights: The legacy of individualism and its impact on American Indian tribes. *Political Studies* 273: 421–39.

Sweedenburg, Ted. 1995. *Memories of revolt: The 1936–39 rebellion and the Palestinian national past.* Minneapolis: University of Minnesota Press.

Tibawi, Ahmed. 1956. *Arab education in mandatory Palestine: A study of three decades of British administration.* London: Luzac.

Tomasi, John. 1995. Kymlicka, liberalism, and respect for cultural minorities. *Ethics* 1053: 580–603.

Torstrick, Rebecca. 2001. *The limits of co-existence: Identity politics in Israel.* Ann Arbor: University of Michigan Press.

Totah, Khalil, and Ma'roof al-Rasafi. 1921. *Collection of school chants* (in Arabic). Jerusalem: al-Quds.

Tilly, James. 1994. Aboriginal property and western theory: Recovering a middle ground. *Social Philosophy and Policy* 112: 153–80.

Tufaha, Fouzi Fathi, ed. 1947. *Collection of national chants* (in Arabic). Jerusalem: al-Khalil.

Volkov, Shulamit. 2002. *In the bewitched circle: Jews, anti-Semites, and other Germans* (in Hebrew). Tel Aviv: Am Oved.

Waltzer, Michael. 1983. *Spheres of justice: A defence of pluralism and equality.* Oxford: Basil Blackwell.

————, ed. 1982. *The politics of ethnicity.* Cambridge: Harvard University Press.

Williams, Melissa. 1994. Group inequality and the public culture of justice. In *Group rights,* ed. Judith Baker. Toronto: University of Toronto Press.

Yiftachel, Oren. 1994. Spatial planning, land control, and Jewish-Arab relations in Galilee (in Hebrew). *City and Region* 23: 55–98.

————. 1997. Israeli society and Jewish-Palestinian reconciliation: "Ethnocracy" and its territorial contradictions. *Middle East Journal* 51, no. 4: 505–19.

————. 1999. Land Day. In *Fifty to forty-eight: Critical moments in the history of the state of Israel* (in Hebrew), ed. Adi Ophir, pp. 279–91. Tel Aviv: Hakibbutz Hameukhad and the Jerusalem Van Leer Foundation.

Yiftachel, Oren, and Alexander Kedar. 2000. Landed power: The making of the Israeli land regime. *Theory and Criticism* (in Hebrew), 16: 67–100.

Yiftachel, Oren, Rasem Khamaisi, and Sandy Kedar. 2000. Land Issues. In *After the rift: New directions for government policy towards the Arab population in Israel. An emergency report by an inter-university research team, submitted to Mr. Ehud Barak, prime minister of Israel, November 2000,* ed. Dan Rabinowitz, As'ad Ghanem, and Oren Yiftachel. Be'er-Sheva: self-published by the editors, with the help of the European Commission in Israel and Shatil.

Zahalka, Jamal. 2001. Here is not Sweden. In *Real time: Al-Aqsa Intifada and the Israeli left,* ed. Adi Ophir, pp. 243–49. Tel Aviv: Keter.

Ziad, Tawfik. 1959. Samar fi al-sijin (Talk into the night in prison). In *Ashud 'ala aydekum* (I support your hands). Haifa: al-Itihad.

Zidani, Sa'ed. 1998. Arabs in a Jewish state: Their status at present and in the future. In *Arabs in Israeli politics: Identity dilemmas* (in Hebrew), ed. Eli Reches, pp. 111–116. Tel Aviv: Dayan Center.

Zureik, Elia. 1979. *The Palestinians in Israel: A study in internal colonialism.* London: Routledge and Kegan Paul.

————. 1988. Crime, justice, and development: The Palestinians under Israeli control. *International Journal of Middle East Studies* 20: 411–42.

About the Authors

DAN RABINOWITZ, PH.D., an anthropologist, is a Senior Lecturer at the Department of Sociology and Anthropology at Tel Aviv University and a regular contributor to the op-ed page of *Haaretz* on politics, environmental issues, and society in Israel and the Middle East. Born in Haifa, he was educated in London and Cambridge. His books include *12 Families in Israel* (Hakibbutz Hameukhad, 1988), *Overlooking Nazareth* (Cambridge University Press, 1997), *Anthropology and the Palestinians* (Institute of Israeli-Arab Studies, 1998) and *The Cross-Israel Highway* (provisional title; Hakibbutz Hameukhad, forthcoming). He publishes regularly in academic journals on anthropology, sociology, and Middle East studies.

KHAWLA ABU-BAKER, PH.D., family therapist, is a Senior Lecturer at the Department of Behavioral Science at Emek Yezreel College, Galilee. Born in Acre and educated at the Hebrew University in Jerusalem, the University of Haifa, and Nova Southeastern University in Florida, she works with Palestinian society and families, especially with women—individuals as well as organizations—in Israel and the Palestinian Authority. Her book *A Rocky Road: Arab Women as Political Leaders in Israel* was published in 1998 by the Institute for Israeli-Arab Studies. She publishes regularly in academic journals on sociology, mental health, family therapy, women's studies, and Middle East studies.

Index

Text: 10/14 Palatino
Display: Bauer Bodoni
Compositor, printer, and binder: Sheridan Books, Inc.